EUROPEAN ECONOMIC AND POLITICAL ISSUES SERIES

INNOVATIVE REGULATORY APPROACHES COPING WITH SCANDINAVIAN AND EUROPEAN UNION POLICIES

EUROPEAN ECONOMIC AND POLITICAL ISSUES SERIES

European Economic and Political Issues, Volume 1
Frank Columbus, (Editor)
ISBN: 1-56072-686-5

European Economic and Political Issues, Volume 2
Frank Columbus, (Editor)
ISBN: 1-56072-793-4

European Economic and Political Issues, Volume 3
Frank H. Columbus, (Editor)
2001. ISBN 1-56072-908-2

European Economic and Political Issues Volume 4
Frank H. Columbus, (Editor)
2002. ISBN: 1-59033-137-0

European Economic and Political Issues Volume 5
Frank H. Columbus, (Editor)
2002. ISBN: 1-59033-322-5

European Economic and Political Issues Volume 6
Frank H. Columbus, (Editor)
2002. ISBN: 1-59033-404-3

European Economic and Political Issues, volume 7
Frank H. Columbus, (Editor)
2003. ISBN 1-59033-581-3.

European Economic and Political Issues Volume 8
Frank H. Columbus, (Editor)
2004. ISBN: 1-59033-766-2

European Economic and Political Issues Volume 9
William B. Stickle (Editor)
2009. ISBN: 978-1-60456-267-5

European Economic and Political Issues Volume 9
William B. Stickle. (Editor)
2009. ISBN: 978-1-60876-558-4
Online Book

Innovative Regulatory Approaches Coping with Scandinavian and European Union Policies
Noralv Veggeland (Editor)
2010. ISBN: 978-1-60876-673-4

European Response to the Financial Crisis
Baron L. Whitley (Editor)
2010. ISBN: 978-1-60876-817-2

European Economic and Political Issues Series

Innovative Regulatory Approaches Coping with Scandinavian and European Union Policies

Noralv Veggeland
Editor

Nova Science Publishers, Inc.
New York

LIBRARY OF CONGRESS CATALOGING-IN-PUBLICATION DATA

Innovative regulatory approaches coping with Scandinavian and European Union policies / editor, Noralv Veggeland.
p. cm.
Includes bibliographical references and index.
ISBN 978-1-60876-673-4 (hardcover)
1. Trade regulation--Scandinavia. 2. Trade regulation--European Union counies. I. Veggeland, Noralv, 1941-
HD3616.S232I56 2009
382'.30948--dc22

2009045948

Published by Nova Science Publishers, Inc. † New York

CONTENTS

EDITOR'S PREFACE

This book is the fruit of a kind inquiry from the editor of Nova Science Publishers if I had the opportunity to put together a book on regulatory matters. My answer was yes, and I proposed a focus on the Scandinavian perspective combined with that of the European Union (EU) on regulation because of deep-rooted integration processes in the region. The impetus for the proposal is my belief that the politics of regulation is an under-researched area, especially outside the United States. To my mind, this dual perspective is compelling for several reasons, and the authors of the seven chapters of this book have all contributed in making those reasons more concrete. The aims of this collection are twofold: first, to contribute to the development of conceptual and analytical studies that shed light on the European variant of the regulatory state, and secondly, to examine the politics of regulation in the age of governance.

In many respects, the organization of the EU and its governing of its member states appear to correspond to traditional definitions of the regulatory state. However, at this time, one cannot by any stretch characterize the EU as a federal entity, but only as a con-federal European power. This feature helps to substantiate the view that the EU clearly deviates from, for instance, the regulatory state of the United States. Accordingly, in chapter one I try to redefine the European variants of the regulatory state order by giving a brief introduction into the issue. I do this by describing and analysing the characteristics of the European regulatory state, trends of dominance, prevailing strategies of governance, transformations, regulatory innovations, and dilemmas of governance.

Taking into consideration that the five Nordic countries are very much interwoven in the EU, either as full member states (Sweden, Denmark, and Finland) or as members of the European Economic Area (EEA) (Norway and Iceland), it is of interest to analyse their adoptions of EU laws and regulations. How do these countries interpret and translate the different regulations nationally, which deliberately involves their penetration into the administrative structures? Further, how do they adapt to the principles of the regulatory state in general? The five countries belong to the Scandinavian administrative tradition and welfare-state model, which in many senses deviate clearly from the Anglo-Saxon and the Continental counterparts. The translations and implementations of EU regulations and other regulatory measures in Scandinavia become coloured by traditions and path-dependencies particular to this region. As a result, the EU seems to have become be a mixture of these traditions.

An attempt to understanding the importance of these processes and of the sometimes conflicting administrative traditions in the European regulatory state requires a combining of theoretical approaches with the study of cases. Chapters two to seven fulfil this demand. These chapters deal with different cases and regulatory reforms, and in that way further our understanding of the regulatory state of Europe and the politics of regulation within the frameworks of administrative traditions and governance.

Chapter two gives an introduction to translation theory and to the distinction between government and governance by using empirical data from a study on Scandinavian local government. Chapter three is a study of the regulatory cooperation on trade between the EU and Canada, and emphasizes the importance of soft regulation. Chapter four introduces a cultural perspective on the regulation of European borders. This contribution illustrates how the dream of creating a borderless Europe through acts of deregulations is often thwarted because borders of different kinds are not easily removed. The next chapter discusses the Scandinavian tradition of involving interest organizations in the formation of public policy, and how in the age of governance this tradition has been challenged and heavily eroded. Chapter six discusses how, despite EU single-market regulations, Norway, a world-leading producer of oil and gas, has managed to retain national control over its petroleum resources and revenues through the central government's planning tools and organizational innovations. Chapter seven discusses Norway's establishment of an international investment fund, the Norwegian Pension Fund – Global (formerly the Norwegian Petroleum Fund), based on the enormous revenues from its oil and gas industry. Ethical guidelines were set up for the proper use and investment of the Fund worldwide. This chapter analyses these guidelines and their relation to international climatic investments, and concludes that living up to these guidelines is challenging in a complex and highly interconnected economic world.

This collection aspires to demonstrate to the reader the manifoldness of the concept of the regulatory state and the issues that it engenders. Accordingly, this book reflects the hope that it will inspire further research on the regulatory state and its implications in various contexts and administrative traditions.

ACKNOWLEDGEMENTS

I would like to thank very much all the contributors of this book for offering their academic knowledge to the study of the issue of the regulatory state by analysing the diversity of developments in the integrated Europe, with a special focus on Scandinavia. I would also like to express my gratitude to my colleagues at the Centre for Public Policy Innovation (CPPI) at Lillehammer University College, for generously offering their time to discuss and advise me on the often under-communicated research field of public innovation. I thank also to Lillehammer University College for giving me the opportunity to write and edit. Further, I am obliged to D. Phil. Candidate, Steven Connolley, for very important, helpful, and effective technical assistance.

Noralv Veggeland
Lillehammer, Norway, August 2009

In: Innovative Regulatory Approaches ...
Ed: Noralv Veggeland

ISBN: 978-1-60876-673-4

Chapter 1

THE 'REGULATORY STATE' IN THE STUDY OF SCANDINAVIAN AND EUROPEAN GOVERNANCE:[1] INTRODUCTORY ASPECTS

Noralv Veggeland

Unelected bodies include central banks, independent risk management bodies, independent economies and ethics regulators, regimes of inspection and audit and new types of appeal bodies (Vibert 2007:5).

APPROACHES

Since the 1980s, owing to the influence of advice from the Organization for Economic Co-operation and Development (OECD) and the penetration of regulations from the European Union (EU), regulatory measures and regulatory agencies and bodies have burgeoned through the extension of institutional innovations into new areas of national economic and social life.[2] The items we buy, the utilities we demand, the work conditions we accept, the welfare services we are offered, the public management we are subordinate to – all of these have become increasingly subject to regulations and legal controls, which specialized agencies usually administer. The institutional self-regulation of the past has been transformed.

---

[1] Google generates 18 300 000 hits for the term of 'regulatory state', and Google Scholar indicates 2 160 000 (last accessed 9 February 2009).

[2] According to the Norwegian search engine Kvasir, there are 46 governmental regulatory agencies in the small state of Norway (last accessed 3 February 2009). Their functions are limited solely to control and surveillance. Among others, this number does not include the European Surveillance Agency (ESA) and its subsidiaries. If we add decentralised subsidiaries by multiplying that number with the number of Norwegian counties, 19, the total number increases to 874 agencies. Other regulators in the form of independent boards of arm's-length bodies producing ordinary public services are also not included.

Markets, societal sectors, organizations, and institutions are de-regulated – and re-regulated. Even knowledge-creating institutions like universities are now subject to statutory innovations in the form of new regulations that have replaced the traditional self-governance of the 'command-and-control' type of bureaucracy (Rhodes 1997). National public administrations organized as a unified, hierarchical state bureaucracy of the Weberian pattern have also been partly replaced. This bureaucracy attempted to manage the whole polity and to pursue the redistribution of resources. It was a process by which the social and individual worlds were increasingly subject to rational action through financial interventions, public monopolies, central planning, formal procedures, and non-discretionary decision-making. Accordingly, the state was believed to be building the ability to exercise widespread command and control.

In contrast, the regulatory state stresses legal interventions in the construction of command and control. The approach of 'steering without rowing', that is, the withdrawal of the state from both the direct participation in the allocation of resources and the role of being owner, has become the general and prevailing idea of dominance.[3] The goals are to correct particular irregularities and market failures through regulatory interventions and to co-ordinate actions through the regulatory form of negotiated legal agreements and contracts. The stress of regulations spreads to the securing of safety (food, work, health, poverty, etc.), the diminishing of risks (unknowable in their occurrence and collective in their incidence; pandemics, technology, etc.), the avoidance of discrimination (gender, race, religion, age etc.), the handling of scandals (corruption, risks of business, medical malpractice, etc.), the counteracting of and recovery from crises (financial, employment, hunger, malnutrition, etc.), the safeguarding of the environment (pollution, global warming, deforestation, etc.), and the programming of co-operation (development programmes, research programmes, partnerships, etc.) (Hood, Rothstein, and Baldwin 2004). The social philosopher Jürgen Habermas (1987) has expressed his scepticism towards the ever increasing reach of the 'systems world', and has argued that we need to protect the privacy of the 'life-world'. However, we cannot ignore the systems world of regulations, and we must, therefore, set the 'taming of the regulatory state' on the scholarly agenda (Veggeland 2009).

By referring to Cass (2005: 60-1), Roger King (2007: 5) has pointed out the usefulness of distinguishing between 'rules' and 'regulations'. On the one hand, legal 'rules tend to be non-discretionary acts of wide application in legally-sustained decision-making'; on the other, 'regulation, however, although, like rules, also guiding and patterning individual behaviours, tends to be much broader in its sources and in its inclusion of both public and private institutions'. Thus rules provide a high degree of predictability in the realm of management and public administration, much like intentions behind the bureaucracy described by Max Weber. Regulations, including legal agreements and contracts, may, however, be much more flexible than rules and can be introduced and modified accordingly to fit changing circumstances. These characteristics are quite unlike what should happen according to Weber's neutral and rational bureaucracy.

The term of 'regulatory state' first came into scholarly use in the study of European politics with the publication in 1994 of Giandomenico Majone's milestone article, 'The

3 The current financial crisis, which has caused economic recession globally, has restored the state back in both allocation and ownership matters through different gigantic governmental packages of different kinds. The prevailing ideology, though, suggests that the involvement is to be temporary.

Emergence of the Regulatory State in Europe' (Majone 1994). Three years later, his next contribution, 'The rise of the regulatory state' (Majone 1997),[4] elaborated the context of the same issue. Here, Majone observes that traditional forms of bureaucratic regulation and control, inherited from the interventionist state, were being broken down in the face of powerful technological, economic, and ideological forces. Majone also ascribed three major functions of the interventionist Keynesian state: redistribution of resources, economic stabilization, and social regulation. It is the rise of the regulatory state that involves the escalation of the third function at the expense of the other two (Veggeland 2009).

New forms of regulation and planning have arisen to serve a wide range of different social goals of control, management, and change in order to facilitate efficiency and innovation in both private and public sectors. In the European Economic Area (EEA), the passing of laws and the publication of the EU directives and programmes have increased dramatically. Far-reaching laws and powers of authority have come to dominate Western polities in general, whereby management through objectives, programming, measurements of goal-attainment, quality-securing systems of measurement, reporting, and auditing actions etc. have been adopted, all of which are typical steering instruments supported by the ideals of New Public Management (NPM).

Naturally, social planning is a part of NPM but not in the form of the traditional, holistic, state central planning. Instead, planning in the regulatory state takes place as fragmented acts. This mode of planning occurs in the context of the transformation of self-regulation as an independent professional activity; each act must be planned by rules and regulations so that both the achievement of goals and the measurement of results might be practically possible. In fact, regulatory action and controls, which are meant to facilitate the realization of specific goals and results, require more extensively detailed and thorough planning than is the case with governance based upon standardized, patterned, and centralized planning activities.

After the great international stagflation crisis of the mid-1970s, the Western states were struggling to reconstruct their economies and to increase the efficiency of the public-sector institutions so that they could adapt to the pressures of global competition. Moreover, the states were increasingly bound to external regulatory systems and agreements pursuing mutually beneficial obligations. These institutional innovations and revolutionary reconstructions were the most important developments that led to the regulatory state of today.

What does the introduction of the regulatory state mean with regard to the contemporary polity? Majone has offered a succinct answer: 'Privatisation and deregulation have created the conditions for the rise of the regulatory state to replace the dirigiste state of the past' (1994:77). Further, 'Reliance on regulation – rather than public ownership, planning or centralised administration – characterises the methods of the regulatory state'.

Other scholars have formulated broader definitions of regulation that invoke either positive or negative societal values. Phillip Selznick, for instance, argues that the central meaning of regulation 'refers to sustained and focused control exercised by a public agency over activities that are valued by a community', and this role is important because 'the regulatory effort helps to uphold public standards, ethics and norms' (Selznick 1985: 363). On the other hand, Michael Moran has taken a much dimmer view, insisting that 'the features of the new kind of state … [are] its persistent interventionism, its drive to ever more

[4] This article has been cited 387 times, according to Google Scholar (last accessed 19 January 2009).

systematic surveillance, its colonization of new regulatory spheres … [thus] perversions of its essential purpose' (Moran 2003: 6). In addition, increasing transactional costs connected to the regulatory state strengthen this negative perspective (Veggeland 2009). Regulation by agreements and contracting out are part of this regime and relate to network management (Baldwin and Cave 1999: 46). Some researchers have identified two different forms of this kind of management (Kjær 2004: 45):

- One form is 'game management', a term which denotes the process of interaction between actors within the network that does not really bring about change within the network; instead, the goal is to facilitate agreement from within.
- The other is 'network structuring', referring to the changing of the network itself in order that it may accomplish new goals.

But, in its widest sense, we may define 'regulation' as the totality of all mechanisms of social protection and control (Jordana and Levi-Faur 2004: 3), including its negative repercussions. This book addresses this totality of regulatory mechanisms.

In our context, we may put forward five explanatory conceptions of regulation (Baldwin, Scott & Hood, 1998):

[1] Law-directed conception: regulation as authoritative rules.
[2] Economics-directed conception: regulation as efforts of state agencies to manage the economy.
[3] Politics-directed conception: regulation as mechanisms of steering and democratic control.
[4] Partnership-directed concept: regulation by agreements and contracts to extend multi-level governance and network co-ordination.
[5] Sustainability-directed conception: regulation as a means of eliminating environmental threats and the 'risk society of the new modernity' in general (Beck 1992).

These conceptions articulated by Baldwin et al. point to an evolution from a narrow, judicial notion of regulation to a much broader one, which both theory and practice account for, that encompasses values and normative and agreement-based actions. This more comprehensive approach, moreover, distinguishes between external and internal regulatory orders and employs comparative analyses to make sense of organizational differences concerning the translation and implementation of regulatory ideas (Pedersen 2009). Chapter 2 focuses on these aspects and presents an analysis of local governments that features examples of Scandinavian municipalities.

Modes Of Regulation

In the regulatory state, the notion of regulation as an assemblage of authoritative rules and agreed normative actions leads to the important distinction between *soft regulation* and *hard regulation*, both of which relate to how different regulation techniques can contribute to the functioning of markets, social stability, the reduction of risk, and sustainability. Soft regulatory instruments are voluntary mechanisms used to achieve a set of regulatory goals, including the goal of minimizing trade barriers. Soft regulatory instruments have their basis on so-called soft law, that is, voluntary documents such as guidelines, declarations, and recommendations. Soft regulatory instruments may also include such procedural mechanisms as benchmarking, open methods of co-ordination, training programmes for regulators, mutual visits and audits, the sharing and exchanging information, and the involvement of trading partners as relevant stakeholders in the different stages of regulation.

Soft regulatory instruments may be used as alternatives, as well as supplements and complements, to hard regulatory instruments, the set of instruments based on binding agreements and mandatory rules. Hard regulation requires legal actions and mechanisms of enforcement to bring about adherence and imposes sanctions when there is a failure to comply (May 2002). This approach contrasts with soft regulation, which is sometimes viewed as regulation through persuasion and deliberative discourse, with agreement being the preferred outcome (Streeck 1995, Amdam and Veggeland 1998). Soft regulation both turns to deliberative solutions (McGowan and Wallace 1996) and allows for commitments between parties not to be strictly legally binding, which gives actors more leeway on how they achieve regulatory goals and development objectives (Mörth 2004)

The soft regulatory strand comprises guidelines with various forms of incentives to achieve desired outcomes, but this approach means that the rules can vary, say, across national borders, just as long as it is possible to determine that the rules fulfil some common objectives that have been satisfactorily agreed upon. The use of these instruments entails the intentional striving for agreement-based regulations, which the European Union has termed 'the open method of coordination' since the launching of the Lisbon Process in 2000. Briefly, soft regulation connotes the following:

- Deliberative work on identifying both the 'best solutions' and the 'best practices'.
- An approach based on the exchange of information and the sharing of development programmes.
- Mutual confidence and some sort of compatibility between regulatory systems.
- A high degree of institutional interaction between regulators.[5]
- The foundation of the networking and partnership-building society (Castells 1996, Veggeland 2003).

The main research questions in chapter 3 focus on the role of soft regulatory instruments that are used to facilitate trade and the functioning of markets. This chapter examines the regulation of trade between the EU and Canada to illustrate these activities, and its analysis of the results takes into consideration the characteristics of the two economies. More specifically, the authors ask:

- What characterizes the regulatory co-operation between the EU and Canada, particularly with respect to the soft instruments employed to create greater compatibility between regulatory systems for the sake of facilitating trade?

[5] Two chapters of this book discuss how and why soft regulation is important in cases of cross-border co-operation.

- What mechanisms are at play within the EU-Canadian regulatory co-operation regarding the effectiveness of soft regulatory instruments as ways to facilitate trade?

Thus, chapter 3 explores the development of trade relations between the EU and Canada with an emphasis on the use of soft regulatory instruments within their framework for trade. The role of soft regulatory instruments in this case offers a useful contrast with the role of hard regulatory instruments. Furthermore, this chapter assesses the effectiveness of soft regulatory instruments to facilitate trade.

Chapter 4 focuses on the role of soft regulation in another arena, the border-transcending sector of culture. This chapter gives an overview of the so-called discursive turn in border studies of the mid- to late 1990s. Here, the famous member of the Frankfurt School, Walter Benjamin, plays an introductory symbolic role. This chapter then develops the argument that this literature has not sufficiently contemplated the issue of normative politics, which would allow for an assessment of different regulatory regimes and their concomitant effects of power. Drawing on the Annales School tradition, the author develops a spatial vocabulary that makes possible a more nuanced approach to the workings of culture and soft power in Europe's regulated borderlands. Several case studies round out the analysis.

Trends of Dominance

According to Majone (1997), Baldwin and Cave (1999), Moran (2001), Black (2005), Braithwaite 2008, Veggeland (2009) and other scholars, there are certain key trends that are dictating the development of the regulatory state. Here a presentation of four of them:

Trend 1: The Use of Legal Authority

The regulatory state's use of legal authority or regulation as supreme tools of policy-making has superseded the Keynesian interventionist-state strategies of stabilization and distribution through the policy of effective demand. As we have already seen, the latter attempted to manage the welfare state by financial and planning measures and pursued development, the redistribution of resources, and the provision of social security accordingly. The regulatory state stresses instead legal interventions either to create markets through deregulation or to correct markets by re-regulation. The latter practice embodies new regulations to deal with negative externalities and, in particular, policy failures (Scharpf 1999). Hence, the concept of re-regulation normally relates to regulatory innovations (Black, Lodge, & Thatcher, 2005), that is, innovations directed to take precautions against imbalances, disorders, risks, and threats to safety.

Consequently, taking control and introducing such precautions require innovative policies, and governments now prefer re-regulation as the main tool for these tasks. Ulrich Beck (1992) has introduced the term 'risk society', and has claimed that the modern industrial society has set up a vast range of grave technological, economic, and social risks. The results are unknowable, and incidents have repercussions on a vast collective scale. Pandemics, technological failures, crises of food safety (e.g., bovine spongiform encephalopathy, BSE), systemic crises, vulnerable communication systems, are only some examples. As individuals, we can hardly do anything to safeguard against these kinds of events, but collectively we can limit their impact through regulatory actions.

Re-regulation is also necessary for facilitating policies that aim to discourage acts of discrimination relating to ethnicity, gender, race, religion, age, etc., and to combat corruption of every kind, high-risk activities of enterprises, medical malpractice, illegal or uncontrolled migration, social dumping, regional and urban development, and so on. In the European Union there is a growing focus on regulatory measures concerning migration and immigration due to two factors: the pressure on external borders due to globalization, and the pressure on internal borders and welfare arrangements following the integration of the labour markets of 27 member states, some wealthy and other poor, plus three states included in the EEA. Consequently, the standardization of regulations has become complicated. Migration policies affect how immigrants perceive a given country as one that provides opportunities or as one that sets up obstacles to immigration (van der Velde and van Houtum 2004). This aspect affects not only the number of immigrants and asylum seekers who seek to enter the country but also the extent to which these immigrants are able to integrate into a very different society.

Lastly, there is need for innovative re-regulation and the institutional ability to steer clear of local, national, and international crises, like the financial crisis of the late 2000s and its attendant disorder, imbalance and risk. Consequently, there is much talk about the international economic recession and the need for the regulation of financial transactions across borders, state interventions, and credit policies (Stiglitz 2009). The financial crisis introduces a dramatic increase in unemployment, negative economic growth, and social imbalance. These results impose very clearly the need to think in new ways about many different issues, not only work, housing, and social-security policies, but also interest rates, taxes, and credit policies in the economic sphere and the role of interventionist versus regulatory policies in the political sphere. Even more, the persistence all over the world of famines, malnutrition among children, diseases, and poverty leads to demands for a new order of international regulations and conventions, as does the threat of global warming, pollution, and nuclear waste. It is hardly surprising, then, that re-regulation is more than ever a prominent element in proposed solutions to contemporary problems.

Trend 2: The Expanding Role of the EU

The expanding role of the EU's regulatory and monetary measures in the absence of other measures (Veggeland 2009), especially the absence of budgetary tools (Majone 1997), facilitates the approach of supranational and intergovernmental regulation by law and by derivatives of intergovernmental agreements. In a global perspective the EU is an exceptional organization, partly a supranational power and partly an intergovernmental organization (Wallace, Wallace, & Pollack, 2004).

The EU's own budget, financial means, and capability of development investments and distribution of resources are relatively small compared to the GNP of an average member state. Its budget mainly allocates financial support of European agriculture and structural policies. The legislative assemblies, the European Parliament and Council of Ministers, and the executive agency, the Commission, can only exercise influence and dominance by working indirectly as regulatory bodies on behalf of the member states. Whatever the limitations it faces, the EU wields its influence effectively through a wide range of acts of de-regulations and re-regulation and in manifold scopes and scales. The regulations penetrate administrations at all level of the European governance system, which includes also the three non-member countries of the EEA and the European Free Trade Agreement (EFTA), Norway, Iceland, and Lichtenstein.

In other words, the EU facilitates development through regulations, but extends its executive role and displaces its costs down to national and sub-national levels. The adoption and implementation of the common European regulations do not necessarily create national institutional convergence, but normally the divergence remains.[6] This effect is due to the fact that the legal acts are subjected to interpretation and tend to be translated in accordance with national frameworks and administrative traditions in a discretionary process that is, of course, under legal surveillance (Knill 2001, Veggeland 2007, Røvik 2007). The member state's translations are innovative, and indicate a resistance against copying other member states and a preference for acting in its own interests. The Commission's only opportunity to augment its influence continues to be the expansion of the scope and scale of its regulatory activities and resources of surveillance. Alternatively, convergence may be achieved by extending 'soft regulation', that is, regulation by persuasion, programmes, values, and ethics into the sphere of 'hard regulation'. Currently, we can see this happening as a shift from the so-called 'hard community method of regulation' to the 'soft method of coordination' (see chapter 3).

Trend 3: The Contributions of Regulators

As more flexible regulation replaces non-discretionary rule-based governance, the regulatory state of the EU inevitably becomes intertwined with and dependent upon an array of national 'unelected' bodies, including both civil and non-governmental regulators (Vibert 2007). In a narrow perspective, these institutions appear limited compared to the building of the many marketized new government bodies and surveillance agencies of the regulatory state (Pollitt and Bouckaert 2004). A wider perspective, however, reveals the regulatory state being organized and biased in a way that vests responsibility and steering capacity in individual or collective regulators (e.g., professional bodies, boards of arm's-length bodies, etc.). This arrangement tends to generate regulatory innovation (Black 2005).

With reference to a study of the British regulatory state, Michael Moran (2001:21-22) explains why and how the '"personalisation" of regulation has created a corps of high-profile political entrepreneurs, the regulators, who have begun to exert an independent influence of their own in setting regulatory agendas – an unsurprising outcome, since they rapidly acquire authority and expertise in their regulated area'. This development expands the extent and variety of political entrepreneurial approaches as well as the number of agencies participating in regulatory processes. Regulatory scope and scale are important in the context of facilitating innovative ability (see Fig. 1 below).

Trend 4: The Audit Explosion

Some researchers have suggested that efforts by the state and the public authorities to regain social control and trust in an era marked by growing institutional innovations, risks, vulnerability, and complexity through increased levels of information have created the 'audit society' (Power 1997), whereby skilled external inspections and controls are replacing internal, self-regulatory, and communicative forms of trusted surveillance and endorsement. The image of the audit explosion describes an accelerating 'spill-over' process of a neo-

[6] The scholarly debate on convergence versus divergence in the European Union is a lasting one (Pierre (ed.) 2001).

functionalistic character (Pollack 2005) typical of the emerging regulatory state in the OECD area since the 1980s. Relatively recently, the word 'audit' had connotations of a technical activity relating mostly to the examination of public budgets and accounts of firms. A satisfactory audit meant an endorsement of honest and responsible activities and a reflection of good management.

The 'audit explosion' has transformed this meaning so that 'audit' now refers to an ever expanding activity that seeks to secure good governance and accountability by inspection, not only in public and private finances and budgetary balances, but also in related administrations and in new social sectors. Auditing as a mechanism of the regulatory state appears in social arenas as different as universities, health and social care, public-service corporations, local government (the Audit of the Municipalities), and national government (the Audit of the Government).

Of course, audits of the local and national governments still encompass the examination of budgets and accounts, but what is a fairly recent institutional mechanism is the inspection of implementations of democratically made decisions and rules, including checking for the proper execution of implementations in order to avoid failures. In the wake of NPM reforms, municipalities and public-service institutions are now bound to report to regulatory bodies their achievements of quantitative and qualitative results, measured according to fixed goals, programmes, agreements, and contracts. The rationale for this requirement is twofold: financial according to the concept of result-based allocations, and benchmarking according to the concept of determining the winners. The Audits of the municipalities and the government have an obligation to inspect and check the accuracy of reported data and achievements.

Altogether, these types of audits clearly represent regulatory innovations, but they also expand considerably the basic knowledge of the diversity of arenas. And it ought not to be forgotten that the expansion of auditing also entails a great expansion of regulatory powers and the creation of new regulatory bodies and departments, which in itself represent institutional innovations.

Trend 5: The Weakening of Corporatist Institutions

In the regulatory state, traditional corporatist institutions no longer provide public decision-makers' need for flexibility. Consequently decision-makers tend both to demand greater latitude in the formative process of internal regulations (see chapter 2 below) and to negotiate individual social and labour market contracts, thus rejecting collective arrangements (Veggeland 2009).

It is difficult, however, to change conflicting legal regulations and contracts because the courts – and neither corporatist institutions nor trade unions – effect such changes. The relations between the unions of interest groups and the state arose during the twentieth century; in Scandinavia, these relations were in accordance with traditions of consensual policy-making (see chapter 5 below). During recent decades the role of interest groups in policy-making has weakened. Privileged groups are no longer invited to important deliberations on public policies. They only gain access when decision-makers assess that the benefits will exceed the costs of closely involving interest groups. This development has consequences for democratic procedures: on the one hand, more social groups present a broader set of inputs to the administrative and political process of decision-making; on the other hand, the price is a less transparent process of policy-making that is typical of the regulatory state.

Prevailing Governance Strategies of the Regulatory State

It has become a commonplace to state that we live in the age of the regulatory state. This regime features the following: (1) *regulation* through modernization of public-sector activity (Pollitt and Bouckaert 2004: 188-196); (2) *agencification* by the establishment of the 'unelected' (Vibert 2007) arm's-length agencies and regulatory bodies and authorities;[7] (3) *transformation of institutional self-regulation from internal to external*; (4) *formalization of relationships* within policy domains, through legal agreements and contract-based relationships.

The Strategy of Modernization

Modernization is perhaps the most obvious cause of the regulatory boom (Moran 2001). According to Pollitt and Bouchaert (2004), the policy of privatization as a part of the strategy of modernization has led to the trend of minimizing the public administrative apparatus, which involves the handing over of as many tasks as possible to the market sector directly through privatization and indirectly through contracting out, that is, outsourcing. It has been called the 'hollowing-out' of the state apparatus, a social-institutional arrangement in which social security and public services of all kinds, such as social and health services, telecommunications, electricity, railways, energy, and even military services, are drastically reduced. The privatization of essential infrastructural services is significant given that these sectors have been widely viewed as essential of the modern state's responsibility.

The ideas of Schumpeter were clearly evident in this strategy: spur economic growth by reducing the rigid state machine through a minimizing strategy and replace it with innovative market actors that are exposed to 'creative destruction' (Schumpeter (1942/1979) but still remain under regulatory control. Such actors intensify the direct contact between the political system and the market economy, unmediated by rigid, Weberian bureaucratic structures. Minimalists categorically reject the idea that governments can be made to act in the best interests of the economy and the public in general. In Schumpeter's world, rulers are judged 'able' because they win votes, not because they have governed or will govern well (Kuper 2004: 98). But the minimalists also use the measurements calibrated for the regulatory state. Policies for tax cuts and low interest rates that target an increase in aggregated consumption and investment followed by private-law regulations accompany the minimizing strategy. In sum, the minimizing strategy represents the political economy of the regulatory state (Veggeland 2009).

The marketizing of the administrative system was an alternative strategy for instituting as many Market-Type Mechanisms (MTMs) as possible within the public sector. This marketizing strategy implies not only a redefinition of the economic rules of the state but also a transformed perspective on governments and their roles as regulatory authorities.

The marketizing strategy of New Public Management (NPM) basically created the so-called Public-Law Agencies (PLAs) and Private-Law Bodies (PLBs), which are steered indirectly by law, regulation, and financial means (OECD 2002). In a democratic framework,

---

[7] Other notions used in the same frameworks and with the same defined meanings are 'non-majoritarian institutions' (Moran 2003), 'Distributed governance bodies' (OECD 2002), and 'Executives' (Christensen and Lægreid 2006).

they have acquired the label of 'unelected bodies' (Vibert 2007). There is an emphasis on the achievement of results through the means of flexible organizational structures and competition. This approach dovetails the Schumpeter's idea that innovation only becomes beneficial through competition in markets corrected for externalities. Hence, public-sector organizations should likewise be made flexible and competitive but under the supervision of law, management by objectives, and regulations. Besides, it would increase efficiency and encourage the users to value the individual freedom to choose.

Like the minimizing strategy, the marketizing strategy prepared the way for policies for tax cuts and low interest rates that were supposed to effect an increase in the aggregated consume and investment, and thereby economic growth. The marketizing strategy has turned out to be characteristic of the government of the regulatory state, namely, 'steering without rowing', that is, steering indirectly by law and regulation and not by central planning and public ownership. With regard to political economy, the administrations subscribing to NPM, especially in the Anglo-American tradition from the beginning of the 1980s, adopted this strategy extensively (Knill 2001, Veggeland 2007).

With respect to political economy, the modernization of the administrative system was to introduce faster, more flexible ways of budgeting, managing, and delivering services to the users by applying regulatory measures. Unelected arm's-length bodies were organized and set into motion as market actors or pseudo-market actors. It was predicated on the distinctiveness of public provision, that is, 'services of general interest'; it was necessary to distinguish between 'non-commercial services' – in-house services under Weberian bureaucratic protection and control – and 'commercial services', marketized services under public or private-law supervision (EU green paper 2003).

Broadly speaking, some have interpreted the arrival of the regulatory state in the form of instrumental governance to be an extension of the powers of the state based on standardization through regulation, quantification, and considerable public reporting (Moran 2003). There was a need to strengthen the state innovatively through multi-level governance rather than through the dilution the state. One example was the wave for reducing vertical differentiation that swept over local government.

The reduction of hierarchical levels in the tier unit of municipalities created an organizational vacuum. NPM instruments and regulatory measurements, such as balanced scorecards, internal quasi-markets, value-based management, and steering by contracts, soon filed this vacuum. Chapter 2 offers a comparative study of two local governments in this context: one in Denmark and the other in Norway. This chapter asks the following questions. What are the similarities and differences in internal regulation after the administrative delayering in Danish and Norwegian municipalities? What are the possible explanations of such similarities and differences in the framework of the regulatory state? Did the implementation of the delayered administration strengthen the local government, or did it instead dilute the steering capacity?

The Strategy and Agencification

Agencification may be defined in terms of a large and growing world of 'unelected' arm's-length agencies and regulatory bodies and authorities. Frank Vibert (2007:5) gives this picture of the varied world of 'unelected': 'Unelected bodies include central banks, independent risk management bodies, independent economies and ethics regulators, regimes of inspection and audit and new types of appeal bodies'. As self-governing organizations they are given their mandate by law and have the ability to borrow money, to earn money from financial investments, to hire and employ staff and to contract service suppliers, and to manage their resources. In the regulatory state governments have sought to apply a more marketized approach by organizing them as unelected stakeholders. However, in light of the framework of what the EU defines as providers of 'services of general interest', that is, non-commercial public services, health, education, police etc., the transformation towards 'businesses' remains limited.

In the context of external self-regulation, the 'unelected' implies at least six aspects:

- The strategy of marketizing public services results in institutional agencification. A steering board guided by law and regulations is given autonomy in the governance of each agency.
- In the regulatory state 'clean' audit and control are laid in the hands of a wide range of regulatory agencies.
- Frank Vibert (2007) portrays the 'unelected' regulatory bodies as a sharing of democratic powers with the democratically elected representatives, and he rejects the view that unelected agency regimes are manifestations of increasing 'democratic deficit'. Indeed, Vibert concludes that the processes of agencification strengthen the democracy of the state because of the sharing of the state power. This conclusion may be valid under certain circumstances and within in a particular perspective, but otherwise it is not, because as a universal concept, the rise of the unelected entails the grave fragmentation of and the abdication of representative democracy.
- Obviously, regulatory agencies as unelected and independent, non-majority parts of the state do constitute a reallocation of power bound to the innovative processes of agencification, as Fig. 1 below illustrates. However, these processes have deep consequences for traditional liberal democracy, given the increased dominance of non-majority politics (Lodge 2007).
- There is a dilemma in finding a balance between non-majority and majority politics. The democratic legitimacy of 'the regulatory state' relies on the state's not distributing excessive regulatory authority to non-state bodies (OECD 2002). When that happens, the state suffers from democratic deficit, almost per definition. Put otherwise, the Vibert's perspective is too narrow.
- A judgement of whether or not agencifaction strengthens or dilutes both democracy and good governance demands criteria against which we can assess success or failure. We need criteria to be able to evaluate whether the innovation of regulatory bodies has led to successes or fiascos. Yet, the tackling of this issue is all too rarely done (Black 2005). There is a need to formulate the criteria that can help us to analyse the impacts of the regulatory state both in macro, globally, and in micro, locally.

Transformations

Transformation of Institutional Self-Regulation

Universities were once self-regulated institutions. A knowledge- based channel of professors with an elected rector, a first among equals, and a consensus-based, representative university council directed them. This communicative regime was in command. The autonomy and power of the elected regime had its limitations, however. It was internally under the budgetary control of an administration led by a managing director, and this meant that rector and other elected organs controlled this regime almost completely, except for the bureaucratic surveillance and control of the budget and the implementation of national laws and rules of the university sector. The old regime of the university is an example, in principle, of traditional internal self-regulation of highly profiled professional institutions, such as universities, medical institutions, and numerous others, which has now been transformed. It is important to note that this is an example 'in principle', because although the institutional structure could be organized in various ways, it always had this characteristic: a leadership rooted in the profession of scholars belonging to the actual institution which provides the service, or the professions of experts monitoring themselves. Hence, the key characteristic of internal traditional self-regulation is the right and duty of the institution to establish independently its own regulatory standards and methods of consensus. This form of self-regulation has greatly declined.

The transformation of self-regulation represents a new face of the regulatory state that is very important but rarely noticed: the reconstruction to steering instruments (Moran 2003: 93). Why have so few recognized that old integrated internal hierarchies of public service have been modified in the favour of much more loosely co-ordinated organizations of public agencies and bodies? One reason may very well be that scholars and researchers of academic institutions tend to be adverse to regulatory measures. This group is viscerally 'anti-regulatory'; that is, according to Roger King (2007: 151), 'regulatory scholarship for higher education researchers is regarded as either empirically inapplicable or normatively suspect'. The breakdown of internal hierarchies and control was implemented, and they were replaced by external controls and by external boards that included all kinds of professionals nominated by the government. Acting as professional board members, the same professionals often participate in diverse public-service institutions, and possess skills that are normally different from those of the internal professionals. The aim is to have top-paid, professional managing directors who possess the one supposed skill of professional management: the general leading and controlling of the internal professionals.

In Anglo-Saxon states and in states heavily influenced by this administrative tradition, the notion of the transformed self-regulation tends to indicate certain ideological overtones: independence from the hierarchy, facilitating local empowerment, more efficiency, reduced power of trade unions, the inclusion of interest groups, and equality under the 'law'. This tradition, however, often overlooks the fact that the state plays a large directing role, albeit a regulatory one by establishing, for instance, economic incentives, rules, surveillance, and budgets bound to output and results.

The institutions after the transformation follow the idea of management by objectives. The government sets the objectives, decides the regulatory framework, and allocates financial means in accordance with the reported achievements and regulation, but otherwise there are no interventions. Hence, under the umbrella of the board's decision-making, there are proclamations of enlarged and decentralized institutional autonomy. Profession-based, self-regulating service-providing institutions have become what some have termed 'formal organizations' (Røvik 2007). 'Formal organization' indicates an understanding of organizations as basically universal and similar in structure with respect to mechanisms for command and control. Accordingly, this term implies that management is a universal skill applicable to any professional service, regardless of the substance of the provision and the particular professional skill needed in order to secure quality and the innovation of processes and offers.

Besides transforming the concept of self-regulation, the trend of managing by objectives, that is, the management of formal organizations and governance by contracts, , also takes power away from the trade unions and other interest groups. This feature is particularly pronounced in Anglo-Saxon states, but it also appears in other countries where the regulatory state rules. Chapter 5 describes a Nordic approach to the issue of trade-union power. The Scandinavian countries have traditionally scored high on the different measures for the presence of strong trade unions and their involvement, in short, corporatism. Corporatism is one of the institutions that enhance consensual policy-making. However, as we have noted, traditional corporatist structures are, for several reasons, under erosion. The current inclusion of interest groups in policy-making bodies is much less comparable to the heyday of corporatism in the 1970s, and the inclusion of interest groups in policy-implementing bodies varies greatly. Chapter 5 concludes that while they are still strong in Denmark, they have been strongly reduced in Norway, and Sweden is somewhere in the middle. The question is if and to which extent this development is a sign of the withering away of consensual politics or if it is only a sign of greater flexibility in the way political and bureaucratic actors interfere with strong interest groups. Answers derived from this comparative analysis highlight the self-regulatory concept.

The strong attachment of the people, politicians, and scholars to the idea of self-regulation makes the idea extremely powerful across the Western democracies. As a consequence, it is common to hear the invocation of the traditional language of self-regulation to justify the institutional arrangements that currently characterize the regulatory state. We may not, however, by any sense or imagination equate the term of 'self-regulation' of today with the traditional term of self-regulation. The earlier use of the term refers to the regulatory state principle of 'steering by rowing', while the new use refers to the opposite principle of 'steering without rowing'. These principles are contextually defined and must be used accordingly.

Few self-regulatory agreements were immune to change. Nor was the earlier, internal, professional self-regulation of higher education and university research. The reorganization of this self-regulatory system regarding the state funding of research was launched and executed over the last ten years. The Nordic countries also became involved in this process of innovation. In Norway, it was not before 2006 that a substantial change came into force with a self-regulatory model of incentives for scientific publishing. The rules of the model set requirements for the inclusion of publications and the extra scoring for publications of high quality. The rules decide, not professional referees (Gabrielsen, Kaarbøe, Lommerud, Risa, & Vagstad 2007).

Formalization of Relationships

The formalization of relationships within domains of regulated policy is a notion that entails legal agreements and contract-based relationships. This notion suggests that the deliberative discourses and the discretionary powers have been reduced in the current multi-level system of governance.

The reduction of discretionary powers has been due partly to the importance of European law and rules penetrating local and national levels without deliberation and without being decided in elected assemblies, partly to the role of new public management and processes of agencification, which create unelected regulatory agencies, and partly to the trend of formalizing relationships in the public sector as public-public or public-private partnerships, or of contracting out the provision of public services. Not only are formal laws and rules closely bound to the regulatory state order, partnership formations and contract-based governance are as well.

THE STUDY OF REGULATORY INNOVATION

Thus, the study of regulation[8] in the broad field of politics has concentrated on four interrelated policy choices (Lodge 2003): the privatization of services formerly provided by public institutions and organizations, the emergence of self-regulatory unelected agencies, which also have quasi-legislative power for economic regulation of marketized activities, and the formalization of relationships such as contract-based partnerships within particular policy domain. Linked to the marketizing and formalization choices has been the growing use of outsourcing of public-service provisions, for example, public tendering procedures. In these interrelated fields the growing presence and importance of EU legislation are significant. Thus, studies of the supranational level of the EU and corresponding national levels of analyses have focused on the organizational forms of the regulatory state (arm's-length agencies and bodies, including partnerships), or processes of multi-level governance and regulatory change and innovation (Kjær 2004). Finally, the studies concentrate on selective sectoral approaches with the goal of taming the 'risk society' (Beck 92, Veggeland 2009). The long list of cases of risk globally involves economic, social, ethnic, and environmental problems, such as ethics and challenges to bad governance (Rothstein and Torell 2005).

According to Charles Edquist,[9] innovation in its broadest sense was traditionally viewed to take place as a consequence of processes leading to either new goods, new technologies, organizational change or new private service provisions, all being products that are successful in the market, see Figure 1 below. The public sector and its actors of infrastructure and service providers were not part of this production order because of their being organized beyond market competition and driven by political objectives and budgetary allocations. Central planning and predictive bureaucratic administration ought not to give any room for innovative actions. However, in the contemporary modernized society, the public sector has

---

[8] The idea of 'regulation' as a political process is arguably rooted in its etymology. The term 'regulation' is rooted in the Latin 'regulare' (to control by rule) and appears in the English language just before the Westphalian Treaty of 1648. By 1715, 'regulation' was defined as 'rule for management'. A regulator was established as a member of a commission or board to manage governance.

[9] Lecture held at Lillehammer University College, Norway, 28 January 2009.

moved far away from the Weberian ideal of bureaucracy and has been brought into accordance with the principles of NPM (Kjær 2004). This transformation into hybrid and self-regulatory organizations results in new conditions for innovation and for innovative activity in the public sector for the production of services and the processes leading up to them.

Among other, LSE Public Policy Group, UK, (2008:6) expands this trend and talks about innovations as new ideas which are: 'New to world/UK, New to public sector/voluntary sector, New to region/locality, New to this government organization'. Furthermore, the arrival of the regulatory state has expanded the perspective on regulation in general. Regulation has come to mean a new sort of necessary societal service, a kind of product of public governance and steering. Studies have made it clear that each regulation is best understood as an impetus for an unspecified range of new regulations, in other words, 'hyper' regulatory innovations for the sake of realizing the original one, with explanatory references to spill-over processes (Moran 2001). Consequently, given the growing number of regulations to be administrated and implemented, we also see the introduction of the new regulatory agencies and bodies, that is, agencification as organizational innovation.

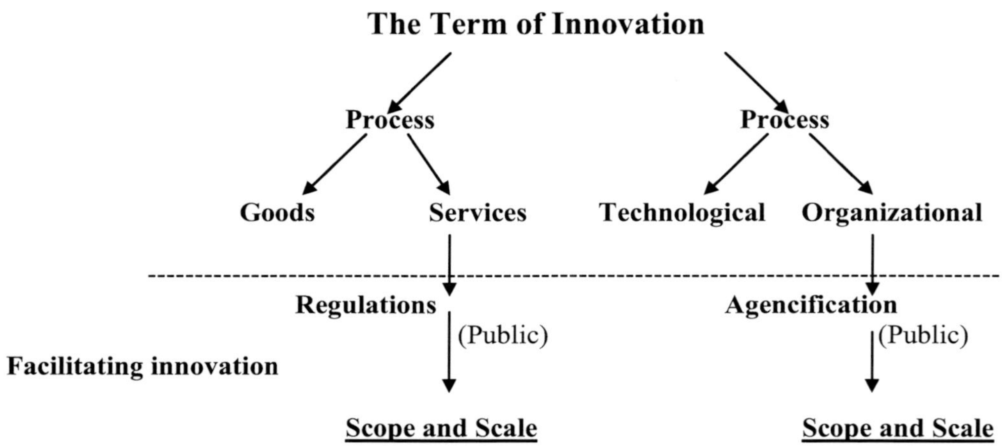

Figure 1. Innovation in the regulatory state, a new perspective

The EU offers a good example. The EU's regulatory and monetary measure system is closely linked to European agencies and bodies. They certainly have a legal role in the economic and social domains of its member states. At the national level regulation is followed up by the bodies responsible for implementation and the agencies responsible for surveillance and control. They also represent organizational innovations. According to Black, Lodge and Thatcher (2005), 'regulatory innovation' is part of the extended terms of references in the framework of innovation in the private and public domains. Figure 1 illustrates this broad perspective on innovation.

Figure 1 indicates: In the regulatory state regulation represents in itself a kind of service making, by scope and scale, markets, institutions and communities functioning. Regulation is understood as the deliberate and sustained attempt to alter the behaviour of others towards standards and goals that are mostly produced by public-sector actors but processed by agencies and other governmental bodies. The proposed model of innovation has a focus on regulation that facilitates innovation and may fit with state activities involved in processes of regulatory delivery and processes of making contracts between actors, for instance, partnership contracts. However, it needs adjustment to apply regulations in a wider sense. We have already drawn attention to five explanatory conceptions of regulation that point to five key areas benefiting from regulatory services. These are regulations (1) as authoritative rules, (2) as efforts of state agencies to manage the economy, (3) as mechanisms of steering and performing legal control, (4) as extensions of multi-level governance and network co-ordination, and (5) as means and measures to handle environmental threats and the 'risk society of the new modernity' in general (Beck 1992). To sum up, we are talking about innovations in regulatory processes, in risk identification and reduction, and in risk analysis and management (Sparrow 2000). It is fully feasible to study the intensity and inclination of innovation in this context. Studies focused on the scope and scale of newly implemented regulations may indicate quite effectively the degree of innovative ability and performance related to the three listed fields or aspects of state governance and areas of responsibility (Veggeland 2007).

Agencification performance, Figure 1, is a key element of the regulatory state order. Our presentation of four characteristics of this order included the marketizing of public-sector services. Marketizing relates closely to the other characteristics, that is, the establishment of 'unelected' arm's-length agencies and regulatory bodies, the transformation of institutional self-regulation into external control, and the formalization of relationships within policy domains, embodied as institutionalizing agreements and contract-based relationships. We may label these collectively as parts of the processes of 'agencification', illustrated in Figure 1. The study of innovation of the regulatory state in this respect focuses on processes favouring new scopes and scales regarding not only public surveillance and control, but also service provision and management linked to agencies. There is, then a concentration on legal European and national acts and institutional changes and reforms within the framework of regulatory governance and goal-achievement. The ability to innovate in the public sector is measurable by its political acceptance and functionality, and innovative frequency gives an indication on innovative intensity (Mørth, 2004).

Innovation of Institutions and Regulations

If we define all innovation simply as change, then we must conclude that all changes are innovative. This definition, however, is unsatisfactory and leads to an equally unsatisfactory conclusion. This lack of precision has inspired studies on the criteria of change and innovation. One aspect relates to the distinction between subjectivity and objectivity. An innovation may be an individual and personal experience of subjective change. An individual changes his or her work routine according to a given labour regulation and adjusts to it in a way that best suits his or her daily life. Though the regulation may not at all be an innovation and instead one adopted by diffusion from somewhere else, the personal experience might very well be one of innovation. In contrast, from a perspective of governance, there is more focus on the fact that innovation is an objective experience that can be empirically measured as change of progress of a significant magnitude. Researchers can identify laws and regulations that introduce new work routines for environmental treatment, improvement of productivity or hospital care, for instance, and count them conveniently as technological innovations (Black, Lodge, Thatcher 2005).

The concept of innovation differs from the concept of invention. Innovation, both subjective and objective, differs from policy inventions or ideas that have not been implemented (Rogers 2003). What characterize innovation are the efforts to rejuvenate and the presence of benevolent motives. In this view, regulations are service goods produced to help stabilize a society and to counteract risks or to offer another way of organizing the society by agencifications, namely, unelected agencies and other arm's-length bodies (see Figure 1). Hence, regulatory innovations have two faces.

In the regulatory state, institutional innovations are part of the organizational changes of processes as indicated by Figure 1. Innovation in institutional structures and organizational processes includes the creation of new organizations in the form of agencies, and the innovation of regulatory services when the norms, rules, and standards of operating procedures undergo change. In simple terms, innovation denotes the use of new solutions for old problems, or of old solutions to address 'new' problems. Generally, innovation is a facet of the modernist project of rationalization, systematization, and ordering (Meyer 2000).

Regulatory innovations take place in different contexts, such as different administrative traditions and models like the Anglo-Saxon, Continental, and Scandinavian or Nordic traditions (Knill 2001, Veggeland 2007). One can measure innovation in the particular context of a geographical area (state, region or municipality), or a policy domain (welfare, social, and physical environment), some other unit of analysis (organizational or individual), or a mixture of different regulatory approaches. The last approach could be a study on the economic regulations in the EU, social regulations in Scandinavia or environmental regulations in the Arctic region.

Regulatory Innovation – A Case of Scandinavian Involvement with the EU

The diffusion of EU law and regulations impinge on the national states under the dominance of this supranational, multi-level regime of governance. Much concern has been directed to the questions of the manner in which the member states pronounce, translate, and implement these regulations and what may be the best way to do so; such questions demand a historical consideration of each state's administrative tradition and welfare-state model (Knill 2001, Iversen 2005, Veggeland 2007). In our context, we may propose two theses (Røvik 2007):

A The copying or imitation thesis: When a state adapts and implements a regulatory act, for instance, a European Union directive, the state may very well take the act literally, and each member state imitates and copies the style of implementation from others, most often from the most dominant states and ideologies within the Community. Such copying activities do not lead to regulatory innovation.

B The innovation thesis: The public authorities of a given member state that administer the legal aspects and the implementation of European Union regulations recognize their own administrative traditions. Hence, their translation aims for adjustments through reformulations, that is, re-regulations. They do so in order to achieve national or local political objectives in a legally sound manner. We may name this practice as modernization by regulatory innovations (Black et al., 2005).

Let us consider these theses more closely by examining a Scandinavian case. First, we must describe an EU-adopted regulation on public procurement from the early 1990s. This regulation demands that all public purchases that are not in-house provisions of goods and services over the marginal cost level of 200 000 Euros are required to be exposed to market competition through tendering and outsourcing. This exposure is to take the form of open or partly open tendering and bidding rounds and the contracting out of the provisions to the private providers who win each of the many bidding rounds.

Next, we must account briefly for the background. We are focusing here on the EEA negotiations at the beginning of 1990 between EFTA countries and the EU in regard to an agreement for access to the single market of the EU. The countries in question entered into the EEA agreement, but Sweden, then an EFTA country, instead became an EU member in 1994 while Norway continued its status as an EEA country. The EEA agreement included the EU's supranational set of rules and directives regarding the public purchasing of products and services. Procedures with, at that time, a dividing line of 200 000 Euros (1 600 000 Norwegian krones (NOK)) were established for such purchases. Purchases for lower values did not require competition and bidding; purchases over this value were included in the directive. Moreover, in order to ensure compliance, Norway was placed under the EFTA Surveillance Agency (ESA).

As with many other EU member states there were substantial obstacles and scepticism towards the introduction of outsourcing in the public sector in Scandinavian societies (Veggeland 2004). This reticence was due to path-dependency, popular and social-democratic concerns about private-sector involvement in traditional public activities. The other concern was related to the fact that, despite the great technical variety, from the Scandinavian perspective of a universal welfare state, very few services would not be liable to outsourcing. The lack of clarity on the issue of which 'services of general interest'[10] (EU Green paper 2003) ought to remain in-house provisions or to be exposed to competition became defined as an attack on the universal welfare state. The challenge to existing public-service provision also triggered resistance from affected public employees, unions, and their political allies. Finally, some perceived the outsourcing game as one where private big businesses would come out as winners and consequently unbalance the Scandinavian mixed economy by enervating small- and medium-sized businesses (SMBs) and hurting local and regional economies.

This general scepticism towards expanding the outsourcing concept and bringing it in accordance with the EU directive had considerable implications. The Scandinavian states introduced innovative re-regulation, which was influenced by the EEA agreement and also probably by the traditions of 'small is beautiful' and the welfare state. Norway and Sweden set the dividing line for bidding much lower than what the EU regime required,

---

[10] The EU defines the term 'services of general interest' as public services, which the government provides and ought to provide under universal obligation. The diversification of this type of services for in-house provision or outsourcing still heavily disputed within the Union (see the dispute on the 'service directive').

NOK 200,000[11] and SEK 200,000, respectively. The decision resulted in a much more extensive use of bidding and outsourcing than if the EU's marginal value for public purchasing had been applied. The decision was legal because the EU directive had no restrictions against lower national limits for biddings and competition, and, therefore, the directive was open to interpretation and translation (Veggeland 2005). Obviously, a great deal of public purchases would exceed this amount owing to the relatively high levels of prices and costs in the two Scandinavian countries.

Why, then, does this adaptation and setting of a lower limit count as an instance of regulatory innovation? It counts because the authorities in both countries recognized and adhered to their administrative traditions and models. This fact thus lends support to thesis B. Likewise, the authorities neither copied nor imitated the EU regulation of public procurements and the use of outsourcing, but made instead a decision quite of their own making – a re-regulation that points to innovation thesis B.

What resulted from this independent and innovative turn on outsourcing and the two Scandinavian regulatory solutions in the wake of this specific Europeanization mode of institutional penetration? The innovation entailed both positive and negative impacts according to certain criteria. On the positive side was the incentive for SMBs to participate in the markets created by the use of this particular outsourcing concept of public administration. Small providers with limited resources for investment gained the opportunity to participate and adjust its activities to the competition for public procurement and tendering owing to the low level of regulatory cost. Numerous and flexible SMBs came out as winners in a large number of bidding rounds. In their becoming contractors, they contributed to a significant creation of employment, and private and public services spread all over in the two Scandinavian countries, thereby sustaining territorial and social balance in the states' mixed economies (Veggeland 2007). The negative side of this re-regulation gradually became apparent as rising transactional costs began to emerge. The transactional costs rose in the public sector owing to the extensive administration required for each rounds of bidding, the evaluation of offers from the many providers, and the ensuing procedures related to contracting and control. Also, for many providers allotted many resources in vain because the participation in the many rounds of bidding could not always turn out successfully (Scharpf 1997, Veggeland 2004).

In short, these empirical facts from this Scandinavian example support the thesis B of innovation: the regulatory public authorities in the two countries acted innovatively in relation to the EU's regulatory regime. It was a path-dependent, contextual innovation, and not an imitation.

Dilemmas of the Regulatory State

The regulatory state order is not only of interest as a subject for empirical exploration, but it is also the site of significant dilemmas, which highlight crucial issues affecting states globally. This section explores four dilemmas of the regulatory state that not only suggest

---

[11] In 2005, the amount was increased to NOK 500 000 by the government.

reasons for instability with policy and democratic deficits, but also more fundamental dysfunctions.

The Dilemma of the Numerous Regulatory Agencies

The huge number of so-called public or semi-public 'unelected' bodies (Vibert 2007) that wield power in the structures of modern democratic states comes often as a surprise to many. It should not, however, because the appearance of such bodies is closely connected to the arrival of the regulatory state (OECD 2002). Different terminology is used to describe these bodies. Many are named 'regulatory agencies', meaning that either they are regulated producers of services or they are legally empowered to be auditing and controlling agencies (Braithwaite 2008: 56). The intention of the international and national central authorities is in line with the regulatory state order to 'govern without rowing', that is, not to act as executives but as regulators. The bodies may operate with different degrees of autonomy and also take different legal forms, depending on their being subject to public or private law, or 'Public Law Agencies' (PLAs) or 'Private Law Bodies' (PLBs), respectively (OECD 2002: 18-19).

This first dilemma emerges from the political element of the regulatory process. Governments are behind the granting of arm's-length autonomy, that is to say, a certain distance from direct political interests and involvements; this arrangement is at best a vulnerable construction. In the regulatory state politicians decide goals and budgets, but grant regulatory bodies full authority over specific decisions and promise more or less their 'abdication' in certain fields. In exchange, the politicians benefit from proclaiming that they have offered the solution to a given problem to those constituents benefiting from this regulatory regime. The dilemma is connected to the division of responsibility. If something goes wrong, who is to blame? Is it the government or the arm's-length body? In the regulatory state, a certain idiom of politics seems ubiquitous, 'the politics of blame avoidance' (Weaver 1986). The sharing of authority and responsibility makes both of the two shareholders primarily interested in avoiding blame. The politicians tend to take both the responsibility and the honour of regulatory successes, but disavow the regime when failures occur. Consequently, the unelected bodies blame the government for bad budgetary balances, excessively narrow regulatory frameworks, and duplicity when success fails to materialize. Bargaining processes then stagnate and a reduction of innovative capacity affects the public domain.

Furthermore, public-private partnerships, together with the hybrid form of public-public partnership,[12] count as regulatory agencies. In the regulatory state, partnerships are established as institutional instruments aimed at mobilizing and facilitating activity in multi-actor and multi-level settings. 'End-mean' thinking dominates the notion of partnership. In regional politics and planning at the European level and the national level as well, these aspects are quite obvious. Network contacts, negotiations, and bargaining launch processes that target agreements and contracts between public and private regional actors and multi-level administrations. The goal is to reach achievements that are made feasible through co-operation and increased steering capacity, the latter embedded in the agreements. The sharing of authority and responsibility makes the shareholders interested in co-operation rather than

---

12 The notion of public-public partnership actually indicates a hybrid organization even though it is all public, because public administrations and public service providers have been split up and made independent arm's-length bodies furnished with the legal authority to sign agreements and contracts.

competition. The concept of regional partnerships is the government's preferred policy for extending territorial competition within the regulatory state.

The dilemma here is that judicial agreement-based governance and regulatory mechanisms move the direction from traditional democratic governance, which derives its legitimacy from the representative decision-making of the elected, to a model where legitimacy depends on the partnership's capacity to accomplish goals and achieve results; in short, legitimacy becomes a legitimacy of output (Veggeland 2003). There are two conflicting regimes, and the balance between them is hard to strike. But there is no doubt that the regulatory state has a bias for the output model. Still, the friction between the two may disrupt settled agreements and decrease innovative capacity at the regional and local levels. Chapter 2 makes a contribution to the understanding of the role of management by objectives and the dilemmas this role reveals. This chapter gives an introduction on the use of this type of NPM governance in the Scandinavian administrative model, and this comparative case study from Denmark and Norway makes it possible to widen the perspective on types of local administration and democracy.

The Dilemma of Hyper-Regulation Leading to Hyper-Innovation

Regulation in one sector or on one level of administration tends to generate new regulations as 'spill-over' in the neo-functionalist sense (Strøby Jensen 2004). The creation of regulatory measures and means generates further regulatory innovations. The dilemma, then, is that innovation tends to create hyper-innovation in the regulatory state. Michael Moran's thesis (2003:26) is that innovation in institutional affairs has been a 'fiasco' that has engendered more innovation in an ever ascending, or more accurately descending, spiral. He argues that in the United Kingdom over the last 30 or so years have been an era of 'hyper-innovation', 'the frenetic selection of new institutional modes, and their equally frenetic replacement by alternatives' (Moran 2003:26).

Consequences of these trends are multiple. One is the growing lack of transparency regarding regulatory administrations due to the number of regulations and innovations and the frequency of institutional changes. Holistic approaches become lost and as do the possibilities of political co-ordination and steering ability. Rising transactional costs connected to fragmented administrative functions are a well-known repercussion (Scharpf 1997). We may observe in Scandinavia and the rest of Europe a direction of reforms since the 1980s towards more hierarchy, more formality, and more state control, 'These observations can be reconciled with prevailing images of the regulatory state, but at tremendous intellectual cost', concludes Moran (2003: 9).

In the regulatory state there seems to be a need for criteria in order to evaluate outcomes. As we have seen above, if we wish to be able to determine whether or not regulatory innovations have led to 'successes' or 'fiascos', good or bad governance, even though it is difficult and too rarely done, we need some criteria against which we can make these assessments. The criteria might be formulated either as standards, social rights or as ethical norms and values (Veggeland 2009). The last chapter of this book presents an example of research that critically analyses such criteria with reference to international investment funds.

The Dilemma of Exponential Rise of Transactional Costs

An OECD report from 2002 (2002: 21-26) drew its conclusions about the dilemmas connected to the regulatory state, and another report, 'Modernising Government: the way forward' (OECD 2005) analysed them further. These reports have raised the following points:

- In most countries, and in line with the new democratic principles, priorities have moved away from the inclination to create new independent and separate bodies. Now the challenge seems to be finding the right balance between accountability, autonomy, and management of the existing independent agencies and bodies through more openness and transparency, as well as by strengthening the steering capacity of governments.
- The new unelected technocratic entities allow governments to avoid taking political decisions or to take decisions guided only by technical expertise on issues that require a political choice and that are at the core of political responsibility.
- The lack of clarity about the differences between the various types of agencies, authorities, and corporations makes it unclear whether the best organizational forms have been chosen for the various purposes of government. Instead, there has been the implementation of standardizing measures.
- Governmental monitoring efforts and control of the independent public entities are becoming more difficult. Despite the presence of reporting procedures and of neutral agencies for legal surveillance, the different types of relationships and mechanisms of control and accountability make accurate control almost impossible.
- The lack of clarity of the institutional system potentially undermines citizens' trust in the systems functions.
- There is an acknowledgement of the need for clearer criteria for establishing different types of boards – advisory, management or governing boards, and their respective responsibilities. There has been criticism of the lack of transparency surrounding the appointments of board members, their salaries, and other benefits. Other criticisms have focused on the lack of representative status of the members with respect to gender, ethnic, and local background.
- The independent bodies are seen as functioning outside political debate, as with little oversight from ministers and ministries, and as having weak arrangements for accountability. The parliaments are neglected, and so are individuals and institutions of civil society. The conclusion is that weak mechanisms of accountability undermine the legitimacy of governments and parliaments.
- Finally, weak mechanisms of co-ordination and failures of coherence threaten effective public-service production in relation to the 'best value' for individuals, social groups, and corporate interests because of fragmented governance.

With regard to the last point on weak co-ordinating mechanisms, we may refer to what has been called Scharpf's Law (Hooghe and Marks (2001:5)): 'As the number of affected parties increases .... negotiated solutions incur exponentially rising and eventually prohibitive transaction costs' (Scharpf 1997:70). In the regulatory state system, according to this law, the problems of technical, communicative or legal co-ordination connected to the involvement of the many actors and bodies escalate immensely with the growing numbers, and the transactional costs will ultimately be prohibitive. Scharpf's Law insists that the weak co-ordinating mechanisms of the reporting countries are not evidence of poor performance of public governance, but actually a *consequence* of the regulatory state itself because of its inclination to spur hyper-regulation and hyper-innovation (Veggeland 2009).

Therefore, according to the earlier of the two OECD reports (2002), there is a growing focus on *good governance and more coherent public services*, that is, on solutions of policy and structural coherence, including having the autonomous bodies collaborate on joint projects and in public-public partnerships. Further, the focus of the states in the study is reported to be on these following endeavours: (a) the attempt to avoid the creation of new independent agencies, public service enterprises, and autonomous bodies; (b) the increased involvement of civil society and the governments in governance; (c) the improvement of parliamentary control over activities to achieve more holistic responsibility; and finally, (d) the recognition of a growing political will to make the overall system more legible and accessible to citizens, and the accountability mechanisms, activities, and performance more easily controllable by parliaments on all tiers and in accordance with the principle of subsidiarity.

The European Union seems now to take this last principle seriously. According to the EU, decision-making on all fields in the Union should be on the lowest possible but effective level. The Treaty of Maastricht of 1993 introduced this principle of subsidiarity more as a political guideline than as a juridical norm because of the elasticity of the formula. The new Treaty of Lisbon, whose ratification is expected in 2010, will transform subsidiarity into a hard regulation, which means that conflicts of the member states with the Union on issues of competence may be brought to the European Court of Justice to get a solution. It is clear, then, that there is a political will to make the overall system of the future more transparent and more resistant to the development of more hierarchical structures.

The Dilemma of Democratic and Legitimacy Deficits

As we have seen the unelected public agencies and bodies in the regulatory state have become so pervasive that we take them for granted and rarely reflect on how they fit together and relate more broadly to the principles of democratic government and good governance. Regulations and the regulatory state order have been widely utilized to apply frameworks taken from elsewhere and therefore have been used as 'dependent variables'. Such an approach sets the regulatory state as a dependent variable of the defined liberal representative democracy and its legitimacy. In this context the regulatory state appears to suffer from a deficit of democracy and legitimacy: less government *by* the people, more government *for* the people (Scharpf 1999, Veggeland 2004). The regulatory state of EU is a typical case.

The elected European Parliament is still a politically weak governmental institution, and remote from the arenas where the most crucial decisions are made. Even so, innumerable laws and regulations are decided every year and implemented in the EU member and associate states. The national governments have become instruments subordinated to unelected regulatory bodies that implement regulations, which penetrate administrations from the national to the local levels. Contextually, the issue of democratic deficit appears per definition, but in what sense?

As a general phenomenon of the regulatory state, democratic deficit implies that elected tier assemblies and governments have become politically weakened, while technocratic regulatory and executive authorities have gained more dominance. Accordingly, the weakening of representative political authorities creates a deficit of input democracy, accountability, and legitimacy – in short, a deficit of the government *by* the people (Scharpf 1999). Regulatory governance for the people and legal partnership institutions are replacing representative government institutions. As Michael Keating (1998:47) quipped, 'governance is what exists when government is weak and fragmented', in the sense that unelected agencies and authorities are replacing the more traditional governments with political holistic responsibilities.

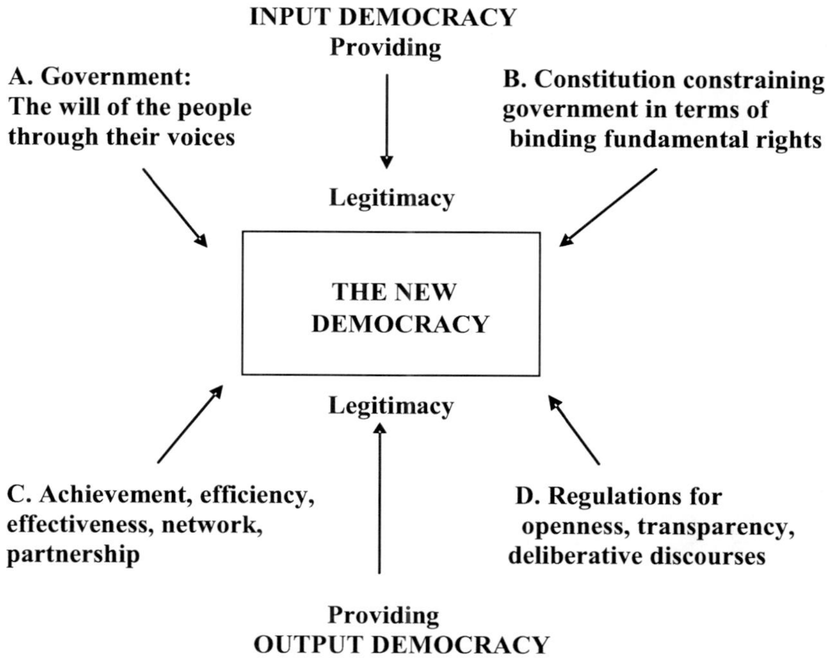

Figure 2. Characteristics of the New Democracy

In the regulatory state, policies gain their legitimacy first and foremost from achievements, efficiency, and effectiveness, that is, from the output or outcome of agencies and executives (Lane and Ersson 2003:183-209). This output legitimacy challenges the traditional principles of parliamentary democracy and the liberal values of openness, transparency, and deliberative decision-making (Scharpf 1999, Veggeland 2004). Figure 2 illustrates some basic principles of both the input and output democratic orders (Veggeland 2003).

According to Figure 2 the regulatory state constitutes both dependent and independent variables. The side of input democracy, together with the constraints of the Constitution, substantiates parliamentary democracy. But the function and legitimacy of these input elements depend very much on the organization of the regulatory state. Keating's (1998) statement that governance is what exists when government is weak and fragmented indicates that regulatory governance challenges and threatens the input democratic order. The solution would appear, then, to involve the restoration of this order by the building of strong and less fragmented government. Politically this strategy is feasible in the European multi-level system of government and would increase the legitimacy of the new double-sided democracy.

On the other hand, the European regulatory state will basically continue to rely on an output democratic order owing to the new democratic order, which the bottom half of Figure 2 shows. We must, then, consider the output order in itself as an independent variable, which affects dependent variables like achievements, efficiency, effectiveness, networks, and partnerships. However, this output or outcome democracy faces two threats: one from the unelected regulatory type of agencies and bodies and the other from their 'locked-in' management that undermines the principles of openness, transparency, and deliberative discourse. In the new democracy, a strong political will is crucial to secure and strengthen these dependent variables.

Obviously, there are several reasons behind the deficit of input and output democracy described here, but generally the deficit is linked to the 'borderless' network-society syndrome, the processes of globalization, and the approach of multi-level governance characteristic of the regulatory states (Habermas 1999, Scharpf 1999, Veggeland 2009).

REGULATION THROUGH ETHICS

Public innovation is a key part of the debate on 'reinventing government' (Osborne and Gaebler 1993) and 'rediscovering institutions' (March and Olsen 1989). National loan capital-driven economies, as some economists (e.g., Lordon 2003) predicted years ago, are in a state of disorder. A serious international financial crisis surfaced in 2008, initially triggered by the largely deficit-driven US economy. And worse, these developments have debilitated monetarist manoeuvres to regulate the economy on the national level because of the international interdependence of financial markets, capital movements, free-trade arrangements, and more (Jordana and Levi-Faur, 2004). What, then, will be the monetarists' measures or manoeuvres? It is inconceivable to imagine the regulatory approach and the arm's-length agencies of the national states that have proliferated in the recent decades will now begin to retreat. On the contrary, the best prediction is that state regulation, backed by law, will grow in importance (Stiglitz 2009). Further, a transformation of national regulatory measures into global ones, which seemingly is a necessary response to this particular crisis, would not be surprising. Innovation in the form of supranational regulation of financial policy could start with international negotiations and agreements that lead to new agencies and a swarm of regulations – or the strengthening of old global agencies, like we see happening today with the International Monetary Fund (IMF).

Can we suppose that such measures will tame the regulatory state that is currently in trouble? Frédéric Lordon, economist and the author of *Et la vertu sauvera le monde... Après la débâcle financière, le salut par l'« éthique »?* [*And virtue is going to save the world....After the financial catastrophe, the salvation by "ethics"?*] (2003), gives this introduction to the character of the new crisis, a crisis rooted in the techno-economic system of the regulatory state. In his analysis he foreshadows the current financial troubles and identifies the failures that triggered them (Lordon 2008:1). According to Lordon there is a need for an ethical regulatory approach in order to tame and rescue Western supply-side economics from a vast recession. There is much to the notion of ethics viewed as part of economic policy and dynamics, even if it has for the most been overlooked.

Certainly, ethics was neither part of the Keynesian-investment and effective-demand policy nor part of the Schumpeterian, market-driven idea of 'creative-destruction' that spurs economic growth. But in the thinking about revitalizing modes of welfare-state economies since the 1970s, ethics in the sense of favouring social equality and security as basic for good economic governance, along with the fight against corruption, has come into much greater focus (Veggeland 2009; Iversen, 2005; Taylor-Gooby, 2004).

In the petroleum-producing state of Norway, revenues from the production are put into a fund for investment abroad. In 2004, the government took action in order to regulate this investment fund. Chapter 6 discusses how the Norwegian government established and developed the Norwegian petroleum industry by creating its own oil company, Statoil, (now StatoilHydro) and by giving attractive concessions and regulatory protection to the Norwegian supply industry since the 1970s. This chapter especially emphasizes the natural-gas sector. Government policy and structures gradually changed as the industry matured and the conditions of markets, international petroleum policies, and technologies have changed (Austvik 2003).

The Norwegian petroleum sector now consists of more companies with the ability to compete on the international scale. The state plays a more regulative role, but remains the main rent collector and capitalist in this sector. Chapter 6 also addresses the role of the petroleum fund, and considers what might have happened if the Norwegian petroleum resources had been founded under the more liberal international economic regime of today. It also compares how the UK, Canada, and Russia have arranged their petroleum industries, and takes into consideration the current international financial crisis. This chapter, moreover, discusses further how Norway's integration with the EU has affected that country's Scandinavian administrative tradition of implementing in general a policy of strong involvement of the state in the oil and gas sector, and the state's role both as regulator and as a receiver of revenues from the sector. Chapter 6 analyses to which degree a nation-state can adjust its powerful interventionist policy to the EU's more liberal organization and regulation of economic activities while simultaneously maintaining nationally defined goals.

Chapter 7 offers an analysis of the ethical aspects of international investment funds, with the Norwegian Petroleum Fund as a case. In 2004 the Storting (the Norwegian Parliament) adopted regulatory ethical guidelines to help ensure the integrity of the investments of the 'Government Petroleum Fund'. Two years later, the government renamed this fund the 'Government Pension Fund – Global', in order to reflect a social-institutional change guided with ethical intentions. According to this chapter, the primary objective of the fund's ethical guidelines is to ensure that current and future generations in Norway will benefit from good returns from the fund. The government thus channels the return yielded by the fund into the state budget to cover state debt. The government will continue to do this for the foreseeable future. The upper limit for annual use in the real economy is the entire return. The return has been around four per cent on average in recent years (90 billion NOK). The Minister of Finance has called this policy 'generational solidarity'.

Ethically, this 'solidarity' expresses the government's wish to avoid encumbering the owners, that is, the citizens, with debt. Ideally, the current generation and future generations in Norway will be free of debt as a result of this strategy. For the many nations currently finding themselves in a deep debt crisis, being free from debt is in itself an almost unachievable privilege.

International commentators have stated that the fund's ethical dimensions represent the gold standard among major institutional investments funds around the world (Time 2008). The government has identified itself with this lofty aim on several occasions. The Report to the Storting, No. 16 (2006-2007), confidently states that 'the fund shall be the best in the world'. The Ministry of Foreign Affairs insists that Norway has become a world leader with regard to taking ethical considerations into the management of the Norwegian Government Pension Fund (Ministry of Foreign Affairs 2008). A political statement, which shall not be easy to follow up in a world where complex economic interests rule. Only future research can make judgements on that matter, and only after criteria have been formulated and international conventions agreed upon for what is good governance and sustained regulatory approaches, based on innovative and effective hard and soft regulations.

References

Amdam, J. & Veggeland, N. (1998). *Teorier om samfunnsplanlegging* [*Theories on Social Planning*]. Oslo: Universitetsforlaget.

Austvik, O.A. (2003). *Norwegian natural gas: Liberalization of the European gas market.* Oslo: Europa-programmet.

Baldwin, R. and Cave, M. (1999). *Understanding regulation: Theory, strategy, and practice.* Oxford: Oxford University Press.

Baldwin, R., Scott, C., & Hood, C. (Eds.) 1998). *A reader on regulation.* Oxford: Oxford University Press.

Beck, U. (1992). *Risk society: Towards a new modernity.* London: Sage Publications.

Black, J. (2005). What is regulatory innovation? In J. Black, M. Lodge, & M. Thatcher (Eds.), *Regulatory innovation: A comparative analysis.* Cheltenham, UK: Edward Elgar.

Black, J., Lodge, M., & Thatcher, M. (Eds.) (2005). *Regulatory innovation: A comparative analysis.* Cheltenham, UK: Edward Elgar Publishing.

Braithwaite, J. (2008). *Regulatory capitalism: How it works, ideas for making it work better.* Cheltenham, UK: Edward Elgar.

Castells, M. (1996). *The Rise of the Network Society.* Oxford: Blackwell.

Cass, D. (2005). *The constitutionalization of the World Trade Organization: Legitimacy, democracy and community in the international trading system.* Oxford: Oxford University Press.

Christensen, T. & Lægreid, P. (Eds.). (2006). *Autonomy and regulations: Coping with agencies in the modern state.* Cheltenham, UK: Edward Elgar.

EU green paper. (2003). *Services of General Interest.* Brussels: COM (2003) 270 European Commission.

Gabrielsen, T. S., Kaarbøe, O., Lommerud, K. E., Risa, A. E., & Vagstad, S. (2007). *Finansieringssystemet for universitets- og høyskolesektoren - teoretiske vurderinger* [*The Financial System for the University and College Sector: Theoretical Evaluations*]. Bergen: University of Bergen

Habermas, J. (1987). *The Theory of Communicative Action.* Cambridge: Polity Press.

Hood, Chr., Rothstein, H., & Baldwin, R. (2004). *The government of risk: Understanding risk regulation regimes*. Oxford: Oxford University Press.

Hooghe, L. & Marks, G. (2001). Types of multi-level governance. *European Integration Online Papers, 5* (11).

Iversen, T. (2005). *Capitalism, democracy and welfare*. Cambridge: Cambridge University Press.

Jensen Strøby, C. (2004). Neo-functionalism. In M. Cini (Ed.), *European Union politics* (pp. 80-93) Oxford: Oxford University Press.

Jordana, J. & Levi-Faur, D. (Eds.) (2004). *The politics of regulation: Institutions' and regulatory reforms for the age of governance*. Cheltenham, UK: Edward Elgar.

Keating, M. (1998). *The new regionalism: Territorial restructuring and political change*. Cheltenham, UK: Edward Elgar.

King, R. (2007). *The regulatory state in an age of governance: Soft words and big sticks*. New York: Palgrave.

Kjær, A. M. (2004). *Governance*. Cambridge: Polity Press.

Knill, C. (2001). *The Europeanization of national administrations*. Cambridge: Cambridge University Press.

Kuper, A. (2004). *Democracy beyond borders: Justice and representation in global institutions*. Oxford: Oxford University Press.

Lane, J.E. and Ersson, S. (2003). *Democracy: A comparative approach*. London and New York: Routledge.

Lodge, J.E. (2003). Institutional choice and policy transfer: Reforming British and German railway regulation. *Governance, 16* (2), 159-78.

Lodge, M. (2007). *Regulation in regulatory state and European politics*. *www.aei.pitt.edu/7951/*

Lordon, F. (2003). *Et la vertu sauvera le monde... Après la débâcle financière, le salut par l'« éthique »?* [*And virtue is going to save the world....After the financial catastrophe, the salvation by "ethics"?*] Paris: Raisons d'agir.

LSE Public Policy Group (2008). *Innovation in government organizations and public sector agencies and public service NGOs: Draft working paper*. London: NESTA.

March, J. & Olsen, J.P. (1989). *Rediscovering institutions: The organizational basis of politics*. New York: Free Press.

May, P. (2002). *Regulations and motivations: Hard versus soft regulatory paths*. Paper presented at the 2002 Annual Meeting of the American Political Science Association, Boston.

Majone, G. (1994). The rise of the regulatory state in Europe. *West European Politics, 17* (3), 77-101.

Majone, G. (1997). From the positive to the regulatory state: causes and consequences of change in the mode of government. *Journal of Public Policy, 17* (3), 139-89.

McGowan, F. & Wallace, H. (1996). Towards a European regulatory state. *Journal of European Public Policy, 3* (4), 560-76.

Moran, M. (2001). The rise of the regulatory state in Britain. *Parliamentary Affairs, 54*, 19-34.

Moran, M. (2003). *The British regulatory State: High modernism and hyper-innovation*. Oxford: Oxford University Press.

Mørth, U. (Ed.) (2004). *Soft law in governance and regulation: An interdisciplinary analysis*. Cheltenham, UK: Edward Elgar.

OECD (2002). *Distributed public governance: Agencies, authorities and other government bodies*. Paris: OECD.

OECD (2005). *Modernising government: The way forward*. Paris: OECD.

Osborne, D. & Gaebler, T. (1993). *Reinventing government*. New York: Plume.

Pollitt, C. & Bouckaert, G. (2004). *Public management reform: A comparative analysis*. Oxford: Oxford University Press.

Pedersen, T.H. (2009). *Fra kommunale forvaltninger til 'forvaltningsløse' kommuner [From municipal administration to 'administration-free' municipalities]*. Tromsø: Tromsø Universitet.

Pierre, J. (Ed.) 2001. *Debating governance: Authority, steering and democracy*. Oxford: Oxford University Press.

Pollack, M.A. (2005). Theorizing EU Policy-Making. In H. Wallace, W. Wallace, & M.A. Pollack (Eds.), *Policy-making in the European Union* (pp. 13-49). Oxford: Oxford University Press.

Power, M. (1997). *The audit society: Rituals of verification*. Oxford: Oxford University Press.

Rodes, R.A.W. (1997). *Understanding governance*. Buckingham and Philadelphia: Open University Press.

Rogers, E.M. (2003). *Diffusion of innovations* (5th edn). New York: Free Press

Rothstein, B. & Torell (2005). *What quality of Government?* Paper presented to the Göteborg University Conference: Quality of Government.

Røvik, K.A. (2007) *Trender og translasjoner: Ideer som formet det 21. århundrets organisasjon* [*Trends and translations: Ideas that formed organizations of the twenty-first century*]. Oslo: Universitetsforlaget.

Scharpf, F. (1997). *Games real actors play: Actor-centred institutionalism in policy research*. Boulder: Westview Press.

Scharpf, F. (1999). *Governing in Europe: Effective and democratic?* Oxford: Oxford University Press.

Schumpeter, J.A. (1942/1979). *Capitalism, socialism and democracy*. London: Allen & Unwin.

Selznick, P. (1985). Focusing Organizational Research on Regulation. In R. Noll (Ed.). *Regulatory policy and the social sciences* (363-7). Berkeley: University of California Press.

Sparrow, M.K. (2000). *The regulatory craft: Controlling risks, solving problems and managing compliance*. Washington DC: Brookings Press.

Stiglitz, J. (2009). Spring is here, but contain your excitement. www.bepress.com/ev

Streeck, W. (1995). Neo-voluntarism: a new European social policy regime?. *European Law Journal, 1*, 31-59.

Time Magazine, 11 June 2008.

Taylor-Gooby, P. (Ed.) (2004). *New risks, new welfare: The transformation of the European welfare state*. Oxford: Oxford University Press.

van der Velde, M. & van Houtum, H. (2004). De-politicizing labour market indifference and immobility in the European Union. In O. Kramsch & B. Hooper (Eds.). *Cross-border governance in the European Union*. London: Routledge.

Veggeland, N. (2003). *Det nye demokratiet: et politisk laboratorium for partnerskap* [*The New Democracy: A Political Laboratory for Partnership*]. Kristiansand: Norwegian Academic Press.

Veggeland, N. (2004). *The competitive society: How democratic and effective?* Kristiansand: Norwegian Academic Press.

Veggeland. N. (2005). *Europapolitikk, innenrikspolitikk og kommunene [European politics, domestic politics, and the municipalities*]. Oslo: Kommuneforlaget.

Veggeland, N. (2007), *Paths and public innovation in the global age*, Cheltenham, UK: Edward Elgar.

Veggeland, N. (2009). *Taming the regulatory state: Politics and ethics*. Cheltenham, UK: Edward Elgar.

Vibert, F. (2007). *The rise of the unelected: Democracy and the new separation of powers*. Cambridge: Cambridge University Press.

Wallace, H., Wallace, W., & Pollack, M.A. (2005). *Policy-making in the European Union*. Oxford: Oxford University Press.

Weaver, R.K. (1986). The politics of blame avoidance. *Journal of Public Policy, 6* (4), 371-398.

In: Innovative Regulatory Approaches …
Ed: Noralv Veggeland

ISBN: 978-1-60876-673-4

Chapter 2

TRANSLATIONS AND INTERNAL REGULATIONS: SCANDINAVIAN LOCAL GOVERNMENTS[1]

Tor Helge Pedersen

This chapter focuses on internal regulation in Scandinavian local governments. Although internal regulation with respect to contracts and performance measurement is connected to institutional economics, the approach here holds that such studies can benefit from using other theoretical perspectives, in this case, historical institutionalism and theories of translation. By using two Norwegian and two Danish empirical examples, this chapter demonstrates how these two perspectives contribute to the study of internal regulation. First, we start by presenting central argument, national contexts, concepts, and theoretical perspectives. Next, we shall briefly present the four empirical examples, and then apply these observations to demonstrate the usefulness of these theoretical perspectives.

INTRODUCTION

Survey data of large firms indicates that the reduction of vertical differentiation (also called 'delayering') has been widespread across the countries of the Organisation for Economic Co-operation and Development (OECD) (e.g., Littler et al. 2003). In many Scandinavian local governments, contracts and other regulatory tools followed this wave. The reduction of hierarchical levels opened an organizational vacuum where different regulatory tools were introduced. Some examples of such tools are management by objectives, balanced scorecards, value-based management, contract steering, and so on. These tools are also examples of PMIs (Popular Management Ideas).

This chapter examines internal regulations in Danish and Norwegian local governments as empirical examples of how regulation tools are translated and transformed in different

[1] The data was collected in connection of the author's doctoral thesis (Pedersen 2009), which has a different focus and theme. This chapter makes use of supplementary material from that collection of data. The four empirical examples presented in this paper are based on interviews in 2005 with employees and managers and on different written internal materials. They are not in the literature list, but the source for each quotation in the text is indicated.

organizational settings. Three guiding questions will be addressed and answered: (i) How are the tools translated? (ii) How does internal regulation occur in the local governments after reducing the vertical differentiation? (iii) What aspects or activities are regulated? The reasons for discussing and analysing internal regulation in Norwegian and Danish municipalities are threefold. First, we need to know more about how internal regulation occurs and is exercised in municipal organizations following the delayering measures. Although internal regulation can illuminate the organizational effects of delayering, there are few studies on contract steering that employ a comparative framework (Ejersbo and Greve (2005:9).Secondly, the rationale behind different tools of internal regulation has its roots in institutional economics (Moe 1984). Yet, these theories are not necessarily optimal for analysing this aspect of political organizations. Some empirical studies suggest that both historical institutionalism and theories of translation could be fruitful. But there are very few efforts that try to link historical institutionalism to the notion of translation. Because of the flexible distinction of historical institutionalism, one may integrate this perspective with other versions of new institutionalism (Peters 1999/2001:76).

A point long established in the literature on the new institutionalism is that 'institutions matter' (Scott 1995); institutions significantly impact our lives owing to their regulative, normative, and cognitive structures that shape and guide human action. Various studies with different theoretical points of departure have concluded that we need to know more about how translations occur within national or organizational contexts (e.g., Veggeland 2007). The theoretical development within the new institutional tradition has also moved towards an interest in the differential reception of ideas (Gammal, Powell & Simard 2005). In other directions of institutionalism, Campbell (2004:80) has also argued for further studies of translations. He argues that studies of diffusion fail to recognize that when institutional principles and practices travel from one site to another, the recipients implement them in different ways and to a greater or lesser extent depending on the social and institutional context.

A satisfactory examination of translations involves and implies a focus on the translator, the activities and operations of the translation (such as the rules, the unit of translation, the behaviour, and modus operandi), and the context. Moreover, one must consider the type of ideas and contexts that promote explicitation and implicitation (which are discussed below). It is not, then, only a question of the different interpretation of ideas but also the adoption of different activities.

THE NATIONAL AND LOCAL CONTEXTS

The Scandinavian countries of Sweden, Denmark, and Norway share not only a common history but also a number of important societal features, such as culture, language, religion and belief-systems, and ethnic composition. Different outside-in approaches have accordingly emphasized similarities on dimensions concerning culture (Hofstede 1979, 1980), welfare models (Esping-Andersen 1990; Veggeland 2007), and managerial practices (Lawrence, Schramm, Nielsen & Sivesind 2004). There are also some parallels in the way in which the political and administrative systems have developed, were constructed, and work, even today.

Still, there are differences. Some scholars have emphasized the variations between the traditions of public administration (e.g., Lægreid & Pedersen 1999) and between the models of local government (Mouritzen & Svara 2002; Pedersen 2009). The former is the distinction between the East-Nordic and the West-Nordic traditions of public administration, with Norwegian and Danish municipalities in the latter. This distinction also reflects a difference in constitutional heritage. The different models of local government enable the identification of different institutionalized forms of government. Mouritzen and Svara (2002) argue that the organizational and governmental structure in local governments in most countries have evolved in a way that reflects national conditions and preferences, although these have not been explicitly labelled. Mouritzen and Svara (2002:51) have identified and constructed four ideal-types of governmental forms that assign different weights to three different organizing principles (or values): layman rule, political leadership, and professionalism. This construction describes different local governments in different countries according to one of four of these ideal types (ibid: 55). This chapter employs these forms as the contexts in which translations occur.

The first of these ideal-types is the *strong-mayor* form that emphasizes the principle of political leadership, which has empirical examples in France, Spain, and Italy. Here, the other principles (i.e., the layman rule and professionalism) are accommodated to strong political leadership. In this ideal type, the elected mayor controls the majority of the city council and is in full charge, both de jure and de facto, of all executive functions (Mouritzen & Svara 2002:55). The chief executive officer (CEO) of the administrative organization serves at the mayor's will and can be hired and fired without the consent of any other politicians or political bodies. According to Mouritzen and Svara (2002), the mayor can hire political appointees to help with any function.

The second ideal-type is the *committee-leader* form, which points to empirical examples in Denmark, Sweden, and Great Britain. Here, one person is the clear but not dominating political leader of the municipality. As Mouritzen and Svara (2002:56) write, 'He or she may or may not control the council. Executive powers are shared. The political leader may have responsibility for some executive functions but others will rest with collegiate bodies, that is, standing committees composed of elected politicians, and with the CEO'.

The third ideal-type is the *collective* form, which has empirical examples from Belgium and the Netherlands. "The decision center is one collegiate body, the executive committee that is responsible for all executive functions. The executive committee consists of locally elected politicians and the mayor, who presides. In this form, greater emphasis is given the layman principle (albeit a select body of laymen), and political leadership and professionalism are accommodated to it (Mouritzen & Svara 2002: 56).

The fourth ideal-type is the *council-manager* form where all the executive functions are in the hands of a professional administrator, which Mouritzen and Svara find in the USA, Australia, Ireland, Finland, and Norway. The city council appoints this professional administrator, also called the city manager. The city council has general authority over policy but is restricted from becoming involved in administrative matters. The council, furthermore, is a relatively small body, headed by a mayor who formally has presiding and ceremonial functions only. According to Mouritzen and Svara (2002:56) the emphasis is on professionalism, with constricted layman rule and limited political leadership.

Another part of the local context in the municipalities is the administrative models. Examples of such models are department-based models, agency-based models (the result-unit model, the two-level model) and purchaser-provider models. The purchaser-provider model has been used in some Swedish municipalities for the production of technical services since the early 1980s (Montin 1993). Somewhat later this model was also adopted in Danish and Norwegian municipalities and also implemented in more soft municipal services. The model has, however, been translated in different ways in different municipalities (Blomquist 1994).

The Empirical Phenomenon and Theoretical Construction

Different studies of regulation have focused on and described the trend towards a regulatory state, entailing the emergence of a more horizontal and fragmented state structure. This structure involves of the expansion of regulation by autonomous agencies and a more indirect and control-oriented approach rather than the traditionally integrated and interventionist approach of the welfare state (Majone 1997; Veggeland 2009). Majone's *The Agency Model: The Growth of Regulation and Regulatory Institutions in the European Union*, one of the most frequently quoted and seminal works on the regulatory state, defines regulation and the regulatory state as the '(…) reliance on regulation – rather than public ownership, planning or centralized administration – characterizes the methods of the regulatory state' (1994:77). Philip Selznick (1985:363), moreover, defines regulation as "sustained and focused control exercised by a public agency over activities that are valued by a community". The state structure finds its parallel in the local governmental structure. Some scholars have employed the concept of regulation in relation to internal organization, that is, regulation inside governments (Lægreid, Roness & Rubecksen 2006). Yet, according to Hood et al. (1999), there is no generally accepted framework for characterizing the tools or instruments of internal regulation.

Vertical differentiation refers, in general, to the number of hierarchical levels of organization (Blau & Schoenherr 1971), and delayering is the doctrine of reducing hierarchical levels (Littler et al. 2003). The popularity of this doctrine is reflected also in other popular ones, such as 'downsizing' and 'business process re-engineering'. Delayering, however, also relates to arm's-length agencies (also called the 'agency fever') at different level of public administration (Pollitt, Talbot, Caulfield & Smullen 2004), to the regulatory state (Majone 1997), and to ideas of New Public Management (NPM). Pollitt and Bouckaert (2000:86) write, for example, that: 'The ideal public sector agency, as envisaged by the enthusiasts and visionaries of the NPM and reinventing government movement, will be "flat", flexible, specialized ("focused") and decentralized, and therefore quite small'.

Theoretical Approaches: Two Complementary Perspectives

Internal regulation can be understood in different ways. One possible – and dominant – theoretical point of departure to internal and external contracting is institutional economics (e.g., Moe 1984). When Terry Moe introduced what he called the 'new economics of organization' to political science, he pointed out that these new contributions differed from the pioneering works of the 1960s on public-choice theory (e.g., Downs 1967), which basically assumes that officials are driven by self-interest, broadly speaking. According to Moe (1984:739), the new approach embodies three key elements: a contractual perspective on organizational relationships, a theoretical focus on hierarchical control, and formal analyses via principal-agent models. This line of thinking continues not only to dominate this field of study, but also the rationale behind internal regulation. This approach, however, is not necessarily the best way of studying internal regulation. One reason for this argument is the differentiated reception of regulatory tools in organizations. Organizations may very well adopt the labels, but not necessarily reproduce the actual practices (Røvik 2007). The practices behind the labels may also be modified according to factors such as historical and constitutional legacies and local contexts.

The first alternative theoretical point of departure of this chapter is historical institutionalism (e.g., Pierson & Skocpol 2002). This perspective emphasizes the element of stability in processes of change. Although, as mentioned above, historical institutionalism lacks sharp distinctions, we can note some features of this theoretical tradition. One feature is a focus on traditional categories of political science such as power and asymmetrical relations of power. Hall and Taylor (1996:940) have pointed out that this characteristic reflects its roots in group theories of politics. Exogenous shocks or institutional breakdowns offer possible examples of situations where the concept of power is useful. As Thelen and Steinmo (1992:15) explain:

> (…) at the moment of institutional breakdown, the logic of the argument is reversed from "institutions shape politics to politics shape institutions" (1992:15).

The reform of 2005-2006 in Denmark when five new regions were created to replace the existing counties and reduced the number of municipalities from 271 to 98 offers such an instance of politics shaping institutions. Many of the existing county tasks were transferred to either the state or the new municipalities, and the right to levy taxes at the regional level was removed (though it has remained at the local, municipal level).

A second feature of historical institutionalism is the image of social causation as path-dependent in the sense that it 'rejects the traditional postulate that the same operative forces will generate the same results everywhere' (Hall & Taylor 1996:941). Historical institutionalism champions the view that 'the effect of such forces will be mediated by contextual forces of a given situation, often inherited from the past' (Hall & Taylor 1996:941). Much of the work in historical institutionalism thus consists of cross-national comparisons of public policy, 'typically emphasising the impact of national political institutions structuring relations among legislators, organized interests, the electorate and the judiciary' (Hall & Taylor 1996:938).

A third feature is that historical institutionalists rarely make firm assumptions about the relationship between institutions and individuals. As mentioned earlier, this chapter attempts to bridge the gap between historical institutionalism and theories of translation. Using these theories, we can say that complementary approaches are one possible way of relating institutions and individuals (i.e., translators). One reason for taking these theoretical steps is found in the following critique of the historical institutional perspective:

> We could continue to pile up examples of how organization theory could inform this version of institutionalism, but the basic point should be clear. Focusing on the decision

making and the roles played by actors within is crucial for giving the historical institutionalist logic more explanatory power (Peters, Pierre & King 2005:1285).

This chapter holds that a focus on translations can lead to improved explanatory power. Instead of focusing on the decisions, we can focus on the ways actors in organizations choose to incorporate with external ideas. We may call this activity 'translation', which will be presented later in this chapter. We may also say that while decisions give us information about the plan, translation gives us information about the actors' activities when encountering and dealing with new ideas.

With respect to the four different ideal-types of local governments, this perspective expects that the adoption of new or circulating ideas will be shaped according to these paths and trajectories. Indeed, research on other trends, such as the decentralizing components within the NPM, shows that decentralization follows different paths in different national contexts, such as the highly centralized UK, the federal USA and the highly decentralized Germany (Wollmann 2001; Pollitt 2005:382).

As mentioned earlier, there has been more attention paid to the effects of the introduction of ideas and tools into new national and organizational contexts. John Campbell (2004:28), for example, argues that one needs to recognize that these changes rarely start from scratch in order to be able to understand better how institutional change occurs in path-dependent ways and through diffusion; in other words, change involves a recombination of new and old elements for translation. Campbell calls changes which involve a recombination of old elements for translation 'bricolage'. Campbell argues that both the concept of bricolage and translation provide insights into the mechanisms in different processes of change.

The notion of translation emerged in organizational studies during the late 1980s (Czarniawska-Joerges & Joerges 1990), a development that was especially inspired by the French sociologist Bruno Latour (1986) who views translation as a way of understanding the role of science and technology in the structuring of power relationships. Czarniawska-Joerges and Joerges (1990:37) argue for an importation of the concept into organization analysis:

> The translation model helps us reconcile the fact that a text is at the same time object-like and yet is read in different ways. The translation mechanism makes us understand the first paradox connected to fashion: that fashion is created while it is followed. It is the subsequent translations which at the same time produce variations on fashion and reproduce it. Hence the second paradox: fashion followers act differently due to the attempt to act in the same way (Czarniawska-Joerges & Joerges 1990:37).

Since the 1990s several scholars involved in the field of organizational science have made great use of translation theory (e.g., Czarniawska & Joerges 1996) and in different ways. Some have argued that local translations of global ideas are more or less unique (e.g., Czarniawska & Joerges 1996). Others have insisted that translations, in one way or another, are guided by sorts of rules (e.g., Sahlin-Andersson 1996). Nonetheless, they all address to what degree and in what way organizations and actors can manipulate regulatory tools. This means that these theories try to account for what actors like internal 'translators', can do with such tools and other ideas. Because managerial tools are ideas, not fixed, physical objects, they are continually translated and transformed into new local versions. In short, this theory squarely recognizes the differentiated reception of ideas or tools.

Another source of inspiration for translation theory is new institutionalism (e.g., DiMaggio & Powell 1983). One important development within the new institutional tradition has been a focus on the differential reception of ideas in organizations. Gammal et al. (2005) have provided a model study of this theme on their research on non-profit organizations in the San Francisco Bay Area. Inspired by the Scandinavian tradition and the focus on the differential reception of ideas, Gammal et al. (2005) conducted interviews with leaders of non-profit organizations and constructed five ideal-types of ways that actors or organizations receive new ideas: (i) the enthusiastic adopter, those that actively seek out new business models and best-practices; (ii) the converted innocent, those that wake up to discover their *modus operandi* has undergone a marked transformation; (iii) the engaged translator, those that are intent on putting their own stamp on new business tools; (iv) the reluctant conformer, those forced to consider new practices, only to find themselves rebuffed by the very proponents who urged the effort; and (v) the active resistor, those determined to remain distinctive and willing to reject fashionable ideas in order to hew to their original historical mission.

As mentioned earlier, we cannot talk about one translation theory, but several approaches which involve the use of this concept. It is important to note that the different theories of translation which have been developed over the last decade have their bases on different ontological and epistemological assumptions about the translation process. On the one hand, we have those who argue that local translations of global ideas are more or less unique (Latour 1986; Czarniawska & Joerges 1996; Scheuer 2003). On the other hand, we have those who argue that, in one way or another, they are guided by some sorts of rules (Sahlin-Andersson 1996; Sevon 1996; Røvik 1998, 2007). Choosing a translation approach implies choosing among different assumptions about translation, and this has implications for the study.

Some similarities between the different approaches are, however, the following. These theories address to what degree and in what way organizations and actors can manipulate regulatory tools. This means that these theories try to account for what actors, like internal 'translators', can do to such tools and other ideas. The point of departure is that managerial tools are ideas, not physical objects, and hence they do not have fixed or final forms. When managerial ideas spread, they are continually translated and transformed into new local versions. In other words, these theories are open for differentiated reception of ideas and tools. Some may adopt the name of the idea or practice, and others take the practice, with many other possibilities in between.

The latest development of this analytical approach is the work of Kjell Arne Røvik (2007) who calls his position 'pragmatic institutionalism' owing to the influence from American pragmatic philosophy, the pragmatic tone in Scandinavian institutionalism, and especially the theory of literal translation, drawn from the research field of translation studies. There are several new elements in this framework. (i) There is a distinction between two main forms of translation: de-contextualization and contextualization. This distinction has its roots in Czarniawska and Joerges (1996), and also Giddens's (1990) *The Consequences of Modernity* in which he discusses "disembedding" and "reembedding". Disembedding refers to the '"lifting out" of social relations from local context of interaction and their restructuring across indefinite spans of time-space' (Giddens 1990:21). Reembedding, on the other hand, is '(...) the re-appropriation or recasting of disembedded social relations so as pin them down to local conditions of time and space' (Giddens 1990:80). (ii) Another distinction exists between rules of inscription and rules of translation and transformation. (iii) There are concepts referring to different modi operandi in translation, meaning that the translation and transformation may vary between reproduction, modification, and a radical modus operandi. (iv) The introduction of new concepts also takes place in order to describe the activity of translation, that is, the rules of translation: copying, subtraction, adding, alteration, and theoretical translation phenomena such as explicitation and implicitation.

Table 1 summarizes these rules of translation, as well as alteration and recombining, in the context of Popular Management Ideas.

Table 1. Rules and operations of translation

Rule/operation	Empirical features	Modus
Copying	Attempts to recreate the PMI in the local setting	Reproducing
Subtraction	Neglecting or omitting elements of PMIs	Moderate
Adding	Adding elements or integrating elements from local traditions	Moderate
Implicitation	Reducing information that is present in the original idea	Moderate
Explicitation	Introducing information that is absent or implicitly present in the original idea	Moderate
Alteration	Severe local reshaping	Radical
Recombining	Bricolage – Recombination of existing elements	Moderate or radical

Outlining rules, modi operandi, and operations are ways of describing the activity of translation or the translating behaviour. Vinay and Darbelnet have described the phenomena or operations of explicitation and implicitation as twin concepts and antonyms (1958/1995:342). They defined explicitation as 'the process of introducing information into target language which is present only implicitly in the source language, but which can be derived from the context or the situation' (1958/1995:8). This operation has later been formulated as the 'explicitation hypothesis' (Blum-Kulka 1986). On the other hand, according to Klaudy & Károly (2005:15):

> Implication occurs, for instance, when SL [source-language] unit of more specific meaning is replaced by a TL [target-language] unit of more general meaning; translators draw together the meaning of several words, and thus SL units consisting from two or more words are replaced by a TL unit consisting of one word; meaningful lexical elements of the SL text are dropped; two or more sentences in the SL are conjoined into one sentence in the TL; or when SL clauses or reduced to phrases in the TL, etc. (Klaudy & Károly 2005:15).

Explication and implication are concepts which cover operations that are conscious or automatic, obligatory or operational. Kinga Klaudy (1998:82-83) has classified explicitation into obligatory (syntactic and semantic differences between the source language and the target language), optional (differences between text-building strategies and stylistic preferences of the two languages in question), pragmatic (the need to bridge the cultural gap in translation), and translation-inherent (resulting from the process of translation itself). In an organizational context these translation theoretical concepts can describe observations where source information of managerial tools is made either more explicit or more implicit in the translation and the local practice of the tool.

Further, translation is not one of the categories of differentiated reception, but instead captures the different degrees of transformation. Transformations may vary between reproduction of ideas and a more radical transformation. Copying means trying to recreate the idea in a new organizational context; subtraction is neglecting or omitting aspects of the ideas; adding can involve integrating elements of local traditions into the ideas; and alteration involves the extensive local reshaping of the managerial idea (Røvik 2007).

From the translation perspective, with weight on the approach of Røvik (2007), we can expect to find the following in the four different local governments: (i) differentiated receptions and uses of regulatory tools; (ii) identifiable rules of translation and techniques in use; (iii) the degree of transformation of the tools being influenced by the rules already in use and contextual factors; and (iv) organizational effects being influenced by how the tools are translated.

Internal Regulation in Scandinavian Municipalities: Different Tools

The previous section has shown some links between historical institutionalism and theories of translation. In the following sections we shall investigate four empirical examples of internal regulation in Scandinavian municipalities after the reform of reduced vertical differentiation. The two Danish municipalities have 8 000 and 24 000 inhabitants, and the two Norwegian municipalities have 6 000 and 25 000 inhabitants. The municipalities are hereafter called the following: the Danish-small municipality, the Danish-medium municipality, the Norwegian-small municipality, and the Norwegian-medium municipality.

Contract Steering as Regulatory Tool, Denmark

Contracting can be understood as 'the design and implementation of contractual relations between purchasers and suppliers' (Domberger 1998:12; Ejersbo & Greve 2005:1). A contract can be defined as 'an agreement between two or more persons intended to create a legal obligation between them and to be legally enforceable (Drewry 2000:257; Ejersbo & Greve 2005:1). According to Domberger (1998:160-165), there are four advantages connected to performance contracts in the public sector: (i) the separation of purchaser and provider roles, (ii) specifications, (iii) competition in the shape of internal markets, and (iv) the monitoring of contractor performance. In other words, one could say that this involves tighter internal regulation. The motives for introducing contracts are to improve steering and management, followed by better service and quality (Ejersbo & Greve 2005:108).

The earliest example on contract steering was the radical programme of state restructuring undertaken by the fourth Labour Government in New Zealand between 1984 and 1990 (Boston, Martin, Pallot & Walsh 1991). These reforms were inspired by public-choice theory and agency theory (principal/agent framework) and involved the introduction of contract steering (Walsh & Boston 1991; Boston 1991). Another source of inspiration was the Danish Ministry of Finance's partial imitation of the British Next-Step solutions around 1992 (Ejersbo & Greve 2002:23). Since then, this regulatory tool has been spread to other parts of the Danish public sector such as the Græsted-Gilleleje, Greve, and Assens municipalities (Ejersbo & Greve 2002:26). According to Ejersbo and Greve's (2005:104ff) study of contracting, this tool is most common in municipalities with over 20 000 inhabitants. In this group of municipalities, 71 per cent used internal contracting. The typical Danish translation of contracting was, however, different to the translation in New Zealand (Ejersbo & Greve 2002:218).

Let us now turn to the two Danish municipalities into which this regulatory tool was translated. Both municipalities adopted contract steering in 2001, and both have had a model with four or more departments following the municipality reform of 1970. In both municipalities there were some changes in the early 1990s involved with the introduction of a collegiate team leader. Both municipalities began contract steering in tandem with the introduction of a new organizational model that aimed to reduce vertical differentiation.

Mouritzen and Svara's (2002:60) description of Danish municipalities is useful for understanding the local political context. They describe a typical local government where the committees and the mayor share the executive powers. The standing committee, for example, is responsible for the 'immediate administration' of affairs, while the finance committee supervises all financial matters and prepares the budget. The office of mayor is a full-time position and the chairman of the city council and the finance committee. Two features are central in the committee-leader form. First, the elected mayor is the formal head of the total municipal administration and is responsible for the implementation of decisions taken by the council and other political bodies. Secondly, the standing committees are fully in charge of specific or sectoral, day-to-day administrative matters (Mouritzen & Svara (2000:60). This committee-leader form has survived a number of major reforms, including the reform of 2005-2006.

The central motive for the Danish-small municipality was modernization. The translation process involved adding other ideas, such as value-based management and more operational autonomy. These measures were perceived as successful:

> Our experience is that they have changed their behaviour after they got all the money. They don't use much on temporary help. Some use it on buildings. This is interesting because the sceptical voices said that if they got all the money, they would use it on salaries and then our buildings would be neglected. The opposite seems to have happened. They save in using temporary help (....) then they invest in a new floor in the sports hall, or buy new computers or develop new subordinates (interview, CEO, Danish-small 26.01.2005).

In the Danish-medium municipality they talked about the agencies having had too much latitude for too long. More political steering without the centralization of authority (which is not accepted in Danish municipalities) was necessary. Contracting gradually became the solution. The goals of the adoption of the regulatory tools were steering, transparent administration and service production, political steering, and flexibility. The experiences of the non-profit providers for the care of the elderly, who had been contracting with the municipality for several years, suggested that the implementation of contract steering in the municipality made political steering more difficult and increased the paperwork. (This finding perhaps reflects Domberger's (1998) observation that one difficulty of performance regarding contracts, is the non-contractability of quality.) This conclusion from the internal evaluation captures the political effects:

> The interviews shows that the politicians experience that the performance catalogues are too complex and too big to handle as a steering instrument (KLK, evaluation of the reform, 2001:28).

Important to the local context of the Danish-medium municipality was a reform implemented in 2001 that featured contract steering, delayering, value-based management, balanced scorecards, and further operational autonomy. Further, at the start of the reform, the municipality was practising a method called dialogue-based budgeting. The mayor highlighted the similarity between the existing practice and the new contract-steering concept in an internal news bulletin:

> The important new element is that the dialogue around goals and means is followed up with a contract between the city council and the leader. The contract determines objectives, scope, and conditions for task performance in light of the goals accepted by the city council (the Mayor in Danish-medium, news bulletin, 19 May 1998).

Effectiveness/rationalization is always an issue, but, in connection with contract steering, they agreed in the city council that it should not be a cutback management and personal reform (interview, CEO, Danish-medium 17.11.2004).

In both municipalities, other types of formal and informal regulation seemed to be important. The leaders in the Danish-small municipality appeared to participate mostly outside their own departments and agencies. Examples are external groups of leaders, participation in committees of experts, administrative representatives in political committees, informal meetings with other leaders or external sector groups etc.

New translations, such as value-based contract steering (KL & KTO 2006), combined the two different tools. The politicians in the Danish-medium municipality did not want to allocate extra resources towards a planned controller unit. We can interpret this reticence as an expression of their not intending to reproduce the steering form and organizational model in their entirety. To sum up, one can say that there is a differentiated reception of the regulatory tools. But there are also similarities in connection with how contract steering was translated, which will be discussed later in this chapter.

Balanced Scorecards and Leader Contracts as Regulatory Tools, Norway

According to Marshall Meyer (2002/2009), two articles in the *Harvard Business Review* were significant in connection with the doctrines of performance management and performance measurement. Both Eccles' (1991) 'The Performance Measurement Manifesto' and Kaplan and Norton's (1992) 'The Balanced Scorecard: Measures that Drive Performance' conveyed the message that financial measures alone are insufficient to gauge business performance. The balanced scorecard has dominated discussions of performance measurement subsequently (e.g., Nilsen 2007). This tool defines the 'balance' as measurements in the domains of innovation, internal processes, customer satisfaction, and financial performance. The balanced scorecard is a procedure for improving both performance measurement and internal regulation. The advantages of performance measurement in general are, according to De Bruijn (2002), a broader view of the objectives of an organization instead of only production, more focus on common goals, better visibility on how public resources are spent, and an opportunity to correct unwanted directions in an organization. These conditions contribute both to efficient productivity and to effective goal-achievement.

During the 1990s, the practice of using balanced scorecards emerged in both Danish and Norwegian public-sector organizations, such as various central agencies and hospitals. The balanced scorecard is an example of a modern managerial tool used for the internal regulation of governmental agencies in Norway (Lægreid, Roness & Rubecksen 2006), including local governments (Hovik & Stigen 2008).

We now turn to some central characteristics of the organizational contexts into which this tool was translated. While the committee-leader form dominates Danish municipalities, there are more variations among Norwegian municipalities (Bukve 2001; Hovik & Stigen 2004, 2008). In Norway, excluding the big cities, there are forms that correspond to three of the ideal-types (Mouritzen & Svara (2002:66). Mouritzen and Svara (2002:65) argue that features from the council-manager form, the collective form, and the committee-leader form are present in Norwegian municipalities. They point out that the CEO by law is the formal leader of the municipal administration and can be delegated other powers by the council. Mouritzen and Svara (2002:65) conclude that the CEO's relation downwards in the administrative organization in Norwegian municipalities resembles the council-manager form of government: 'The Norwegian form of government seems to come closest to the council-manager type' (Mouritzen & Svara 2002:66). The Local Government Act of 1992 also strongly recommended the separation between policy and administration. To compensate for the relative freedom instituted by this act, there was the implementation of new provisions concerning internal supervision and control and external auditing. This measure is a typical feature of the regulative state. One example here is the control committee, a new political body, elected by the council, and its exclusive task is to deal with supervision, control, and audits.

Moreover, the executive committee (*formannskapet*) deviates from the ideal-types and is anomalous in an international context. As for administrative organization, practically all Norwegian municipalities adopted a model during the late 1970s and the 1980s, which has many similarities with the models adopted in the Danish municipalities in the 1970s, as a consequence of the growth of the modern welfare state. The principal standing model features a basic structure consisting of four departments or divisions (*etat/avdeling*): education (ages 6-16), health and social care (including elderly care), culture (often including leisure), and technical affairs (i.e., water, sewage, municipal roads, infrastructure, and property housing etc.). In addition to this, the CEO heads the central administration.

We now turn to the introduction of the balanced scorecard as a regulatory tool in the Norwegian municipalities. Both Norwegian municipalities had abandoned a sector-oriented political structure. Also, in the Norwegian-medium municipality, two leaders searched for new accounting system in 1999. They chose the balanced scorecard and tested this system in about four or five departments at the city hall. Two years later a cost reducing management reform was initiated and a new organizational model was chosen and implemented in 2003. The new organizational model sought to reduce vertical differentiation and implemented contracts between the agency manager and the CEO. There were also political reforms.

In the Norwegian-medium municipality, the leader contract states the following about the evaluation of the leader:

> The CEO shall systemically – at least two times a year – carry out a formal dialogue with an emphasis on evaluating the result and other issues in the leader's policy area with regard to the annual performance contract and development plan (performance and development dialogue). In addition to performance evaluation, the dialogue should address relevant issues and document conditions that the leader needs assistance from the CEO to work out (for example development steps) (Norwegian-medium municipality, Leader contract between CEO and kindergarten leader, dated 09.01.2004, page 4).

According to both the agency manager and the vice CEO, who represents the CEO in these issues, dialogue, rather than hard or strict evaluations, characterize the evaluation meetings.

In the Norwegian-small municipality, there were earlier attempts to delayer and contract out. In 2001 a cutback of management costs was initiated that involved adopting a new organizational model, delayering, balanced scorecards, and empowerment-projects. In 2003 another reform was implemented that involved contracts between the agency manager and the CEO, along with some political reforms.

According to the informants in both Norwegian municipalities, both municipalities were under fiscal pressure. It is significant that the Norwegian-medium municipality adopted the balanced scorecard before the reduction in the vertical differentiation. But several informants also mentioned that the balanced scorecard was implemented only after the delayering process. The main reason for adopting this tool was that they 'wanted to know more and to guess less'. To sum up, there are some differences with respect to the timing and the order of adoption. There are, however, several similarities in how these tools were translated, which will be discussed later in the chapter.

Analysis: Regulation Inside Local Governments

Table 2 is a summary of the data and the findings. The table shows what tools are translated and in use, what is regulated, and how it is regulated. The Norwegian-small municipality has similarities with what Gammal et al. (2005) calls the 'enthusiastic adopter', and the other municipalities have similarities the 'engaged translator'.

First of all, all municipalities implemented some sort of contracting practice, albeit with different labels and slightly different content. Secondly, the partners in the contracts were systematically different between the Danish and Norwegian municipalities. This pattern matches the observation that different forms of local government are relevant, and supports expectations drawn from historical institutionalism. Thirdly, the translations have both similarities and differences. The Danish translations follow a path of further operational autonomy.

Table 2. Internal regulation: the findings

Local Government	Tools	Regulating how & what
Danish-small	Contracting, value-based management, more operational autonomy	Contract between the elected and the operational leader, written expectations Values more important than the contract, the psychological effect
Danish-medium	Contracting, value-based management , more operational autonomy	Contract between the elected and the operational leader, written expectations Political steering with resources and specific goals
Norwegian-Small	Performance contract Balanced scorecard	Contract between leader and the CEO, written expectations Measuring a part of the planning process and diverse dialogues Performance contract – a planning tools
Norwegian-medium	Leader contract Balanced scorecard	Contract between the operational leader and the CEO, written expectations Measuring a part of the overall planning system Contracts a dialogue instrument

Norwegian and Danish municipal leaders chose different internal regulatory tools during or after the reduction of vertical differentiation in the administrative organization. While they both used the translational rule of adding, they chose different tools. Alternatively, they added the some organizational forms to the regulatory tools. There are more general arguments that the use of contracting and balanced scorecards represents different paths in reforming public organizations (Greve 2000:163). Different paths, interpretations, and meanings – in short, translations – are observed with reforming phenomena. Pollitt (2005:300-302) describes the significance of the historical and constitutional legacy in the example of the decentralizing elements within New Public Management. These components had very different resonances in the highly centralized UK, highly decentralized Germany (Wollmann 2001), and the federal USA. Pollitt writes:

> In the federal USA a pro-business, anti-public sector ideology has meant that decentralization has recently been translated into a massive contracting-out of public services, whereas in federal Germany a very different ideology has seen decentralization strengthen the portfolio of activities carried out by multi-purpose local authorities. Clearly, if authority is highly concentrated, as it is in states such as the France, New Zealand and the UK, then decentralization has "further to go", and may come as a greater shock to the system, than in already extensively decentralized states such as Denmark, Germany and Switzerland (Pollitt 2005:300-302).

The legacy of the past, then, is significant (cf. Peters 1999/2001).

Another striking difference relates to the parties of the internal contracts in these cases. In the Norwegian municipalities the leader contracts were between the agency manager and the CEO. In the Danish municipalities the contracts were between the agency manager and the elected city council. This observation relates to the argument that organizational changes are often closer to recombination than replacement. As Stark (1996:995) notes, 'Change, even fundamental change, of the social world is not the passage from one order to another but rearrangements in the pattern of how multiple orders are interwoven. Organizational innovation in this view is not replacement but recombination'. In other words, earlier decisions and actions are important, and elements from the old practice and form can be added the new ideas and form.

The local translations of the regulatory tools were different in relation to the content and priorities of the regulatory tools and also in relation to the labels and language. The rules of translation they used, however, reveal important similarities across the empirical examples. In all four municipalities the tools were subject to the translational rule of adding. The Danish municipalities combined contracts with value-based steering; the Norwegian municipalities combined the leader contracts with performance measurements, or more precisely, balanced scorecards.

THE SIGNIFICANCE OF IMPLICITATION

The different tools, contracting and balanced scorecards, were subject to the process (or technique) of implicitation. The Danish municipalities, for example, emphasized 'the dialogue aspect' of internal contracting and the experience of the psychological effects on being contracted. There are several studies that indicate that the hard practice and language involved in contracting are made more implicit when these tools are translated into a municipal context (Ejersbo & Greve 2005). Greve's (2000:163) conclusion illustrates this point: 'Denmark pointed the way to an alternative use of contacts in the public sector in the 1990s. The alternative use consisted of introducing contracts from principles of trust and co-operation, and not solely on a principal-agent framework'.

Implicitation is an important operation in translation that tones down the hard elements. In the Norwegian municipality the balanced scorecard was coupled to the overall planning system. The strict or hard performance recording was toned down. Even in the Danish-medium municipality, where internal contracts were subject to systematic implementation, they used contracts without sanctions. This practice reflects the more general conditions in the contracts:

> This contract has no legal status and thus has no valid judicial consequences. The municipality still has the juridical and financial responsibility. The contract is only a statement and a clarification of which direction and spirit the enterprise is to pursue while political objectives and expectation of service level are defined more precisely (contract 2003, page 5).

The CEO referred to the Swedish municipality of Nacka where they had implemented a stricter version of contracts and even closed down purchaser units. This was not the case in the Danish-medium municipality which emphasized dialogue rather than sanctions for internal contracting. There are different explanations for this translation. According to Ejersbo and Greve's (2005) survey of Danish municipalities, there is a pattern that seems to emerge when municipalities use three or more managerial tools: they seldom use contracts. Secondly, informants in both Danish municipalities did not attribute the financial benefits to the introduction of contracts or the new organizational forms; instead they pointed to the implementation of greater operational autonomy.

Another empirical example of implicitation is the principle and doctrine of the steering concept in the Norwegian-small municipality:

> To be successful it is important that more than 80 per cent of our attention is put on values, culture, and attitudes – and less than 20 per cent on structure and models (Norwegian-small municipality, Handbook Steering dialogue, revised version 27.03.2008).

The performance contract for the leaders in the Norwegian-small municipality is another example of implicitation. The harder or more exacting element of the performance measurement was made more implicit and overshadowed with softer elements of planning activities and using the contract as an instrument of dialogue.

Informal Internal Regulation

The leaders in the four municipalities agreed that reduced vertical differentiation increased the dependence on the individual leaders. This result contradicts Keuning and Opheij's (1994) work on the benefits of reducing vertical differentiation in organizations, in which they argue that augmented operational autonomy is an important result of reduced vertical differentiation. This argument appears not to apply well to these municipal organizations. A second organizational effect after eliminating hierarchical levels was the increased level of leader participation outside their own agencies. All leaders reported an increase in the number of tasks, some of which were outside their own agencies. This effect was a possible result of the translation of another part of the four reforms studied here.

The Role oF Politicians

There are differences across the four cases that reflect the different local contexts. These differences include the parties of the contracts, the political interventions, and the forms of communication. Important aspects of the informal internal regulation were the different networks, arenas, and formal and informal meetings. Here we can identify one important difference between the Norwegian and Danish municipalities. In the latter, there are both formal and informal meetings between committee politicians and the local leader and user boards. In fact, the parties of the contract are between the local leader and the politicians. In the former, on the other hand, the parties of the contract are the local leader and the CEO. The politicians keep a distance from the local agencies.

There is one possible historical explanation for this difference. Since the Local Government Act of 1992, some Norwegian municipalities have developed a system of governance based on the principle of separation of functions that seeks to uphold a clear distinction between political and administrative matters. The Act of 1992 stressed the importance of forming a unitary and hierarchical system of management in municipalities and counties. Models reflecting the idea of a clear distinction between policy and administration soon began to circulate. The so-called 'hourglass model' envisioned all communications between the administrative and political areas of local government being channelled through the office of the chief municipal executive, thus reinforcing and expanding the responsibility of this office in all matters relating to personnel politics and administrative organization. Surveys have also confirmed this trend of adopting political structures to the Act of 1992. In addition, they also show the following developments in the period between 1993 and 2004: the increased delegation of responsibilities from the political to the administrative level; the steady reduction in the number of councillors and executive-committee members; and the reduction in the number of standing committees (Hovik & Stigen 2008:24). In other words, there clearly were moves towards a structure that discourages the politicians from interfering in the way the chief municipal executive manages his or her administration in order to achieve better political steering and more transparent service production.

The committee-leader ideal-type is arguably the one that best fits the institution in Danish municipalities. This form has a long history, and it has mostly been unchallenged (cf. Mouritzen & Svara 2002). This can explain why the Danish adoption and translation of the regulatory tools involved more active politicians. The Norwegian municipal executive committee (*formannskapet*) also has a long history and had mostly been unchallenged until the 1980s. This demonstrates the utility of historical institutionalism in studies of internal regulation in different national and organizational contexts.

SUMMARY: SIMILARITIES AD DIFFERENCES

The previous sections and the analysis above show different regulatory tools in use. There are, however, important similarities as well. In all four local governments there were increased informal internal regulations relating to, for example, securing horizontal co-operation for certain activities, dealing with uncertainties, and vertical communication. Table 3 is a summary of the similarities and differences between the four municipalities.

It was not surprising that formal internal regulation increased in all four municipalities during or after the reduction of vertical differentiation. This effect seemed to be a part of the process or effects of delayering reforms.

Table 3.Similarities and differences in Norway and Denmark

	Similarities	Differences
Historical influences (input)	West-Nordic tradition of public administration	Forms of government, variations within Norway
Process	Co-operation before competition Politicians as one group and actor, not different political parties	The Danish politicians were more active in the process. The Norwegian politicians adapted to the change in the administrative structure Different regulatory tools, conformity to field recommendations
Results (output)	More contracts and written documents Increased informal regulation	The parties of the internal contracts were different in the two municipalities The participants in the internal regulatory processes were different

In the Norwegian municipalities, it was clear that the leader contracts and the performance contracts resulted from the adoption of new organizational models which involved reduced vertical differentiation. This interpretation from a vice CEO in the Norwegian municipalities illustrates how contracting became an issue after the levelling process:

> It became clearer and clearer for us the need to concentrate some administrative tasks. (...) And the role of these administrative units has become clearer and clearer. And you end quickly up in a purchaser-provider thinking when you level out the structure (interview vice CEO, Norwegian-medium, 11.11.2005).

The increase in internal contracting and the purchaser-provider mentality in the Norwegian municipalities were unintended consequences of adopting new organizational models. When the four municipalities are compared, we can conclude that the formal internal regulation increased the most in the Danish-medium municipality. Here, they made detailed performance catalogues that were far too detailed for political use.

In both countries, we can observe the increase of informal internal regulation, such as the greater leader participation outside their own agencies in different networks and in different arenas. All in all this lead us to the conclusion that reduced vertical differentiation (without reduced horizontal differentiation) seems to lead to increased formal and informal internal regulation.

CONCLUSION

Although internal regulation is associated with economic perspectives and doctrines on organization, this chapter has argued that studies of internal regulation can benefit from using other perspectives, in this case, historical institutionalism and theories of translation. Historical institutionalism draws our attention to variation in historical and constitutional legacies between nations, sectors, and organizational contexts. The Scandinavian and pragmatic institutionalism leads our attention to the activities and operations within these organizational contexts in relation to the reception and use of regulatory tools.

In this chapter we have examined regulation inside four local governments from the West-Nordic tradition of public administration. The description and analysis in this chapter presented evidence that the four municipalities employed different types of formal internal regulatory tools after the delayering processes. Contract steering was the main tool in the Danish municipalities and the balanced scorecard for the Norwegian ones. Two possible explanations for this difference include: (i) the popularity of contract steering among Danish municipalities (Ejersbo & Greve 2002) and the popularity of the balanced scorecard among Norwegian municipalities (Hovik & Stigen 2004, 2008) and (ii) internal regulation occurred in two different local contexts embedded in two different types of local governments.

One empirical implication from this chapter is that ideas, managerial knowledge, regulations, recommendations, and EU-directives can be and are translated into different national and organizational contexts. EU-directives, for example, are texts that are can be subject to both explicitation and implicitation. Another empirical implication concerns the connection between language and action, in other words, between talk and practice. The overall picture is that the internal regulatory tools are subject to the translational rule of implicitation. On the other hand, we know that talk and labels can influence practices over time (Røvik 2007). This means that the softer regulations can turn into harder regulations. This transformation occurred with the dialogue budgeting in the Danish-medium municipality as a consequence of the ossification of talk and labels over time.

One theoretical implication from this chapter is that historical institutionalism and theories of translation should be developed further. Moreover, this chapter demonstrates how these perspectives can complement each other. More empirical studies exploring and testing the limits of the translational approach are also needed. One fruitful question would be whether it is possible to study translations in government from a greater distance or if it is only possible through case studies that offer an inside look. Another question is whether it is possible to establish and observe translations by studying historical documents or other written materials retrospectively.

REFERENCES

Blau, P.M., & Schoenherr, R. (1971). *The Structure of organizations*. New York: Basic Books

Blomquist, C. (1994). Beställer-utförarmodellen möter politiken [The order-performance modell meets policy]. In Jacobsson, B. (Ed.): *Organisationsexperiment i kommuner och landsting* [*Organizational experiments in municipalities and county-councils*]. Stockholm: Nerenius & Santerus Förlag

Blum-Kulka, S. (1986). Shift of cohesion and coherence in translation. In House, J., & Blum-Kulka, S. (Eds.), *Interlingual and intercultural communication: Discourse and cognition in translation and second language acquisition studies* (pp. 17-35). Tübingen: Gunter Narr

Boston, J. (1991). The theoretical underpinnings of public sector restructuring in New Zealand. In Boston, J., Martin, J., Pallot, J. & Walsh, P. (Eds.), *Reshaping the state: New Zealand's bureaucratic revolution* (pp. 1-26). Auckland: Oxford University Press

Boston, J., Martin, J., Pallot, J. & Walsh, P. (Eds.) (1991). *Reshaping the state: New Zealand's bureaucratic revolution*. Auckland: Oxford University Press

Bukve, O. (2001). Organisasjonsstruktur og leiarskap: En studie av komitëmodell og hovedutvalsmodell som rammer for kommunalt leiarskap [Organizational structure and leadership: A study of the committee model and the main committee model that frames municipal leadership]. In Fimreite, A.L., Larsen, H.O. & Aars, J. (Eds.), *Lekmannstyre under press: Festskrift til Audun Offerdal* [*Layman steering under pressure: Memorial volume for Audun Offerdal*] (pp. 49-74). Oslo: Kommuneforlaget

Campbell, J.L. (2004). *Institutional change and globalization*. Princeton & Oxford: Princeton University Press

Child, J. (1984). *Organization: A guide to problems and practice* (2nd edition). London: Harper & Row publishers

Czarniawska-Joerges, B., & Joerges, B. (1990). Organizational change as materialization of ideas: *Report: Study of power and democracy in Sweden (rapport till maktutredningen, januari 1990)*. Uppsala: Maktutredningen

Czarniawska, B., & Joerges, B. (1996). Travel of ideas. In Czarniawska, B. & G. Sevon (Eds.), *Translating organizational change* (pp. 13-48). Berlin: Walter de Gruyter

De Bruijn, H. (2002). *Managing performance in the public sector*. London: Routledge

DiMaggio, P.J., & Powell, W.W. (1983). The iron cage revisited: institutional isomorphism and collective rationality in organizational fields. *American sociological review*, 48, 147-160

Domberger, S. (1998). *The contracting organization*. Oxford: Oxford University Press

Downs, A. (1967). *Inside bureaucracy*. Boston: Little, Brown

Drewry, G. (2000). The Citizen and the New Contractual Public Management: the Quest for New Forms of Accountability and a New Public Law. In Fortin, Y. & H. van Hassel (Eds.), *Contracting in the New Public Management* (pp. 255-271). Amsterdam: IOS Press

Ejersbo, N., & Greve, C. (2002). *Den offentlige sektor på kontrakt* [*The public sector on contract*]. København: børsens forlag A/S

Esping-Andersen, G. (1990). *Three worlds of welfare capitalism*. Princeton: Princeton University Press

Gammal, D.L., Powell, W.W. & Simard, C. (2005). Close Encounters: The circulation and Reception of Managerial Practices in the San Francisco Bay Area Nonprofit community. In Czarniawska, B. & Sevon, G. (Eds.), *Global ideas: How ideas, objects and practices travel in the global economy* (pp. 233-258). Malmö: Liber & Copenhagen Business School Press

Giddens, A. (1990). *The consequences of modernity*. Cambridge: Cambridge University Press

Greve, C. (2000). Exploring contracts as reinvented institutions in the Danish public sector. *Public Administration* 78 (1), 153-164

Greve, C. & Ejersbo, N. (2005). *Contracts as reinvented institutions in the public sector: A cross-cultural comparison*. Westport, Connecticut & London: Praeger

Hall, P.A. & Taylor, R.C.R. (1996). Political science and the three new institutionalisms. *Political Studies*, XLIV, 936-957

Hofstede, G. (1979). Hierarchical power distance in forty countries. In Lammers, C.J., & Hickson, D.J. (Eds.), *Organizations alike and unlike: International and inter-institutional studies in sociology of organizations* (pp. 97-119). London: Routledge & Kegan Paul

Hofstede, G. (1980). *Culture's consequences*. Beverly Hills, CA: Sage

Hood, C., Scott, C., James, O., Jones, G., & Travers, T. (1999). *Regulation inside government: Waste-watchers, quality Police, and sleaze-busters*. Oxford: Oxford University Press

Hovik, S., & Stigen, I.M. (2004). Kommunal organisering 2004: Redegjørelse for kommunal- og regionaldepartementets organisasjonsdatabase [Municipal organization 2004: Statement for the organization data base of the Ministry of Local Government and Regional Development]. Oslo: *NIBR Notat 2004:124*

Hovik, S., & Stigen, I.M. (2008). Kommunal organisering 2008: Redegjørelse for kommunal- og regionaldepartementets organisasjonsdatabase [Municipal organization 2008: Statement for the organization data base of the Ministry of Local Government and Regional Development]. Oslo: *NIBR-rapport 2008:20*

Keuning, D., & Opheij, W. (1994). *Delayering organizations: How to beat bureaucracy and create a flexible and responsive organization*. London: Financial Times/ Pitman

KL & KTO (2006). *Dialogbaseret kontraktstyring: Kvalificering af kontraktstyring gennem medarbejderinddragelse* [Dialogue-based contract steering: Qualifying of contract steering though association involvement]. Fredriksberg: Kommuneinformation A/S

Klaudy, K. (1998). Implicitation. In Baker, M. (Ed.) *Routledge encyclopedia of translation studies* (pp. 82-84). London: Routledge & Kegan Paul

Klaudy, K., & Károly, K. (2005). Implicitation in translation: Empirical evidence for operational asymmetry in translation. *Across Languages and Cultures* 6(1), 13-28

Latour, B. (1986). The power of association. In Law, J. (Ed.), *Power, action and belief* (pp. 264-280). London: Routledge & Keegan Paul

Lawrence, P., Schramm-Nielsen, J., & Sivesind, K.H. (2004). *Management in Scandinavia: Culture, context and change.* Cheltenham: Edward Elgar

Littler, C.R., Wiesner, R., & Dunford, R. (2003). The dynamics of delayering: Changing management structures in three countries. *Journal of Management Studies,* 40 (2): 225-256

Lægreid, P. & Pedersen, O.K. (1999). *Fra opbygning til ombygning i staten: Organisationsforandringer i tre nordiske lande* [*From constructing to re-constructing the state: Organizational changes in three Nordic countries*]. København: Jurist- og Økonomforbundets forlag

Majone, G. (1997). The agency model: The growth of regulation and regulatory institutions in the European Union. *EIPASCOPE, European Institute of Public Administration 3*,9-14

Meyer, M.W. (2002/2009). *Rethinking performance measurement: beyond the balanced scorecard.* Cambridge: Cambridge University Press

Mouritzen, P.E., & Svara, J.H. (2002). *Leadership at the apex. Politicians and administrators in western local governments.* Pittsburgh, PA: University of Pittsburgh Press

Nilsen, E. (2007). Oversettelsens mikroprosesser: Om å forstå møtet mellom en global idé og lokal praksis som dekontekstualisering, kontekstualisering og nettverksbygging [Microprocesses of translation: On understanding the meeting between a global idea and local practice as decontextualizing, contextualizing, and network-building]. PhD thesis. University of Tromsø, Institute for political science

Pedersen, T.H. (2009). Fra kommunale forvaltninger til "forvaltningløse" kommuner: En komparativ og oversettelsesteoretisk studie av organisatorisk utflating i danske og norske kommuner [From municipal administration to 'administration-free' municipalities: A comparative and translation-theory study of organizational flattening in Danish and Norwegian municipalities]. PhD thesis. Tromsø: University of Tromsø

Peters, B.G. (1999/2001). *Institutional theory in political science: The 'New Institutionalism'.* London & New York: Continuum

Peters, B.G., Pierre, J. & King, D.S. (2005). The politics of path dependency: Political conflict in historical institutionalism. *The Journal of politics*, 67 (4):1275-1300

Pierson, P. & T. Skocpol (2002). Historical institutionalism in contemporary political science. In Katznelson, I. & Milner, H.V. (Eds.), *Political science: The state of the discipline* (pp.445-488). New York: Norton

Pollitt, C. (2005). Decentralization: A central concept in contemporary public management. In Ferlie, E., Lynn, L.E jr & Pollitt, C. (Eds.), *The Oxford handbook of public management* (pp. 371-397). Oxford & New York: Oxford University Press

Pollitt, C., & Bouckaert, G. (2000). *Public management reform: A comparative analysis.* Oxford: Oxford University Press

Pollitt, C., Talbot, C., Caulfield, J., & Smullen, A. (2004). *Agencies: How government do things through semi-autonomous organizations*. New York: Palgrave Macmillan

Røvik, K.A. (1998). *Moderne organisasjoner* [*Modern organizations*] Bergen: Fagbokforlaget

Røvik, K.A. (2007). *Trender og translasjoner* [Trends and translations] Oslo: Universitetsforlaget

Sahlin-Andersson, K. (1996). Imitating by editing success: The construction of organizational fields. In Czarniawska, B. & G. Sevon (Eds.), *Translating organizational change* (pp.69-92). Berlin: Walter de Gruyter

Scheuer, J.D. (2003). Patientforløb i praksis – en analyse af en idés oversættelse i mødet med praksis [Patient follow-up: An analysis of an idea's translation in practice]. PhD thesis. København: Handelshøjskolen i København

Scott, W.R. (1995/2001). *Institutions and organizations*. Beverly Hills: Sage

Selznick, P. (1985). Focusing organizational research on regulation. In R.G. Noll (Ed.): *Regulatory policy and the social sciences* (pp.363-367). Berkeley: University of California Press

Sevon, G. (1996). Organizational imitation in identity transformation. In Czarniawska, B. & Sevon, G. (Eds.). *Translating organizational change* (pp. 49-67). Berlin: Walter de Gruyter

Stark, D. (1996). Recombiant property in East European capitalism. *The American Journal of Sociology*, vol.101 (4):993-1027

Thelen, K. & Steinmo, S. (1992). Historical institutionalism in comparative politics. In Steinmo, S., Thelen, K., & Longstreth, F. (Eds.): *Structuring politics: Historical institutionalism in comparative analysis* (pp. 1-32). Cambridge: Cambridge University Press

Tullock, G. (1965). *The politics of bureaucracy*. Washington, DC: Public Affairs Press

Veggeland, N. (2007). *Paths of public innovation in the global age*. Cheltenham, UK: Edward Elgar

Veggeland, N. (2009). Taming the regulatory state: Politics and ethics. Cheltenham, UK: Edward Elgar

Vinay, J-P. & Darbelnet, J. (1958/1995). *Comparative stylistics of French and English: A methodology of translation*. Amsterdam: John Benjamins Publishing Company

Walsh, P. & J. Boston (1991). Introduction. In Boston, J., Martin, J., Pallot, J., & Walsh, P. (Eds.) (1991): *Reshaping the state: New Zealand's bureaucratic revolution* (pp. ix-xii). Auckland: Oxford University Press

Wollmann, H. (2001). Germany's trajectory of public sector modernisation: continuities and discontinuities. *Policy & Politics* 29 (2):151-170

In: Innovative Regulatory Approaches …
Ed: Noralv Veggeland

ISBN: 978-1-60876-673-4

Chapter 3

USING A SOFT MODE OF GOVERNANCE TO FACILITATE TRADE: REGULATORY CO-OPERATION BETWEEN THE EU AND CANADA

Christel Elvestad and Frode Veggeland

INTRODUCTION

The increasing transactions of the flow of goods, money, people, and services across international boundaries lead to interdependence in world politics (Keohane & Nye, 2001). This development has resulted in the establishment of a significant number of international institutions that aim for states to realize their mutual economic interests. In the area of trade, the Word Trade Organization (WTO) provides a multilateral regime that regulates international trade relations and lowers trade barriers between its 153 members. Also, there has been a considerable growth in free-trade agreements at the regional and bilateral level since the early 1990s (Oatley, 2004). More than 400 free-trade agreements are expected to be in operation within 2010.[1] The establishment of legally binding agreements is thus the most common way of reducing barriers to trade. However, a new trend is emerging. In contrast to the 'hard bargaining route' that leads to legally binding agreements, the new soft initiatives follow an alternative path to the reduction of trade barriers through voluntary co-operation. While international legal agreements rest on binding rules and often coercive mechanisms to sanction non-compliance[2] (so-called hard law), soft modes of governance feature voluntary co-ordination of action and social incentive structures, for example, 'peer pressure' to promote compliance (so-called soft law) (see e.g., Abbot & Snidal, 2000).

As tariff levels have been progressively reduced through international negotiations, there has been a growth in non-tariff barriers to trade (Grieco, 1990). The new soft instruments are especially directed towards reducing so-called 'red tape', that is, various bureaucratic or legal

---

1 See the WTO homepage at: http://www.wto.org/english/tratop_e/region_e/region_e.htm), accessed 25 June 2009.

2 The WTO dispute-settlement system has inter alia an important role in clarifying and enforcing the legal obligation of the various WTO agreements.

issues that can hinder trade, and preventing and reducing trade barriers caused by unnecessary regulatory divergences between markets.

In this chapter, we draw on the relevant literature and use the regulatory co-operation between the EU and Canada as an illustration of the *potential effects, advantages, and challenges of applying soft governance* in a context of trade facilitation. The EU and Canada are at the forefront with regard to applying soft modes of governance, and their co-operation exemplifies how soft instruments work between states at the same level of development of regulatory systems and policies that are not radically different at the outset.

This chapter first provides a short presentation of how various forms of regulatory co-operation can reduce non-tariff barriers to trade. Next, we elaborate on EU-Canada bilateral trade relations, emphasizing the soft mechanisms at play within the EU-Canada regulatory co-operation. We then examine the effects of these measures on facilitating trade before we discuss what lessons the EU-Canada model offers, emphasizing the advantages as well as challenges and limitations of applying a soft approach.

Our main conclusion is that the key advantage of applying a soft mode of governance relates to the adaptability and flexibility of soft regulatory co-operation in contrast to hard-law agreements. Regulatory frameworks provide close contact between regulators at every step of the regulatory process, which represents a clear advantage with respect to resolving trade irritants as they appear and preventing regulatory trade barriers from emerging in the first place. Furthermore, we emphasize the confidence-building effects of soft regulatory co-operation as the main reason why governments would do well to apply a soft mode of governance or in combination with hard-law instruments in order to facilitate trade. However, the limitations of applying soft modes of governance for facilitating trade relate to conditions such as the symmetry of market power for the parties involved, the compatibility of regulatory systems, and the degree of conflict over the trade issue at hand.

The empirical basis of our analysis rests mainly on qualitative data, that is, systematic reviews and analyses of documents, literature and interviews conducted with relevant government officials.[3] The interview data have first and foremost been used for background information and as a means to validate information obtained from relevant written documentation. However, we have applied selected anonymous citations from interviews in the text in order to illustrate certain analytical points. We have also benefited from insights from other studies on different types of instruments of trade facilitation by various authors (Elvestad, 2002; Elvestad & Veggeland, 2005; Veggeland, 2006; Veggeland & Elvestad, 2004).

The persistence of non-tariff barriers and the important role of regulators in minimizing such barriers have led to the description of regulators as 'the new diplomats' (Slaughter, 2004). The issue of regulation has traditionally been a domain of domestic policy-making, but regulation is increasingly becoming trans-national in the sense that it 'structures, guides and

[3] Interviews have been conducted with officials from the EU's delegation to the WTO's Sanitary and Phytosanitary (SPS) Committee, officials from the European Commission's Directorate General for Health and Consumer Affairs (DG SANCO), DG Trade, DG Agriculture and DG Enterprise, officials from the Canadian delegation to the WTO's SPS and Technical Barriers to Trade (TBT) Committees and the Canadian permanent mission to the WTO and to the EU as well as the Treasury Board of Canada Secretariat. Interviews were conducted in October 2005, February, March, and June 2006, and in June and September 2008. Some interviews were conducted over the phone; the others were conducted face-to-face in Geneva and Brussels.

controls human and social activities and interactions beyond, across and within national territories' (Dejlic & Sahlin-Andersson, 2006:6).

TRADE FACILITATION: REDUCING NON-TARIFF BARRIERS TO TRADE (NTMS)

To use the phrase by Slaughter (2004), interaction between regulators across national borders and the establishment of regulatory co-operation have become part of a 'new world order'.

Non-tariff barriers to trade (NTBs) can be defined as various forms of regulation other than tariffs that affect and distort the trade of goods, services, and factors of production (Beghin, 2008). Inter alia the cost of complying with different product requirements in different markets can be a heavy burden for exporters. However, it may not be desirable or feasible to remove all national differences. Some forms of differences could be 'good heterogeneity' in that it may reflect acceptable and desirable regulatory differences between nations with regard to geography, incomes or tastes, for example. However, regulatory heterogeneity 'driven by protectionist capture, bureaucratic indifference or information failures' may be undesirable (Sykes, 1999:52,57). In relation to the potential ways of dealing with non-tariff barriers to trade, we apply the concept of trade facilitation, defined as the: 'methods and tools used to prevent, reduce or eliminate the transaction costs[4] associated with regulation, enforcement and administration of trade policies' (Staples, 2004:140). Below, we shall give a brief overview of both hard-law and soft law instruments that can be applied to eliminate or reduce unnecessary regulatory burdens and regulatory divergences between markets in order to facilitate trade.

HARD INSTRUMENTS TO FACILITATE TRADE

A wide range of different tools can be used to reduce regulatory divergence (see e.g., Egan, 2001) and thereby to facilitate trade. *Full harmonization* is the elimination of all regulatory differences between markets through binding agreements where options for local deviations are prohibited and compliance is mandatory. The most obvious example is the development of EU law, which takes place within the framework of negotiated treaties between the member states. EU law covers total harmonization between the EU member states on a large number of regulatory areas, such as competition, food safety, and consumer protection. An alternative to total harmonization is *partial harmonization*. With this option, harmonization and mandatory compliance are reserved to trans-border trade, while compliance is optional in local markets.

However, there are other hard-law tools that aim to avoid problems of regulatory divergence while allowing for some regulatory differences, such as *equivalence* and *mutual recognition* (Elvestad, 2002; Veggeland, 2006; Veggeland & Elvestad, 2004). The principle

[4] Transaction costs are costs associated with making an economic exchange, e.g., costs related to compliance with regulations.

of equivalence allows trade to flow freely even though there may be differences between regulatory systems. More specifically, the determination of *equivalence* means that the parties involved accept that the rules are different as long as it is possible to determine that the rules fulfil some commonly stated objective in a satisfactory way. Thus, the concept of equivalence refers to the 'likeness' (not 'sameness') of different rules with regard to some predetermined parameter. In the EU, the 'mutual-recognition principle' ensures that goods which are lawfully produced in one member state must be accepted for sale in the territory of another member state, even if it is produced in accordance with technical or quality specifications different from those applied by the importing state. The application of the mutual-recognition principle thus guarantees the free movement of certain goods and services without the need to harmonize member states' national legislation. Outside the EU, the principle of mutual recognition is most often applied through so-called Mutual Recognition Agreements (MRAs). MRAs normally include some sort of acceptance of each other's systems of conformity assessment. For instance, signatories could be obliged to recognize certificates issued by each other's conformity-assessment bodies in order to eliminate the need to test products both in the exporting and in the importing country. Hence, mutual recognition 'more or less exempts foreign suppliers from regulations in the importing country, and the attendant cost of compliance' (Sykes, 1999:67).

Another option is to avoid regulatory divergence by including *references to private, public or intergovernmental standards* instead of including detailed requirements in the national law that could obstruct trade. This practice presupposes the existence of harmonized standards for the area in question, or at least the existence of standards that all trading partners recognize as legitimate. One of the objectives of the so-called new approach of the EU is to make it possible for the EC legislators to concentrate on the 'essential requirements' (e.g., the protection of health and safety) specified in framework directives while European standards bodies draw up the corresponding technical specifications. Thus, basing national regulations on this standard is an effective way of conforming to the essential requirements specified in mandatory directives. Hence, the aim is not total harmonization, but a degree of flexibility that allows regulations to be different as long as they fulfil the essential requirements specified.

Soft Instruments to Facilitate Trade

Equivalence, mutual recognition, and reference to standards all allow some differences between national regulatory systems to exist. However, these three tools are not soft instruments for facilitating trade, since they are normally used in connection with either binding agreements (equivalence agreements, MRAs) or binding decisions (references to standards in national law) (Howse, 2006:383). As mentioned in the introduction, applying soft-law instruments means that objectives, for instance, regulatory convergence to avoid trade problems are pursued on a voluntary basis without resorting to legislation or negotiations of binding agreements. However, the establishment of soft-law agreements has traditionally been viewed as 'second-best' solutions when the negotiations of hard-law agreements have failed. The prevailing idea is that while the best option is to have hard-law agreements, it is better to have a non-binding agreement than no agreement at all. For instance, Schäfer suggests this lower status by pointing out that 'international organisations select soft law less for its effectiveness than for its capacity to foster compromises' (Schäfer, 2006:194). Furthermore, soft-law arrangements are often viewed as transitional, a mere a step to what should preferably turn into hard law (Mörth, 2004). Nevertheless, other parts of the literature emphasize that the use of soft law 'avoids some of the costs of hard law and has certain advantages of its own' (Abbot & Snidal, 2000:423).

In order to understand the nature and potential advantages of soft co-operative instruments, it is necessary to look more closely into the types of social mechanisms involved. Eberlein and Kerwer argue that there is often a lack of in-depth understanding of the procedural mechanism inherent in soft-law instruments (Eberlein & Kerwer, 2004, p. 131). Soft instruments that facilitate trade compose a diverse group of soft law arrangements based on 'procedures that are voluntary, open, consensual, deliberative and informative' in nature (Caporaso & Wittenbrinck, 2006, p. 472). The so-called open method of coordination (OMC) of the EU rests inter alia on non-binding objectives and guidelines with specific timetables for achieving goals, qualitative and quantitative indicators, and the use of benchmarks as means of comparing best practices between countries. Furthermore, periodic monitoring, evaluation and peer review are organized as mutual learning processes. A main point is that the transfer of knowledge and the mutual learning inherent in the processes of soft instruments can create a common understanding of problems and solutions (Jacobsson, 2004), and lead to the convergence of goals and instruments (López-Santana, 2006). Hence, by learning from each others different regulatory systems may thus move towards greater compatibility without having to come to binding agreements. In the next sections, we shall explore in more detail the soft mechanisms at play within the regulatory co-operation between the EU and Canada.

The EU-Canada Bilateral Trade Relations: Main Features of the Regulatory Co-Operation

The EU and Canada have a long-standing tradition of bilateral co-operation. They have established a large number of co-operative arrangements. The formal economic co-operation between the EU and Canada dates back to 1976 with the conclusion of the 'Framework Agreement for Commercial and Economic Cooperation' (European Commission, 2003:3). This agreement was actually the EU's first co-operative agreement with an industrialised country, and it still provides the principal legal basis for the formal relationship between the EU and Canada.

Today, Canada is the EU's eleventh most important trading partner (in Euros) whereas the EU is Canada's second most important trading partner after the United States, with a 9.8 per cent share of Canada's total external trade. Trade with Canada comprised 1.8 per cent of the EU's total trade with the rest of the world (European Commission, 2008). Trade between the EU and Canada is important for both economies, and thus both parties have a clear interest in minimizing unnecessary trade barriers caused by regulatory differences. However, it took some time before there was the realization of concrete actions in the regulatory area.

In 1996, the EU and Canada entered a new phase in their relationship with the adoption of the 'Joint Action Plan'. In 1998, the EU-Canada Trade Initiative (ECTI) was established as a follow-up to the stated goal of enhancing economic and trade relations (European Commission, 2003:6). This initiative addressed a large range of issues, including regulatory ones. In order to identify remaining barriers to bilateral trade and investment, and the appropriate means to remove them, the European Commission and the Canadian government agreed in 2001 to conduct parallel business studies. These studies showed that barriers such as tariffs and quotas only played a minor role in bilateral trade whereas regulatory barriers were the foremost impediments to EU-Canada trade and investment. Thus, the EU and Canada agreed at a summit in December 2002 to intensify their regulatory dialogue and to work towards a new framework in this field.

The two parties subsequently decided to prepare a new plan of action for regulatory co-operation and to re-launch their regulatory dialogue that would also involve representatives for other stakeholders. In May 2003, a 'Joint Action Plan' for regulatory co-operation was adopted at an EU-Canada summit (EU-Canada, 2003). The plan identified measures to implement the political commitment to strengthen the regulatory co-operation between the two parties. These measures included holding a seminar to discuss the need for regulatory co-operation, producing an inventory of existing areas of EU-Canada regulatory co-operation as well as identifying new areas of co-operation, and making a review of relevant regulatory tools. In 2004, the two parties adopted a new regulatory co-operative framework[5] designed to 'promote a more systematic dialogue between EU and Canadian regulators during the early stages of the development of regulatory proposals for all goods' (European Commission, 2004). This voluntary framework is a soft-law document that is not legally binding to the Canadian government, the European Commission or the EU as a whole. The 2004 framework is a comprehensive plan for intensifying the regulatory dialogue and co-operation between the two parties, complemented by a 'Regulatory Cooperation Roadmap' as a means to implement fully the commitments for all the areas included in the framework[6] (EU-Canada, 2007a, 2007b).

Table 1 EU-Canada arrangements including regulatory co-operation[7]

The EU-Canada Joint Action Plan (1996)
The EU-Canada Trade Initiative (ECTI) (1998)
The Joint Action Plan on Regulatory Cooperation (2003)
The Framework on Regulatory Cooperation and Transparency (2004)
The EC-Canada Regulatory Cooperation Roadmap (2007)

[5] A confidential arrangement for information-sharing and an implementation plan of co-operative projects were also concluded in relation to the framework document on 'Regulatory Co-operation and Transparency'.

[6] The issues originally covered are chemicals, electrical and electronic equipment and waste (e-waste), organics equivalency, the Canada-EC Veterinary Agreement, pesticides, pharmaceuticals, radiation-emitting devices, chemical contaminants in food, food-allergen labelling, and incident prevention.

[7] There are also several hard-law agreements such as the Agreement on Customs Co-operation and Mutual Assistance (1997), the Agreement on Mutual Recognition of Conformity Assessment (MRA) (1998), the Veterinary Agreement, and the Competition Agreement (both 1999).

The Institutional Set-Up

In order to create favorable conditions for the implementation of the voluntary framework, the EU and Canada have created an institutional set-up for interaction between policy-makers, regulators, and technical experts at all levels. Regulators have established working groups on issues of common concern in their respective areas of competence, which have been agreed upon voluntarily between the two parties. Further, focused websites, teleconferences, joint seminars and workshops, and different arenas for exchanging and sharing information relevant for regulation-making and strategies of compliance are important. The Canada-EC Regulatory Co-operation Committee established for this purpose regularly follow up the functioning of the framework and progress on identified regulatory projects. This committee discusses horizontal issues, plans seminars on regulatory issues, identifies areas for improvement, disseminates best practices, and facilitates implementation of the framework in areas of mutual concern. The regulatory framework includes a number of tools to prevent and eliminate unnecessary barriers to trade. In the following sections, we shall highlight some of main procedural mechanisms involved.

Procedures for Information-Sharing and Regulatory Consultations

EU and Canadian regulators are encouraged to interact and exchange information as early as possible in the regulation-making process. Information and consultation about changes in the regulatory structure in the respective jurisdictions and upcoming legislative issues are especially important. In particular, with regard to the development of regulations and mechanisms of compliance that may have trade implications, for example, proposed technical or sanitary and phytosanitary measures,[8] the framework encourages regulators to consult each other and exchange information throughout all the stages of regulation. It is explicitly stated that the earlier that such exchanges and consultations can take place, the better. The framework even allows the opportunity for regulators to share non-public, sensitive information (cf. 'A Model Confidentiality Arrangement'). Furthermore, regulators are encouraged periodically to exchange information, such as annual work programmes on ongoing or planned regulations. Regulators are encouraged to provide, upon request by their counterparts, copies of proposed regulations and also to allow time for interested parties to provide comments. Hence, the EU and Canada are able to prepare comments and proposals for amendments to the respective regulators. When annual work programmes are exchanged, the framework encourages regulators to supplement the programme with other useful information such as potential benefits and costs and other impacts of the regulatory approach under consideration in order to make the process more transparent.

[8] In the WTO, these measures are covered by the Agreement on Technical Barriers to Trade (The TBT Agreement) and the Agreement on the Application of Sanitary and Phytosanitary Measures (The SPS Agreement).

PROCEDURES FOR EXCHANGING EXPERIENCES AND IDENTIFYING BEST PRACTICES

An important part of the framework concentrates on identifying good regulatory practice to promote better regulation. This work also involves exchange of experiences and benchmarking processes in order to identify best practices. The framework, for instance, encourages technical experts and regulators to initiate co-operative research agendas and generally to make an effort to establish a common scientific basis, say, by using similar methods of data collection. Joint reviews, staff exchanges or work-sharing activities are other examples of ways of exchanging experiences. The framework also promotes the practice of regulators' exchanging information on regulatory requirements and on choices of regulatory instruments, and stresses that these practices should take place at the earliest stage possible. By exchanging information on the different approaches to regulation, regulators may better understand the rationale behind regulatory choices and may enhance the examination of the potential for greater regulatory convergence on how to determine both the objectives and the scope of regulations. Furthermore, regulators may be in a better situation to compare methods and assumptions that analyses of regulatory proposals employ. Information about impact assessments and strategies of compliance are part of this understanding, including the potential cost-effectiveness of specific regulatory proposals compared to alternative regulatory requirements and approaches. In this context, the potential for minimizing unnecessary divergences in regulations requires examination as well.

THE EFFECTS OF REGULATORY CO-OPERATION

Based on the short presentation above, we now discuss how a soft regulatory instrument like the regulatory co-operative framework can contribute to regulatory convergence and reduction of regulatory trade barriers. In more analytical terms, we ask what possible effect the regulatory co-operative framework as an international institution may produce.[9] Inspired by the literature on international governance (see e.g., Haas, Keohane, & Levy, 1993; Young, 2002), we have categorized possible effects into 'The three C's'– increasing governmental *concern*, building national *capacity*, and enhancing the *contractual* environment. In addition, we apply a fourth 'C category' of effects labelled *confidence-building*. Though the term 'confidence-building' is not applied explicitly in the regime's literature, the role of procedures for information, openness, and communication is essential for the reduction of uncertainty and risk between actors in international relations. Keohane (1982) argues that governments contemplating international co-operation need to know their partners, not merely to know about them, in order to achieve international policy coordination (which would include the reduction of non-tariff trade barriers).

---

[9] We emphasize that this section is not an attempt to evaluate the effectiveness of the regulatory co-operation between the EU and Canada.

Increasing Governmental Concern towards Specific Problems and Relations

Our first point is that the establishment of a soft regulatory co-operation, like the EU-Canada framework, is worthy of attention in several ways. First and foremost, regulatory co-operative frameworks are strategically useful for drawing attention towards important bilateral relations. For instance, in the case of Canada, the main motivation behind the establishment of the regulatory co-operation was to strengthen its relation to the EU as one of its main trading partners. For Canada, a relatively small actor on the scene of international trade, it is vital to get the attention of large actors such as the EU. In this regard, the soft regulatory framework furnishes the systematic attention that can contribute to engaging and retaining the interest of trading partners. In other words, regulatory co-operative frameworks can be important as an active part of foreign policies to raise the profile of important relationships. Moreover, creating a framework for soft regulatory co-operation can help increase the awareness of the specific problems at hand, in this case, trade impediments caused by regulations. The activities initiated through the EU-Canada Framework, for instance, the mapping of problems caused by non-tariff barriers in their bilateral trade, provide a common base of knowledge that generates awareness of the problem at hand. Furthermore, most government agencies have limited resources available, but the regulatory framework can put pressure on departments to prioritize issues of trade facilitation. According to one of our interviewees, 'It's a question of prioritization. All departments are strapped for resources; they have to select their priorities very carefully, so sometimes you need these dialogues or processes to help focus'. Furthermore, co-operative frameworks may be useful in making sure that the necessary linkages are in place to coordinate the attention of relevant departments in order to facilitate trade. In this respect, the EU-Canada regulatory co-operation is an umbrella framework that fosters those linkages both domestically (between sectoral authorities in Canada and within the EU) and trans-nationally (between Canadian and EU regulators).

Building National Capacity to Deal with the Issues at Hand

The second point is that the regulatory co-operative frameworks can also enhance the problem-solving capacity of the governments involved. The EU-Canada framework establishes inter-organizational networks in order to transfer technical and managerial expertise that could mutually strengthen both parties' regulatory capacity. The learning-processes initiated through the framework, for example, mutual visits, exchange of personnel, seminars and different forms of sharing and exchanging information as well as the identification of best practices may contribute to the improvement of regulatory systems. Also, these processes contribute to enhancing the compatibility between systems, which creates a more favourable environment for minimizing trade barriers caused by regulatory differences. The activities of this framework thus contributes to creating a common understanding of the reasons for regulating, what to regulate, and not least the choice of 'the least trade-restrictive' regulatory tools that may help minimize problems related to regulatory trade barriers. This arrangement can also have cost-savings effects through the exchange of risk assessments, for instance. On the practical level, trade problems may not be a result of the trade rules themselves, but of the implementation of these measures. Hence, regulatory co-operative framework augments the capacity of regulators to consider all part of the regulatory process from design to compliance and inspection, and can make it easier to prevent and reduce trade problems at the administrative level. On the other hand, administrative issues may need political attention and backing to be solved, which leads us to the third category of effects.

Enhancing 'The Contractual Environment': Moving Issues Forward

The third aspect of regulatory co-operation is that it can help facilitate the progression of important issues. The dynamics created by the processes of the regulatory co-operative framework provide a certain momentum that can put pressure on decision-making. Normally we see regulators at the sectoral level are neither trade experts nor trade negotiators. However, it may take high-level political attention and coordination to initiate the necessary discussions. While some trade problems caused by regulations can be prevented and reduced at the administrative level, others are long-standing irritants that are very hard to overcome. One of our interviewees' points out that, 'Without political direction, sector departments could have a lot of great conversations, but they won't have (the) mandate or marching orders to actually solve it'. In relation to the EU and Canada, the ministerial meetings within the framework accompany a tangible pressure on a yearly basis to have something concrete to deliver. In Canada, the Department of Foreign Affairs and International Trade would normally push the sectoral departments to meet some objectives in various areas each year in order to facilitate trade. In this way the regulatory framework can offer high-level support to co-operation and thus give the necessary push to move issues forward.

Building Confidence: Preventing and Resolving Problems

The last category of effects relates to how regulatory co-operative frameworks can produce added value with respect to trade facilitation through confidence-building. The potential for trade facilitation may seem to be greatest for preventing future regulations from becoming regulatory trade barriers, rather than for resolving problems relating to regulations already in place. This perception is understandably due to the fact that the main focus of the regulatory co-operation between the EU and Canada is directed towards forthcoming regulations. Through the regulatory framework the parties give each other information much earlier than what is required of them as members of the WTO. Normally, the notification of new regulations in accordance with WTO rules should take place 60-75 days before it comes into effect. However, as regulatory processes can take three to five years to develop, the hard-law commitment to notify is often more of a formality, a 'last chance to comment' since the direction of policy has already been determined, and the regulation is designed and in its final stages of approval. Even though it is possible to modify regulations at this late stage, it is obviously harder than in the early stages of the regulatory process. In many respects it can be easier for the relevant parties to co-operate on forthcoming regulations by talking with each other early in the developmental phase and making sure that regulations are compatible and do not lead to trade barriers in the future. It is important to note that regulatory co-operation is not a part of the classic 'paradigm' of trade negotiation where problems are addressed head on. Even though issues on the agenda relate to trade irritants, the parties do not sit down at the table and negotiate resolutions; trade negotiators from other forums tend to participate in this kind of bargaining. Instead, the activities of trade facilitation take place on the technical administrative level and assume a more co-operative tone. One of our interviewees emphasized that the regulatory co-operation 'is a bit of a different creature than hard-nose negotiations. It is more a positive dialogue to get people thinking along similar lines and to facilitate resolution in these issues.'

Furthermore, the networks that are established through regulatory co-operation reflect a long-term investment in relationship between different systems. Through soft modes of co-operation, the parties may be able to understand the strengths and weaknesses of their own regulatory system in contrast to other systems. The co-operation may also make it easier to monitor each other's regulatory policies, including the quality and performance of regulations, thereby making regulatory activities more transparent. This monitoring can, in turn, make it easier to hold governments accountable for regulations that have the most adverse effects on trade. One of our interviewees pointed out that, 'A network of regulators is very handy; you know who to call, who to talk to about a trade issue, to get information, to get a response about trade irritants. That is important from a practical perspective'. However, equally important is the opportunity to understand the foundation and rationale behind the counterparts' regulations better and to be able to respond by accommodating one's own interests in the process, which could help prevent problems from arising in the first place.

Advantages and Challenges of Applying a Soft Mode of Governance to Facilitate Trade

The EU-Canada co-operative framework illustrates how trading partners can establish comprehensive, systematic, and strategic frameworks for regulatory co-operation by applying a soft mode of governance. A regulatory co-operative framework may provide political support as well as a structure for continuous contact between regulators that can significantly facilitate trade. Instead of dealing with problems related to regulatory trade barriers ad hoc, the parties have made a long-term investment in an institutional framework for promoting regulatory convergence on a voluntary basis.

The key asset of applying a soft mode of governance seems to relate to the procedural nature of these kinds of instruments and the adaptability and flexibility soft co-operative procedures provide. The benefits of close and systematic contact between operative personnel across borders has, for example, been emphasized by Keohane (1982:163) who argues that: '...intergovernmental relationships characterized by ongoing communication among working-level officials, "unauthorized" as well as authorized, are inherently more conducive to information-exchange and agreements than are traditional relationships between internally coherent bureaucracies that effectively control their communication with the external world'. The main challenges with implementing hard-law instruments like equivalence and mutual recognition agreements relate not only to the highly resource-demanding negotiations, but especially to the problem of implementing and maintaining the final agreements in practice. This latter consequence arises from the fact that problems of regulatory divergence and administrative burden are most often highly technical issues that cannot be settled once and for all. Thus, the networks that soft regulatory co-operation provides can enable governments to adjust to regulatory changes and to solve practical problems in a flexible way through regular contact with their counterparts in other countries. This is also one of the main reasons why the EU has more or less 'gone off MRAs' and has put their efforts into regulatory dialogues instead. Hence, through soft regulatory co-operation, lower levels can deal with trade irritants, and there is a higher probability of avoiding trade conflicts stemming regulatory differences. However, it is important to stress that regulatory dialogues between trading partners does not necessarily produce revolutionary results, that is, the removal of all trade-distorting differences between regulatory systems. Yet, they can produce incremental improvements that are of great value on the practical level. Nevertheless, there are important challenges and limitations with regard to applying soft regulatory co-operation to facilitate trade.

Table 2. Potential benefits and challenges of soft regulatory co-operation

Benefits:	**Challenges:**
Provides systematic attention	Incompatibility of regulatory systems
Creates internal and external linkages	Asymmetrical power relations between partners
Enhances problems-solving capacities	Lack of interest
Promotes common understanding of problems and solutions	Lack of resources
Provides momentum to move issues forward	High degree of conflict – 'malignant problems'
Builds confidence and trust	
Prevents and resolves problems	

First, differences in administrative systems and traditions may represent a challenge to regulatory co-operation. Shaffer, for example, points out that the significant institutional asymmetries between the United States' and EC's regulatory systems and cultures create a major challenge for transatlantic regulatory co-operation (Shaffer, 2002:30). In contrast, the regulatory systems of the EU and Canada are more similar at the outset which makes it much easier to produce positive results in trade facilitation.

Even though the EU and Canada give priority to regulatory co-operation with their most important trading partners, they are also interested in increased regulatory convergence with emerging markets, which may have rather different regulatory systems. This factor leads to the important question of symmetry and asymmetry in market power. The relationship between, say, the EU and the USA is a relation between two major actors in global trade, thus both parties have market power to 'impose' its regulatory system on other states – if not on each other. Countries with less market power, on the other hand, are more likely to align their regulatory systems to the requirements of the markets they depend on voluntarily. However, such efforts may be difficult and costly for countries with a regulatory system highly divergent from the systems of large markets, for example, developing countries. Hence, in cases of asymmetrical market power, regulatory co-operation may be lacking reciprocity and mutual learning.

Other types of challenges relate to ensuring that there are sufficient political commitment and resources to move the work of facilitating trade forward. The EU-Canada regulatory framework has benefited from strong political support, which is a precondition for establishing and maintaining a vital regulatory dialogue. However, there have been some challenges on capturing the interests of some regulators and making them play along with the programme of the larger framework, instead of following their own agenda. One of our interviewees emphasized that, 'some of the regulators don't see the utility. Their main concern is resources to facilitate their co-operation, but we don't have anything to offer – other than good intentions'. There may be, then, a need to consider how resources can best be allocated and channelled in order to strengthen incentives.

Applying soft modes of co-operation also has limitations in particular with regard to cases of severe trade conflicts, which can only be solved by trade negotiators in other types of forums. It is clear from the presentation above that applying a soft mode of governance to facilitate trade is applying 'a different kind of logic' than the hard bargaining logic of traditional trade negotiations. The focus is not on resolving trade conflicts but on building the confidence between regulators and regulatory system that could prevent problems from arising and ensure greater regulatory compatibility in the long run.

In conclusion, we emphasize the importance of continuously maintaining and nourishing trust and confidence between regulators in order to avoid inertia and deadlock in trade relations. This point also finds support in the comprehensive literature on trust within and between organizations, which views trust as an important mechanism for policy co-ordination (for an overview see e.g., Lane & Bachmann, 1998), which is vital for achieving regulatory convergence. For instance, if the parties exchange inspection reports and one of the parties find that the quality or thoroughness of inspections or the resulting report is not acceptable, then one 'might cease to rely on the foreign partner's inspections and resume or increase its inspections in that country' (Horton, 1998:713). Hence, an important key to success lies in achieving and maintaining a high level of trust and confidence throughout the entire regulatory process. Trust and confidence, therefore, are essential for the initiation of new regulations, for the inspection and control of agreed solutions, and for the changing and amending of regulations.

The confidence-building effects of soft co-operation are the main reason why governments should apply regulatory co-operation to facilitate trade, either as a soft mode of governance alone or in combination with hard-law instruments. Soft instruments may function as separate means for increasing regulatory compatibility, but they could also constitute a first step towards negotiating binding agreements[10] or help to maintain and implement hard-law agreements. Soft modes of governance for facilitating trade are an important part of the 'trade facilitation tool package', where several tools may be applied simultaneously to supplement and support each other.

REFERENCES

Abbot, K. W., & Snidal, D. (2000). Hard and soft law in international governance. *International organization, 54*(3), 421-456.

[10] The regulatory co-operative framework has been creating favorable conditions for the establishment of hard-law agreements, such as a hard-law regulatory co-operation agreement in connection with the negotiation of a 'Trade and Investment Enhancement Agreement' (TIEA). However, TIEA negotiations halted in May 2006 after a joint decision by the EU and Canada to await the results of the ongoing WTO negotiations.

Beghin, J. C. (2008). Non-tariff barriers. In S. N. Durlauf & L. E. Blume (Eds.), *The new Palgrave dictionary of economics* (Vol. 2nd Edition, pp. 126-129): Palgrave Macmillan LTD.

Caporaso, J., & Wittenbrinck, J. (2006). The new modes of governance and political authority in Europe. *Journal of European Public Policy, 13*(4), 471-480.

Dejlic, M.-L., & Sahlin-Andersson, K. (2006). *Transnational governance: institutional dynamics of regulation*. Cambridge: Cambridge University Press.

Egan, M. (2001). *Constructing a European market: Standards, regulation and governance.* Oxford: Oxford University Press.

Elvestad, C. (2002). Equivalence and mutual recognition agreements in relation to technical measures. *Norwegian agricultural economics research institute, NILF working paper 2002:36.*

Elvestad, C. & Veggeland, F. (2005). International trade and guidelines on equivalence and mutual recognition. *Norwegian agricultural economics research institute, NILF Report 2005-1.*

EU-Canada (2003). The joint action plan on regulatory co-operation. Adopted at the EU-Canada Summit, Athens, 28 May 2003.

EU-Canada (2007a). EC-Canada regulatory cooperation roadmap 2007.2008. Endorsed by the leaders of the EU and Canada at the EU-Canada Summit, Berlin, 4 June 2007.

EU-Canada (2007b). EU-Canada summit statement. Statement from the summit held between the leaders of the EU and Canada in Berlin, 4 June 2007.

European Commission (2003). *On EU-Canada relations: Communication from the Commission. COM (2003) final, Brussels, 13.5.2003.*

European Commission (2004). *Boosting business between EU and Canada. IP/041524. Press release, Brussels, 16.3.2004.*

European Commission (2008). Bilateral trade relations: Canada, from *http://ec.europa.eu/trade/issues/bilateral/countries/canada/index_en.htm, accessed 30 June 2009*

Grieco, J. M. (Ed.). (1990). *Cooperation among nations: Europe, America and non-tariff barriers to trade.* Ithaca and London: Cornell University Press.

Haas, P. M., Keohane, R., & Levy, M. A. (1993). Improving the effectiveness of international environmental institutions In P. M. Haas, R. Keohane & M. A. Levy (Eds.), *Institutions for the earth: Sources of effective international environmental protection.* London: MIT press.

Horton, L. (1998). Mutual recognition agreements and harmonization. *Seton Hall Law Review 29*(2), 692-735.

Howse, R. (2006). A new device for creating international legal normativity. In C. Joerges & E.-U. Petersmann (Eds.), *Constitutionalism, multilevel trade governance and social regulation*. Oxford.

Jacobsson, K. (2004). Soft regulation and the subtle transformation of states: The case of EU employment policy. *Journal of European Social Policy, 14*(4), 355-370.

Keohane, R. O. (1982). The demand for international regimes. *International Organization, 36*(2).

Keohane, R. O., & Nye, J. S. (2001). *Power and interdependence*. New York: Longman.

Lane, C., & Bachmann, R. (1998). *Trust within and between organizations: Conceptual issues and empirical applications*. New York: Oxford University Press.

López-Santana, M. (2006). The domestic implications of European soft law: Framing and transmitting change in employment policy. *Journal of European Public Policy, 13*(4), 481-499.

Mörth, U. (2004). *Soft law in governance and regulation*. Cheltenham: Edward Elgar.

Oatley, T. (2004). *International political economy: Interests and institutions in the global economy*. University of North Carolina at Chapel Hill: Pearson Longman.

Schäfer, A. (2006). Resolving deadlock: Why international organizations introduce soft law. *European Law Journal, 12*(2), 194-208.

Shaffer, G. (2002). Managing U.S.-EU trade relations through mutual recognition and safe harbour agreements: "New" and "global" approaches to transatlantic economic governance". *Robert Schuman Centre, EUI working papers, RSC NO 2002/28.*

Slaughter, A.-M. (2004). *A new world order*. Princeton and Oxford: Princeton University Press.

Staples, B. R. (2004). Trade facilitation: Improving the invisible infrastructure. In M. A. Hoekman B. and English P. (Eds.), *Development, trade and the WTO: A handbook*. Washington, D.C.: The World Bank.

Sykes, A. (1999). The (limited) role of regulatory harmonization in international goods and services markets. *Journal of International Economic Law* (2), 49-70.

Veggeland, F. (2006). Trade facilitation through equivalence and mutual recognition: The EU model. *Norwegian agricultural economics research institute, NILF Report 2006-3.*

Veggeland, F. & Elvestad, C. (2004). Equivalence and mutual recognition in trade arrangements: Relevance for the WTO and Codex Alimenatarius Commission. *Norwegian Agricultural Economics Research Institute, NILF-Report 2004:9.*

Young, O. R. (2002). *The institutional dimensions of environmental change: Fit, interplay and scale*. Massachusetts: The MIT Press.

In: Innovative Regulatory Approaches …
Ed: Noralv Veggeland

ISBN: 978-1-60876-673-4

Chapter 4

REGULATING EUROPEAN BORDERS: A CULTURAL PERSPECTIVE

Olivier Thomas Kramsch

There is no document of *culture* that is not
at the same time a document of *barbarism*.
(Benjamin, 1996: 12)

PRELUDE

Walter Benjamin lies buried on the Spanish side of the Franco-Iberian border in a small cemetery situated on a rocky outcrop overlooking the pale blue waters of the Mediterranean. For the purpose of this chapter it is significant that Benjamin, fleeing the Nazi regime, attempted to cross this border on foot in late September 1940, carrying an old suitcase containing an unfinished manuscript, accompanied by three female companions. He hoped to make it to Lisbon, as a ship was to take him across the Atlantic to New York, where anxious friends had secured a post for him at the New School for Social Research. Despite these efforts, disaster struck. Franco's border guards allowed the female travellers to cross into Spain, but owing to a passport technicality blocked Benjamin's entry. That night, fearing that German police were about to capture him, he took his life in a small hotel room on the French side of the border. The Israeli-born artist, Dani Karavan, commemorated Benjamin's fraught *passage* with an iron sculpture shaped like the mottled ruins of a tunnel, which snakes down the hillside from the cemetery towards the water's edge. As one climbs down the tunnel's stairs, one arrives at a large glass plate with this chapter's epigraph carved onto it. When one turns one's head to retrace one's footsteps, it is as if one were looking up the dark smokestack of a chimney.

INTRODUCTION

To return to Benjamin's *hotel terminus* as a scholar of European borders is an eerie experience.[1] Passport controls at the Franco-Spanish border have long been made unnecessary for European Union citizens. The small town of Port Bou, located in a valley only a stone's throw from the cemetery, is a beehive of cross-border activity with the neighbouring French municipality of Cerbere. Indeed, the larger departmental regions of which Port Bou and Cerbere are a part have over the past decades joined administratively to form a vibrant transboundary region (or *euregio*), which seeks to catalyse the area's cross-border advantages in natural resources and tourism to promote joint strategies of economic development (Hakli, 2004). Such attempts at transboundary regional co-operation resonate now with similar initiatives taking place across the face of the continent. In each of these instances, and through a diverse panoply of funding mechanisms, the European Commission seeks to re-inscribe formerly peripheral and poorly developed areas of nation-states into borderless hubs and gateways of economic growth, where, as self-styled 'laboratories of European integration', they might also serve as platforms for the crystallization of a trans-national, European *demos*.

A maturing academic literature has attempted to conceptualize these emergent cross-border regional dynamics within the broader framework of debates surrounding the impacts of globalization, European integration, and the associated territorial re-scaling of political and economic life (Castells, 2000). Notably, much of the scholarship working within a political-economic horizon traces the emergence of cross-border regionalisms and their associated governance regimes to shifts in strategic state competencies, both upwards to institutions of supra-national governance as well as downwards to sub-national entities such as cities, regions, and their increasingly sprawling hinterlands (Perkmann and Sum, 2002; Jessop, 2002; Sparke, 2000). According to these influential meta-narratives, European member states engage in cross-border institution-building largely in an attempt to generate fresh rounds of capital accumulation in areas formerly bypassed by centralized administrative-economic structures (Perkmann and Sum, 2002). Various notions of agency may be accorded non-economic actors by these accounts, but even in their more flexible neo-Gramscian formulations the primacy of economic class analysis as the primary determinant of cross-border relations persists (Jessop, 2002).

From the early- to mid-1990s a self-consciously described 'postmodern' stream of theorizing boundaries and boundary relations has co-existed parallel to that of Marxist-inspired narratives. Drawing upon social-constructivist understandings of boundary-formation, scholars in this field have been keen to overcome overtly physicalist conceptualizations of borders associated with an earlier naturalist tradition of social scientific theorizing by pointing to the discursive nature of all borders and bordering processes. In this perspective, borders are viewed as complex, tension-filled achievements almost always involving the institutionalization of an Us/Them binary relationship. At the level of nation-state borders, this discursively governed Us/Them relation is produced and reproduced across a range of state-driven actors and media: church, school, newspapers and other arenas of civic life (Paasi, 1996). In this way, borders are products of intricate acts of 'spatial socialization',

---

[1] The author wishes to thank Abel Albet i Mas for accompanying him on a memorable excursion to Walter Benjamin's gravesite in June, 1995.

in which the parties involved on one side of the border tend to crystallize their identities in response to a potentially threatening 'Other' (Paasi, 1996; Newman and Paasi, 1998).

While undeniably capturing important aspects of cross-border governance in contemporary European space, I argue that both Marxists and so-called postmodernist border scholars engage to some degree or other in what George Steinmetz already a decade ago labelled 'foundationalist decontextualization' (Steinmetz, 1999:). Reviewing the existing literature on the study of the state, he meant by this tendency 'a view of human subjectivity as determinable outside its social and historical context' (1999: 20). For Steinmetz the touchstone of foundationalist decontextualization lay in some founding assumption about human nature, be it rooted in some form of instrumental rationality, an inclination towards violence or territorialism. A resultant 'social naturalism' (Rorty, 1979) would go on to postulate some privileged institution – the individual, the market, territory – as being grounded in some predeterminate and presocial foundation. To the extent that more orthodox Marxist accounts have conceived of the state as situated 'above' civil-society relations, historical-materialist accounts have traditionally partaken of this decontextualizing move (Althusser, 1971). Likewise, so-called postmodern border scholars who posit the existence of a unified and static national or ethnic culture ('Us') counterpoised to an undifferentiated national 'Other' ('Them') also traffic in a 'culturalist version of social naturalism' (Steinmetz, 1999: 21). This is quite ironic, given that the very promise of postmodern geography, at least in its most progressive formulations, and the wider 'cultural turn' which accompanied it, argued for a concept of national culture that was anything *but* homogeneous and static; on the contrary, culture was to be viewed as internally heterogeneous and contradictory, fissured, contingent, and riven with power relations (Hall, 1980; hooks, 1994; Bhabha, 1990; in geography, Soja, 1989, 1996; Massey, 1994; Kramsch and Albet i Mas, 1999).

With the significant exception of anthropologically and ethnographically attuned reflections on borders and border transformations in various European contexts (Sahlins, 1989; Donnan and Wilson, 1994), European border studies thus inhabits a rather impoverished conceptual landscape with respect to understanding the properly *cultural* determinants shaping cross-border space. This is partially attributable, I argue, to the degree that boundaries are understood 'in the last instance' by large swathes of the border-studies community as derivative of state territoriality, conceived in broadly social naturalist terms. In the long run, I argue, this has the effect of hindering our ability to identify new and emergent identity constellations, particularly at the outer borders of the EU, where the collapse of the Iron Curtain has ushered a period of great fluidity in the governance of cross-border relations in the cultural sphere. Adherence to the different strands of 'foundational decontextualization' cited above raises the danger of blinding us to the novel cultural spaces opening up on the EU frontier, spaces which in turn may prefigure important underlying transformations within the wider European polity.

To set the stage, Part I sketches the 'state of the art' in state/culture theory, in which various theoretical enframings of the state/cultural nexus as they have developed in recent decades are laid out. Part II attempts to map recent work that has taken seriously the 'cultural turn' in relation to traditional state theory, while making links to the implications this might have for the regulation of European borders, particularly at the outer fringes of EU space. An underlying argument of this section is that one productive pathway into understanding the culture parameters of Europe's borders may be achieved by unpacking the 'black box' of state territoriality itself as constituted through myriad cultural practices, many of which originate 'outside' the state apparatus proper. Part III traces a provisional research agenda that might gain traction were European border studies to take on board some of the precepts of the 'cultural turn' in state theory. Finally, in a somewhat circuitous loop, we return to Benjamin's gravesite for a set of concluding reflections.

I. State of the Art of State/Culture Theory and the Link to European Border Studies

The role of culture in state formation and state transformation has not been elided in mainstream social-scientific treatments of the state, but rather has been analysed in the context of variously contested rounds of debate extending since the Fordist accumulation crisis of the late 1960s and 1970s. This section first analyses conceptual approaches that have addressed culture not as determinate of state practices but as epiphenomenal to and derivative of them. In this view, culture as an analytical category carries little if any purchase for understanding more 'fundamental' state-led processes. This view, I argue, largely informs Marxist understandings of borders and transboundary regionalism, severely curtailing the role cultural influences can play in structuring cross-border developments. A second, neo-Weberian paradigm, while recognizing the constitutive role of culture, has tended to treat culture as largely autonomous of the state apparatus. This has had the effect, I suggest, of reinforcing an Orientalizing analytic which places states and their cultures on a continuum of development defined by a variable geometry of 'substantive rationality', whereby the most highly developed align with the cartography of North Atlantic states. On this account, the influence of culture in relation to the state gains purchase to the degree that it acquires geographical distance from a developed 'core'. A corollary gesture within this approach has been to render culture into a timeless substance undergirded by unified and static national essences. I analyse each of these in turn.

In Marx's earlier, neo-Hegelian writings, the state emerges as a central moment in the production of wide-ranging system of ideological representations (1964; see also Jessop, 1982). Ideology, however, is determined in the last instance by the capitalist mode of production (Marx: 1970a). Though demonstrating some signs of causal effectivity, culture in this view is merely an effect of more fundamental and underlying socio-economic processes. Although Marx attributes more causal power to cultural processes in his later work on the lingering effects of Prussian feudalism or the charismatic influence of Napoleon (1970b), the effects of culture on modern state formation do not shape his work in any systematic way. Subsequent twentieth-century Marxisms were by and large intensively engaged with cultural analysis. In the first half of the century the treatment of culture as made up of symbolic systems shaped by power, inequality, conflict, and structures of domination was signally influential in the work of neo-Marxists such as Lukacs (1971), Gramsci (1971), Benjamin (1969), Horkheimer and Adorno (1944/1972). In the post-war period these themes were carried forward by theorists of 'ideology', as the work of Althusser (1971), Macherey (1978) and Barthes (1957/1972), including the British school of cultural studies, broadly attest (During, 1993). With rare exceptions, however (Anderson, 1976), Marxist state theory has tended to subsume cultural analysis to the imperatives of more 'basic' structural indices, such as capital, class or mode of production, or has attempted to create a spurious separation between things cultural (relegated to the Marxist category of use-value) and things economic (the preserve of system, or exchange-value) (Sayer, 1999).

Recent Marxist scholarship treading onto the field of border studies would seem to corroborate the abovementioned tendency within Marxist state theory. As Barbara Hooper and I already observed over half a decade ago now, for those pursuing a Marxist line of analysis into recent studies of borders and transboundary regionalism, the 'fitful' institutionalization of European cross-border regions is tied to 'their status primarily as outcomes of higher order objectives of economic governance associated with broader shifts in postwar capitalism' (Kramsch and Hooper, 2004: 6). This is evinced, for instance, to the degree that cross-border regions are perceived as the result of wider logics of globalization and neo-liberal state restructuring, or as an attempt to achieve fresh rounds of accumulation on the back of a capital-centric 'spatio-temporal fix' not unlike that accorded regionalization dynamics operating within nation-states (Perkmann and Sum, 2002; Jessop, 2002). The problem of governance in European cross-border regions is thereby defined as a response to the partial weakening or 'hollowing out' of the political-economic regulative capacities of the post-war Keynesian welfare state, the re-allocation of these governance capacities upwards towards supra-national institutions and downwards to the sub-national arenas of cities and regions (Keating, 1997; Jessop, 2000). The proliferation of cross-border regions since the 1980s is thus regarded as a 'contingent effect' of globalization, regionalization, and the end of the Cold War (Perkmann and Sum, 2002: 17). By these accounts, the role of culture in cross-border region-building is limited to the actions of class-based elites who succeed in harnessing the ideological smokescreen of a borderless world so as to better position themselves as global nodes within wider geo-economic networks (Sparke, 2000).

A neo-Weberian response emerged in the 1970s and 1980s, largely in response to the perceived ontological reductionisms of Marxist analysis. Weber's *corpus* seemed at the time to be a promising point of departure for those seeking a more nuanced culturalist understanding of state institutions and practices. Weber, after all, had creatively incorporated hermeneutic methods into his analyses of the imbrication of economic and religious practices under early capitalism (1930). For Weber, traditional or non-Western states in particular were deeply shaped by religious cultural systems; Confucianism as religious system as well as bureaucratic *praxis* became thoroughly entangled with the emergent Chinese state, while Hindu ethics allowed for an endogenous political structure in India (Weber: 1958). In addressing modern state rationality, however, Weber posited as one of its defining features a formal-legal rationality denied to previous instantiations of statehood. Thus, an ideal-typical modern state would distance itself from 'substantively rational' cultural systems that had infused earlier historical manifestations of state power in Europe, as well as non-Western state forms. While eschewing any claims that such a 'pure' state rationality had ever been achieved in the modern world, he nevertheless implicitly held to this ideal whenever engaging in comparative cultural analysis of state formations. To the degree that such an ideal was mapped onto Western European state formations, Weber could be accused of partaking of an 'Orientalist political teleology', one which systematically denied a modern rationality to non-Western state regimes (Steinmetz, 1999: 16).

Such teleological understandings of the genesis of the modern state would largely be recuperated in neo-Weberian conceptual approaches to the state. In this register, an influential 'state-centred' perspective on state theory emanating in the 1970s would not only implicitly frame Western states as inherently rational and non-Western states as suffused with cultural determinations, but would further posit the modern state as largely independent of the interests of dominant social classes (Skocpol, 1979). As notably reflected in the landmark text, *Bringing the state back in* (1985), so as to better deflect neo-Marxist explanations of the state apparatus as a 'collective capitalist', Theda Skocpol and her colleagues sought to underline how the state was not only 'relatively' autonomous from dominant social classes but in some instances were fully autonomous. In this way, neo-Weberian state theory became influential in accounting for anomalies in orthodox Marxist narratives of the state, especially in instances where state structures and policies failed to hew to hegemonic class interests. But by limiting the analytical alternatives to the binary choice between 'state-centred' and 'society-centred' explananda, the neo-Weberian state theoretical paradigm evaded cultural determinants of state action, owing to the fact that most of what was considered culture in an anthropological sense was collapsed into the 'society' domain of the state/society dualism (Steinmetz, 1999). As with Marxism, culture in the neo-Weberian perspective would be perceived ultimately as epiphenomenal to the structural conditions under which statesmen and public officials elided dominant class interests.

Where cultural determinants could not be ignored, neo-Weberian approaches to the state resorted to making 'culture itself into a timeless base by positing the existence of unified and static national (or religious, racial, or ethnic) cultures' (Steinmetz, 1999: 21). The discursive isomorphism of polity and culture had already been made clear in the political anthropology of traditional non-Western states (Balandier, 1962; Geertz, 1980). Curiously, neo-Weberian cultural essentialisms have also crept through the back door of political geographic work on European borders and border regions, in spite of their so-called postmodern theoretical provenance. This is particularly so to the extent that the 1990s produced a substantive body of scholarship on borders, border regions, and border identities emphasizing the changing role of territoriality, nationalism, everyday life, and state power in the production of boundaries (Paasi, 1991, 1996; Newman and Paasi, 1998; Anderson and O'Dowd, 1999). While this literature has opened insightful pathways for thinking about borders and boundaries beyond the physical determinisms of an earlier era, I argue that the socio-cultural approach it deploys, in its overall effect, continues to re-inscribe a static and homogeneous view of culture that is very much at odds with the spirit of the wider cultural and spatial turn in the social sciences (Dirks et al., 1994; Soja, 1999).

The ethico-political project animating much border scholarship in the 1990s is informed by a deep suspicion of globalization's purported role in reducing the salience of borders worldwide, coupled with an abiding scepticism towards the ostensible goal of ushering in a world 'without borders', a goal that is considered uninformed about the 'essential', underlying realities of the contemporary state-system in which people continue to construct their identities on the basis of variously scaled socio-spatial distinctions. Thus, in his seminal volume, Paasi (1996) argues for the central role of language and discourse in the social construction[2] of space. Against the backdrop of the historic implosion of the Iron Curtain in 1989, the reconfiguration of Europe's borderlands in Central and Eastern Europe, and the raging Balkan wars, Paasi insists that:

---

[2] Social constructivism in border studies draws on the larger field of social constructivism, which posits the collaborative nature of individual cognition and learning (Vygotsky, 1978). Within this analytical framework, borders are understood to be produced through inter-subjectively grounded understandings of 'Self' and 'Other'.

> Territorial units are historical products – not merely in their physical materiality but also in their socio-cultural meanings. Hence territories are not eternal units but, as manifestations of various institutional practices, emerge, exist for some time and disappear in the transformation of the world state system.
> (Paasi, 1996)

For Paasi, shifts in the 'territorial organization' and 'ideological landscape' of the late 1980s and early 1990s have accentuated a 'perpetual regional transformation process' (1996: 4), one which has had the effect of re-awakening a dialectic between regional transformation and the 'Other'. 'Boundaries and borders', Paasi affirms, 'no longer play the same role in distinguishing space and place as they [once] did' (1996: 6). Nevertheless, while acknowledging qualitative transformations in the nature of territoriality under the impact of globalization, Paasi hurries to offer a 'more geographical' approach, one that seeks to study 'explicitly the process of the territorialization of space, the construction and signification of demarcation and boundaries' (1996: 7). As this process unfolds:

> Even if the loyalty structures of individuals and groups are becoming both spatially and socially more complicated, one *essential* dimension of the regional transformation still appears to be the *perpetual* restructuring of various demarcations and boundaries, and the struggle over the rights and means to define the new ones as part of a *system of control* maintained over the state or some sub-state entity ... [Q]uestions of nation, state and territory have in fact returned to the top of the world's political agenda.
> (Paasi, 1996: 6; emphasis added)

Reprising these themes a few years later, David Newman and Anssi Paasi (1998), noting the re-emergence of 'questions relating to boundaries and territorial identities' in the wake of broader post-Cold War transformations, claim that:

> Geographers in particular seem to understand boundaries as expressions or manifestations of the *territoriality of states*, not least because geographic processes of socialization have taught us to acknowledge the state system within which we live – a spatial system which is characterized by more or less exclusive boundaries.
> (Newman and Paasi, 1998: 186, 197)

While Newman and Paasi strain to avoid the critique of social naturalism alluded to earlier by asserting that 'boundaries and their meanings are historically contingent... even if they are always more or less arbitrary lines between territorial entities', they do not fail to reinforce the notion that boundaries carry profound symbolic, cultural, historical, and religious meanings for their respective communities (1998: 187-88). Baring a thinly veiled disdain for 'postmodern' geographers who 'seek legitimacy within the wider social scientific context' by arguing for the gradual erosion of boundaries (Newman and Paasi, 1998: 191), the authors assert the continuing importance of territorial 'lines in constructing socio-spatial and national identities' (Newman and Paasi, 1998: 191). Indeed, they conclude, 'the construction and deconstruction, of various types of boundaries is in fact *the very story of human civilization* and of contemporary social transformation' (Newman and Paasi, 1998: 193; emphasis added).

Through these varied pronouncements, Newman and Paasi accomplish several goals with important implications for boundary studies generally. First, the existential act of boundary-making is made conceptually subservient to wider restructuring processes, notably those taking place at the sub-national regional and state territorial scale. The crucial role of the state and nationalism in overdetermining the social construction of boundaries between social collectivities is expressed in Paasi's notion of 'social spatialization', defined as:

> [T]he process through which individual actors and collectivities are socialized as members of specific territorially bounded spatial entities and through which they more ore less actively internalize collective territorial identities and shared traditions. (Paasi, 1996: 7)

Boundaries, in this view, act as the expression of socially constituted and institutionalized wholes. A corollary effect of this stance, while cognizant of the 'real and symbolic' nature of all boundaries, is to train attention on the disciplining and control-orientated aspects of boundary-drawing, focusing on that aspect of dialectical transformation which *divides* and *separates* rather than that which seeks distance from or problematize state power. From this presupposition flows Paasi's multi-tiered analytical schema outlining forms of socio-spatial integration and distinction rooted in a nationalizing 'We/Other' binary relationship (Paasi, 1996: 14).

Despite showing qualified support for the notion that the arena of local everyday life experience is the scale where 'the meanings of (state) boundaries are ultimately reproduced and contested' (Newman and Paasi, 1998: 197), thereby signalling some autonomy from the more generalized socio-spatial consciousness of the nation-state, in the end the 'state still appears to provide the basic frame for discussing boundaries' (Newman and Paasi, 1998: 197). Territorial partitioning, it appears, 'seems to remain the order of the day' (Newman and Paasi, 1998: 199). Furthermore, by evoking a 'perpetual' process of boundary demarcation and delimitation, Paasi renders boundary-making a timeless ritual with no clear geo-historical coordinates by which to measure conjunction-sensitive effects, fields of force, and capacities for negotiation and adaptive resistance to state power. As with Marxist analyses, in the social constructivist literature borders and associated identity dynamics are simply 'read off' larger-scale constructs, notably state territoriality. In short, although Newman and Paasi's social-constructivist framework recognizes that 'questions of power become crucial as far as boundaries are concerned' (1998: 188), they provide no markers for assessing different forms of border-making power, their potentially positive or negative effects and the actual capacities for 'contestation' (to use a much cited word in the literature). As I have argued elsewhere (Kramsch, in press), we seem to be standing before a normative limit in European border studies, whereby a dynamic problematization of culture and power at the border is at once ceaselessly invoked and deferred as analysis continuously reverts to static national cultural essentialisms. This patterned response, I aver, ultimately hinders our ability to grasp the culturally emergent properties at stake in the governance of European borders in the contemporary conjuncture.

II. Towards 'Another Culture'? Border 'Dialectics'

If, with Steinmetz (1999: 23), we agree that '... theorists associated with the cultural turn reject ... simplifying assumptions about human subjectivity, the explanatory primacy of utilitarian or material determinants, the directionality of history, and the inexorable differentiation of politics from broader cultural systems in the process of modernization', then we may be well positioned to search for alternative culture/state articulations that provide more theoretical specificity to borders and border cultures than has been the case thus far. In this respect the work of David Laitin may prove instructive. In his analysis of the workings of the African state dating back to the mid-1980s, Laitin had already posited a 'Janus-faced' approach to national cultures, one which argued that while states, at key foundational moments, may have the capacity to shape the cultural framework of those societies over which they govern, the cultural frames produced in the end have an independent impact on political life outside the remit of the state apparatus proper (Laitin, 1986). As later applied to inter-ethnic boundary politics involving ex-Soviet successor states, this cultural framework was developed in such a way as to suggest a *dialectical* relationship between the nationalizing policies of new states, on the one hand, and societal discourses, on the other (Laitin, 1998, 1999).

Unlike neo-Marxist and social-constructivist border scholars, what makes Laitin's cultural account relevant for this chapter is that it grants analytical primacy neither to the state nor to individual or group actors, or both, in setting the parameters for new identity formations emerging at the borders of ex-Soviet space. 'In extraordinary times', he argues, 'the groupness of culture cannot be taken for granted' (Laitin, 1999: 292). Indeed, and as he convincingly demonstrates in the case of four ex-Soviet republics – Estonia, Latvia, Ukraine, and Kazakhstan – it is in the dialectical tension between 'titular' elites who assumed the mantle of sovereignty following the collapse of the Soviet Union and entrepreneurial groups representing non-titular populations within these new nationalizing formations that 'a new cultural identity – a 'Russian-speaking population', is in formation (Laitin, 1999: 292). Importantly, this Russian-speaking population is different both from what was expressly sought after by those who classify themselves now by a Russian-speaking identity, as well as those state elites who achieved titular sovereignty after the Soviet collapse of 1991.

Laitin hypothesizes that the degree of freedom achieved by this new Russian-speaking identity formation in post-Soviet space is dependent on the extent of hegemony achieved by titular national elites in each host country. This power differed from society to society. The Baltic states were included in the Soviet Union only after WWII and therefore had the interwar experience of sovereignty. Moreover, the Western capitalist world never recognized the Soviet occupation of these states. Their nationalist elites had the choice, then, in 1991 to declare their states as having legal continuity with the inter-war republics. This move gave nationalists from Estonia and Latvia the legal right to exclude all Soviet-era migrants from automatic citizenship in their restored republics (Laitin, 1999: 293). Significantly, this ban extended to the right to vote. In the Ukraine and Kazakhstan, however, titular Ukrainians and Russians had equal claims to receive citizenship. Due to the longer period of Soviet rule, there furthermore existed many Russian-speaking titulars who were not as enthused about aggressive moves towards Ukrainian or Kazakh nationalisms as their peers in the Baltics.

Depending upon the local and national environments cited above, Laitin found that Russians in Soviet successor states were compelled 'by the uncertainties of the transition period to explore new identities, those that made sense to them in a new political context' (1999: 295). In Estonia and Latvia, for instance, the parameters for the novel identity configurations of Russian-speaking publics were established by their respective states' 'culturalist' nationalization programmes, one which offered the choice either of assimilation or a revivalist response. Against these state policies, the leaders of the Russian-speaking population sought to broaden their constituencies as much as possible by integrating Russians, Ukrainians, Belarusans, Poles, and Jews. Thus, ethnic politics in the Baltics is shaped by attempts at boundary expansion by the leaders of the Russian-speaking population, and boundary retraction and splintering by titular state leaders. In Ukraine and Kazakhstan, since governments have taken the 'civic' route towards nation- state formation, cultural politics have shown a different cast. In these republics, leaders of the non-titular subset of the Russian-speaking nationality seek to limit the move towards cultural pluralism, as this would deny them the monopoly ground on which they could speak for 'their' people. Towards this goal, their aim is to create the conditions for a rigid Russian/titular divide in Ukrainian and Kazakh societies. In all the republics under consideration, it is noteworthy that each side strives for its goals through discursive positionings that are by and large autonomous of state bureaucrats or nationalist entrepreneurs. Against this backdrop, to posit an overarching conflict between two pre-defined and fixed identities – nascent titular nationalities and Russians – would be to miss 'the possibilities of new compounds formed and reformed in the "wild frontier" opened up by the "Leninist extinction"' (1999: 314).

III. Looking Up Benjamin's Chimney Hole

Latin's 'wild frontier', of course, applies specifically to the intra-state ethnic boundaries crystallizing *within* ex-Soviet states. But I would argue it would not take a great leap of the imagination to apply the term equally well to the actually existing frontiers separating ex-Soviet states, and between EU states and Russia proper. This is the case, as Ann Kennard has so eloquently documented, because culture is increasingly seen by EU officials as a means of forming a bridgehead between EU and non-EU space (Kennard, 2004, 2006). Any serious consideration of the regulation of identity politics within these fraught borderlands would certainly need to develop a notion of culture that eschews higher order essentialisms and is attuned to the fluid, internally fissured, unstable and power-riven nature of social relations between the Russian-speaking 'beached' diasporas of the ex-Soviet sphere and their Russian cross-border counterparts. Such an approach would of necessity demand a relational understanding of state power, one which not only asserts that states 'are shot through with circuits of meaning that cut across the state-society frontier' (Steinmetz, 1999: 12), but highlights the fact that such 'circuits of meaning' are often located at and beyond the territorial margins of the state proper, in its disruptive borderlands (Tilly, 1999). Such a culturally inflected understanding would also go far in helping to clarify what is at stake in 'taming the regulatory state' within Europe's cross-border regions, as the outward distribution of public-governance capacities to the trans-boundary regional level, at least from the evidence of the Nordic countries, appears to have a detrimental impact on building networks of trans-boundary social capital and trust relations necessary for the endogenous development of such regions (Veggeland, 2009: 125-138).[3]

---

[3] In this context, it might be useful to stage a dialogue between Laitin's conceptualization of 'frontier dialectics' as regards the identity politics of Russian-speaking non-titulars in the Baltic states with Veggeland's reporting on the political tensions involved in establishing a trans-boundary Barents Euro-Arctic Council (BEAC) (Veggeland, 2009: 131-134). In the latter body, indigenous peoples residing in the northernmost parts of Finland, Norway, Sweden, and north-west Russia occupy one seat on the Barents Regional Council and form Working Group of

Such a dialectical understanding of border culture would, moreover, crack open an important epistemological borderland in European border studies. Indeed, such a gesture would move beyond the foundationalist de-contextualizations of Marxist analysis as well as the *a priori* identitarian presuppositions of socially-constructed 'Us/Them' relations to interrogate the very premises upon which the meta-governance of time and space are legitimized at the borders of states. It is to the elaboration of such a redemptive space-time, freed from modernity's nationalizing myths and associated nostrums of universal progress, that Walter Benjamin focused his attention in the final years of his life. The idea of border govern-*mentality* embedded in this strategy would literally be expressed through the drawing of a new politicized border, in which the lost struggles of the past, as well as forgotten spaces, would be called back into a new way of seeing: the 'now of recognizability' (1999: 945; see also Blanqui, 1973). 'It is very easy to establish oppositions, according to determinate points of view, within the various "fields" of any epoch, such that on one side lies the "productive", "forward-looking", "lively", "positive" part of the epoch, and on the other side the abortive, retrograde and obsolescent', Benjamin wrote mid-way through the ruins of his vast Arcades Project (1999: 459). He would add:

> The very contours of the positive element will appear distinctly only insofar as this element is set off against the negative. On the other hand, every negation has its value solely as background for the delineation of the lively, the positive. It is therefore of decisive importance that *a new partition be applied* to this initially excluded, negative component so that, by a displacement of the angle of vision ..., a positive element emerges anew in it too – something different from that previously signified. And so on... until the entire past is brought into the present in a historical apocastasis.
> (Benjamin, 1999: 459; emphasis added)

We may forgive Benjamin, his messianism, his overly poetic style. But crucially, the transformed angle of vision he presaged in the foregoing passage would allow us to break with the tendency towards spatio-temporal continuity in the study of European borders and boundaries, and would renew attention to the 'places where tradition breaks off – hence its peaks and crags, which offer footing to one who would cross over them...' (1999: 474). For as Laitin's study reveals, it is precisely here, in the discontinuities and ruptures characterizing Europe's borders, notably on its eastern frontiers, that unforeseen 'newness' is being secreted. Tragically, Benjamin never made it over the 'peaks and crags' of the Pyrenean borderland where he now lies. In *our* space/time of disorienting transition, where it would appear, once again, 'all that is solid melts into air', it is up to us to recuperate Benjamin's unique power of (in)sight to grasp better what is truly at stake in Europe's emergent cultural borderlands.

ACKNOWLEDGEMENTS

I would like to thank Noralv Veggeland for offering me a congenial space in his book project. Conversations in various pleasant cross-border locales between Nijmegen and Lillehammer helped to clarify some of the ideas presented here.

Indigenous Peoples, which has an advisory role to the Regional Council and the BEAC. A dialectical understanding of indigenous people's orthogonal relationship to their respective nation-state structures might indeed go far in explaining why 'the interaction between these diverse and complex partners tends to contribute to some extent towards making the many partnerships and regulatory bodies non-transparent' (1999: 136).

References

Althusser, L. (1971). Ideology and ideological state apparatuses. In *Lenin and philosophy* (pp.121-72). London: NLB.

Anderson, J., & O'Dowd, L. (1999). Borders, border regions and territoriality: contradictory meanings, changing significance. *Regional Studies, 33.7*, 593-604.

Anderson, P. (1976). *Considerations on Western Marxism*. London: Verso.

Balandier, G. (1962). *Afrique ambigue*. Paris: Plon.

Barthes, R. (1957/1972). *Mythologies*. New York: Hill and Wang.

Benjamin, W. (1996). Seventh thesis on the philosophy of history. In M. Bullock, & M.W. Jennings (Eds.), *Selected writings. Vol I (1913-1926)* (pp.113-127). Cambridge, MA: The Belknap Press of Harvard University Press.

Benjamin, W. (1969). *Illuminations*. New York: Schocken.

Bhabha, H. (1990). *Nation and narration*. London and New York: Routledge.

Blanqui, A. (1973). *Instructions pour une prise d'armes: l'éternité par les astres, hypotheses astronomique, et autres textes*. Paris: Société Encyclopédique Francaise.

Castells, M. (2000). *End of millennium*. Oxford: Blackwell.

Dirks, N.B., Eley, G., & Ortner, S.B. (Eds.) (1994). *Culture/power/history: a reader in contemporary social theory*. Princeton: Princeton University Press.

Donnan, H., & Wilson, T.M. (1994). *Border approaches: anthropological perspectives on frontiers*. Lanham, MD: University Press of America.

During, S. (Ed.) (1993). *The cultural studies reader*. London: Routledge.

Geertz, C. (1980). *Negara: the theatre state in nineteenth century Bali*. Princeton: Princeton University Press.

Gramsci, A. (1971). *Selections from the prison notebooks*. New York: International Publishers.

Hakli, J. (2004). Governing the mountains: cross-border regionalization in Catalonia. In O. Kramsch, & B. Hooper (Eds.), *Cross-border governance in the European Union* (pp. 56-69). London and New York: Routledge.

Hall, S. (1980). *Culture, media, language: working papers in cultural studies, 1872-1979*. Birmingham, UK: Centre for Contemporary Cultural Studies.

Hooks, B. (1994). *Outlaw culture: resisting representations*. New York: Routledge.

Horkheimer, M., & Adorno, T.W. (1944/1972). *Dialectic of enlightenment*. New York: Herder and Herder.

Jessop, B. (2002). The political economy of scale. In M. Perkmann, & N.-L. Sum (Eds.), *Globalization, regionalization and cross-border regions* (pp.45-63). Hampshire: Palgrave.

Jessop, B. (2000). The crisis of the national spatio-temporal fix and the tendential ecological dominance of globalizing capitalism. *International Journal of Urban and Regional Research, 24, 2*, 323-60.

Jessop, B. (1982). *The capitalist state*. New York: New York University Press.

Keating, M. (1997). *The new regionalism in Western Europe: territorial restructuring and political change*. Northampton: Edward Elgar.

Kennard, A. (2006). The EU's new eastern border: will cultural overlap be a force for change? In *Borderland identities: territory and belonging in Central, North and East Europe* (pp.89-108). Förlags ab Gondolin.

Kennard, A. (2004). Culture shift on the future eastern border of the EU. *Perspectives on European Politics and Society, 5, 1*, 1-28.

Kramsch, O. (in press). The Rabelaisian border. *Society & Space: Environment and Planning D.*

Kramsch, O., & B. Hooper (2004). *Cross-border governance in the European Union*. London and New York: Routledge.

Kramsch, O., & Albet i Mas, A. (1999). Space, inequality and difference: 'radical turns' and 'cultural turns'. *European Planning Studies*, *7, 1*, 77-79.

Laitin, D.D. (1999). The cultural elements of ethnically mixed states: nationality re-formation in the Soviet successor states. In G. Steinmetz (Ed.), *State/culture: state formation after the cultural turn* (pp. 291-320). Ithaca and London: Cornell University Press.

Laitin, D.D. (1998). *Identity in formation: the Russian-speaking populations in the near abroad*. Ithaca, NY: Cornell University Press.

Laitin, D.D. (1986). *Hegemony and culture: politics and religious change among the Yoruba*. Chicago: University of Chicago Press.

Lukacs, G. (1971). *History and class consciousness*. Cambridge, MA: MIT Press.

Macherey, P. (1978). *Pour une théorie de la production littéraire*. Paris: Maspero.

Marx, K. (1970a). The German ideology. In *Marx and Engels: selected works*, vol. I (pp. 16-80). Moscow: Progress.

Marx, K. (1970b). The eighteenth Brumaire of Louis Bonaparte. In *Marx and Engels: selected works, vol. I*. (pp. 394-487). Moscow: Progress.

Marx, K. (1964). *Early writings*. New York: McGraw-Hill.

Massey, D. (1994). *Space, place and gender*. Minneapolis: University of Minnesota Press.

Newman, D., & Paasi, A. (1998). Fences and neighbours in the postmodern world: boundary narratives in political geography. *Progress in Human Geography*, *22.2*, 186-207.

Paasi, A. (1996). *Territories, boundaries and consciousness: the changing geographies of the Finnish-Russian border*. Chichester: John Wiley & Sons.

Paasi, A. (1991). Deconstructing regions: notes on the scales of spatial life. *Environment and Planning A*, *23*, 239-56.

Perkmann, M., & Sum, N.-L. (Eds.) (2002). *Globalization, regionalization and cross-border regions*. Hampshire: Palgrave.

Rorty, R. (1979). *Philosophy and the mirror of nature*. Princeton, NJ: Princeton University Press.

Sahlins, P. (1989). *Boundaries: the making of France and Spain in the Pyrenees*. Berkeley: University of California Press.

Sayer, A. (1999). *Culture and economy after the cultural turn*. London: SAGE.

Skocpol, T. (1985). Bringing the state back in: strategies of analysis in current research. In D. Rueschemeyer, P.B. Evans. & T. Skocpol (Eds.), *Bringing the state back in* (pp. 3-43). New York: Cambridge University Press.

Skocpol, T. (1979). *States and social revolutions*. New York: Cambridge University Press.

Soja, E.W. (1999). In different spaces: the cultural turn in urban and regional political economy. *European Planning Studies*, *7, 1*, 65-76.

Soja, E.W. (1996). *Thirdspace: journeys to Los Angeles and other real-and-imagined places*. London: Blackwell.

Soja, E.W. (1989). *Postmodern geographies: the reassertion of space in critical social theory*. London: Verso.

Sparke, M. (2000). Chunnel visions: unpacking the anticipatory geographies of an Anglo-European borderland. *Journal of Borderlands Studies, 15*, 187-219.

Steinmetz, G. (Ed.) (1999). *State/culture: state formation after the cultural turn*. Ithaca and London: Cornell University Press.

Tilly, C. (1999). Epilogue: now where. In G. Steinmetz (Ed.), *State/culture: state formation after the cultural turn* (pp. 407-419). Ithaca and London: Cornell University Press.

Veggeland, N. (2009). *Taming the regulatory state: politics and ethics*. Cheltenham, UK: Edward Elgar.

Vygotsky, L. (1978). *Mind in society*. London: Harvard University Press.

Weber, M. (1958). Politics as a vocation. In H.H. Gerth, & C.W. Mills (Eds.), *From Max Weber* (pp. 18-35). New York: Oxford University Press.

Weber, M. (1930). *The Protestant ethics and the spirit of capitalism*. New York: Scribner.

In: Innovative Regulatory Approaches …
Ed: Noralv Veggeland
ISBN: 978-1-60876-673-4

Chapter 5

FRIENDS FOREVER? INTEREST ORGANIZATIONS, PLURALISM, TRANSPARENCY, AND CONSENSUAL POLICY MAKING IN SCANDINAVIA[1]

Peter Munk Christiansen

INTRODUCTION

In Denmark, Norway, and Sweden, the relations between interest groups and the state were developed during the twentieth century in accordance with Scandinavian traditions of consensual policy-making. During recent decades the role of interest groups in policy-making has changed. Privileged groups are no longer invited to timely deliberations on public policies. They get access when decision-makers assess the benefits to exceed costs of close interest-group involvement. The development has democratic consequences. On the one hand more groups present a broader set of inputs to the administrative and political decision-making process. On the other hand the price is a less transparent policy-making process.

In all the Scandinavian countries old traditions for close involvement of interest organizations in the formation of public policy have been eroded during the last couple of decades. Interest organizations are still important actors when public policies are formulated, but in very different ways than before. There are more interest organizations around, they cover a broader segment of interests, and there are more access points to influence public policy-making. Whereas these changes may enhance public deliberation on policies and thus strengthen democratic processes, a second group of changes may have the opposite consequences: formalized structures of policy preparation have been eroded, and it has become less transparent which interest groups affect which policies in which ways. A broader set of relevant interest groups and a less transparent policy-making process are what this chapter is about.

The three Scandinavian countries traditionally rank among the top group on scales of corporatism. Markus Crepaz and Arend Lijphart (1991) have Norway, Sweden, and Denmark

[1] Most of the empirical material for the chapter relates to Denmark, but where possible the chapter draws on empirical material from Norway and Sweden.

as number two, three, and five in an 18 countries comparison. According to Alan Siaroff (1999: 184) – also based on a review of previous studies – Norway and Sweden come out as 'strongly corporatist' and Denmark as 'moderately-to-strongly corporatist'. Most of the measurements that Crepaz and Lijphart and Siaroff refer to are from the 1970s and 1980s – some of them even older. I show that at least in terms of corporatism in the policy preparation phase, Scandinavian traditions have changed considerably from the 1980s until now. We start by looking at the rise of Scandinavian corporatism.

The Rise of Scandinavian Corporatism

Corporatism is one of the most contested concepts in political science, and it is used to deal with a number of different issues (cf. Molina & Rhodes, 2002; Siaroff, 1999). In a large part of the literature corporatism is analysed as a variant of capitalism, in which strong and centralized labour market organizations settle their disputes under the surveillance and active intervention by the state. Countries with strong and enduring corporatist structures are so-called co-ordinated market economies as opposed to non-coordinated liberal economies. Our interest here is not the economic, but rather the democratic aspects of corporatism. That calls for other aspects of corporatism than centralization of the labour market, wage settlements, and economic outcomes. From a democratic perspective the interesting aspects related to interest groups are how they participate in and affect the political and administrative decision-making process. To what extent are interest groups integrated in the political and administrative decision-making process, and to what extent are interest groups only deliberately included in public policy-making when it fits the demands of decision-makers? Are some interest groups privileged, and others not? How transparent is the political process? Do some groups have *de facto* power to block political or administrative decisions?

By corporatism we understand the institutionalized integration of interest groups in the formulation or implementation, or both, of public policies (cf. Christiansen et al., 2009). Corporatism is opposed to pluralism in which the inclusion of interest groups in policy formulation or policy implementation varies from case to case, that is, a system without interest groups that enjoy a special privileged position.

The development of Scandinavian corporatism is characterized by three traits: First, it developed slowly and not according to a grand plan. In this way corporatism was developed to fit into existing political and administrative institutions. Secondly, corporatism was established in relation to labour-market policy and industrial policies, but moved gradually into other policy areas to cover a broad magnitude of policy areas at the height of corporatism. Thirdly, corporatism served a plurality of purposes, such as increasing legislative legitimacy through adaptation to the preferences of organized interests, involving expertise knowledge in the policy process, parliamentary control of the administration etc. Together these traits support the characteristics of the Scandinavian countries as consensual democracies (cf. Lijphart, 1999: 250).

The literature varies in terms of when Scandinavian corporatism was established, even within each country. It may date as far back as the pre-democratic guild system, but not until the late nineteenth and early twentieth century does the outline of the corporatist system start to emerge. In all three countries various commissions and councils were established from the

1880s and onwards. They mainly dealt with labour-market issues and later on with agriculture, fishery, and manufacturing. The three countries were late industrialists, but the rapid growth of the urban work force gave rise to a number of social problems that the tiny state and municipal administrations had only few resources to handle. The 'social question' or the 'labour problem' (cf. Knudsen & Rothstein, 1994: 212; Nørgaard, 1997; Nordby, 1994) was a challenge to existing institutions. Involving the workers' and employers' organizations in their solution seemingly suited the politically most powerful actors of the time, even if the social democratic parties were weak. At the same time industrial organizations grew stronger, and owing to increasing globalization of trade in agriculture and manufacturing, they demanded a stronger political and administrative focus on their trades and their conditions. An Agricultural Ministry was established in Denmark in 1896 and a Ministry of Trade in 1908 – a time not very different from the other Scandinavian countries.

Prior to World War I the newly established corporatist structures were still fragile. They were not established according to a general decision, but seemed to fit the demands of the day. In Denmark there were 43 committees in 1913. Three out of four had representatives from interest organizations, and two out of three had as main assignment to make suggestions for new political decisions (Christiansen & Nørgaard, 2003: 43). The Great War was probably a major boost to the institutionalization of the committee system and thus the development of corporatist policy-making in all three countries. War-time regulations involved the state in activities – mostly restrictions on trade and consumption – that represented new responsibilities to ministers and civil servants (Nordby, 1994: 42-3). In Denmark the number of committees doubled from 1913 through 1916 (Christiansen & Nørgaard, 2003: 43); and in Norway at least 16 committees were established with duties related to trade, pricing, and consumption on major groups of goods (Nordby, 1994: 43).

Even if the provision of raw materials and goods became liberalized after the war and the commissions for their administration abolished, the corporatist institutions seem to have survived the prosperous 1920s. Corporatist commissions, committees, and councils apparently could be used for many purposes, also in times of prosperity. And if the roaring 20s were not enough, the economic crisis of the 1930s and World War II did the job (cf. Christiansen and Nørgaard, 2003: 41ff.; Nordby, 1994: 43ff.; Rothstein, 1992: 110ff.). After World War II corporatist structures were well developed in all three countries, and the three decades or so following the war became the 'golden era' of Scandinavian corporatism. By way of example, the total number of committees in Denmark had grown to 413 in 1946. And as experienced in the aftermath of World War I, the liberalization of international trade following the war did not lead to the abolishment of the committee system. On the contrary, in the Danish case, the net number of committees grew from 413 in 1946 to 667 in 1975 (Christiansen & Nørgaard, 2003: 59).

To illustrate the point that corporatist institutions were developed to fit existing institutions and dominant political actors let us briefly look at the establishment of the Danish unemployment system in 1907. The proposal had been underway for many years. The still weak Social Democratic Party went for a Ghent system in which state-subsidized unemployment benefits would be administered by the trade unions. The two biggest parties, the Liberals and the Conservatives, had each their reasons for supporting an unemployment system of the Ghent type. The Conservative Party, which in this case represented the urban employers, was eager to have the state pay part of the price for urban peace to avoid fuelling a social revolution. The Liberal Party, representing the peasants, on one hand, did not want the unemployment scheme to spread to the country side, and, on the other hand, had very little trust in the state administration that had been run by the Conservatives until 1901. The Ghent system was an excellent construction to serve the ends of the two dominant political parties. The Conservatives got their insurance system, and the Liberals kept it away from the countryside and did not assist in further enlargement of state bureaucracy (Nørgaard, 1997: Ch. 5). When the labour movement and the Social Democratic Party came to love the Ghent system intensely – and still do today – it is because the system implies a high level of unionization (Scruggs, 2002) and because it is one of the strongest barriers to the drop in unionization that we have witnessed during the last couple of decades in most countries, except the four Ghent countries (Denmark, Sweden, Finland, and Belgium).

Scandinavian corporatism was fitted to work in accordance with, not against, existing political and administrative structures. It was not only subject of influence from the Scandinavian administrative tradition; it also became part of it. It fitted to and became part of a consensual way of policy-making (cf. Lijphart, 1999). Thereby corporatism also became part of the Scandinavian or Nordic administrative model where multi-party systems goes together with state recognition of few well organized groups that are allowed to be quite influential (Kickert, 2002).

Another point about Scandinavian corporatism is that even if it was established within labour-market policy and industrial policy, corporatist structures came to cover a number of policy areas with only one structural prerequisite in common: the existence of interest organizations that represent major actors in the policy sector in question. In the Danish case educational policy was one of the major sectors for penetration of the corporatist way of policy-making in the post World War II period; it was actually the policy area in which most new commissions and committees were established (Christiansen & Nørgaard, 2003: 73-81). In Norway educational policy was even before World War II one of the major sectors for the integration of interest groups in policy formulation and implementation. In 1936 one of five committees belonged to the Church and Educational Ministry, in 1966 the corresponding figure was one out of three (Nordby, 1994: 86). We find the same tendency in Sweden (Rothstein, 1992: 284ff.). The integration of interest groups in the political and administrative decision-making process became a significant element in many policy areas. Bo Rothstein (1992) mentions a large number of such areas in addition to the usual suspects of corporatist policy-making: alcohol policy, environmental policy, and constitutional policy.

Environmental policy entered the agenda in the Scandinavian countries in the late 1960s and the early 1970s. It was a new political issue that in some respects differed considerably from the traditional policy areas; new types of regulations were to be imposed on industry, municipalities, and consumers and with fairly intangible effects. Nevertheless, policies were developed and implemented according to established traditions, but adapted to the new policy regimes. In the formative years of Scandinavian environmental policy – Sweden was a few years ahead of Denmark and Norway – industrial organizations and municipal and regional organizations were heavily involved in designing the new policy areas' institutions and instruments (Christiansen, 1996; Jansen & Osland, 1996; Lundqvist, 1996). Corporatist policy-making was so broadly accepted that no one questioned that interest groups should be heavily integrated into the formulation and implementation of environmental policy. In the formative years environmental groups only played a modest role for the simple reason that they were hardly developed except for very few organizations (Christiansen et al., 2004: Ch. 9). It was only later on that environmental groups became central partners for policy-makers in environmental policy (e.g., Rommetvedt & Opedal, 1995). The inclusion of environmental groups in the environmental policy-making process shows a flexible way of adapting to changing societal conditions, *in casu* the growth of environmental groups. The case of Danish environmental policy and the role of interest organizations in its formulation are expanded below.

The last point to be made about Scandinavian corporatism is that it serves and has served a number of different purposes. The rise of corporatist interest mediation is not an effect of a grand plan or a specific ideology; nor did it come from above because of necessity. Inclusion of interest groups in the policy process was rather an adequate answer to shifting political and administrative demands. Corporatism was introduced, learned, and spread as a consequence of its plasticity. The way corporatism was spelled out in especially Denmark and Norway reflected the demand for a flexible instrument. In Sweden parts of the corporatist structures were slightly more formalized (i.e., the agency governance system), but still with leverage for flexibility.

If we look at the core institutional expression of corporatism, the committee system, the composition and functions may illustrate the multitude of purposes of committees. To be classified as a corporatist body, committees must have at least one interest organization as member. All other elements of their composition may vary, and they do. We find all possible variants of committees with a mix of members from interest organizations, political parties, civil servants, municipal representatives, and experts. Of the 667 Danish committees that existed in 1975, 86 per cent had civil servants as members, 57 per cent had interest groups, 12 per cent politicians, 30 per cent municipal representatives, and 54 per cent experts, including judges (Christiansen & Nørgaard, 2003: 59).

Through the composition of committees, ministers, and top civil servants can meet some and oppress other considerations, and in all kinds of variants. Inclusion of interest groups signals acceptance of partial interests, whereas inclusion of experts signals an analytical demand. In some cases judges are chairmen of corporatist committees such as appeals boards. The combination of a judge and interest organizations as members signals the role of a semi-judicial body in which partial interests' considerations are accepted. The composition of committees including chairman and number of members is a vital instrument in the hands of the principals putting together the committees.

Committees also have very different functions. Some committees have been used for policy-preparation. Norway and Sweden have institutionalized policy-preparation in the NOU system (*Norges Offentlige Utredninger*, Official Norwegian Reports) and the SOU system (*Statens Offentliga Utredningar*, Swedish Government Inquiries), where as the Danish inquiry system is less institutionalized. Policy-preparing committees may serve different political preferences. In some cases committees are established simply to scrutinize problems and their possible solutions in a more or less synoptically rational way. In other cases policy-preparing committees serve more clearly political purposes, depoliticizing an issue, clearing the way for unpopular decisions, or stalling for time to allow the political principals to find their own standpoint.

Other committees implement public policies in the sense that they have administrative duties that might otherwise be performed by traditional bureaucracy, but for some reason it has been decided by law to let a collegial body handle an administrative task. They may be semi-judicial like for instance appeals boards in which the legislator prefers an arm's-length principle typical for the regulatory state (cf. Veggeland, 2009) to the politically controlled bureaucracy. They may be created to let expertise dominate the decisions like for instance research councils, which allocate research grants. Administrative committees may also be created to remove unpleasant decisions from the minister or from the ministerial hierarchy. This is the case with the Danish Refugee Appeals Board. Refugee cases can be quite problematic for a minister because of all the human problems involved. To protect the minister from such cases, individual appeals are handled outside of the ministerial hierarchy.

Committees' main role may also be advisory. In a way policy-preparing committees are also advisory, because their policy recommendations are never more than recommendations. However, there is also a quite large group of committees, many of which have interest groups as members that do not prepare policies and do not have administrative duties. This group also serves different purposes, for instance, forums of general policy discussions between civil servants and interest groups or specialized advisory boards in technically complicated matters, or something in between.

Finally we shall point to the role of committees as checks on the government. Particularly in the early period when mistrust towards civil servants was widespread among the Liberals and the Social Democrats, the opposition parties to some extent used committees to control government (Christiansen & Nørgaard, 2003: Ch. 3). By allowing access through committee membership for organizations that were friendly to the opposition parties, the opposition established an institutional beachhead into the governments' administration. Still today political parties exploit interest groups to act as agents in order to control governmental preparation of decisions or governmental administration. Normally politicians and civil servants are agents of interest groups; the reverse, however, may also be the case (Christiansen & Nørgaard, 2006).

The rise of Scandinavian corporatism during the first three quarters of the twentieth century is a story about a gradual development of a flexible institution of policy formulation and policy administration. It came out of concrete needs for problem-solving, it seems to have been diffused by learning, and it seems to fit a political culture of co-operation and consensus.

The Decline of Scandinavian Corporatism

The literature does not agree about the fate of Scandinavian corporatism in the last quarter of the twentieth century. Alan Siaroff (1999: 198) finds a very marginal reduction of the strength of integration (which he prefers to corporatism) in Denmark and Sweden, but not for Norway from the late 1960s through the mid-1990s. For 24 OECD countries he only finds a very modest average drop in integration in the same period. Hugh Compston (1998) is occupied with the concertation of labour-market policies. He finds that Swedish corporatism has been reduced since 1985, but that labour-market corporatism has increased in Denmark and Norway in the same period. These two authors mainly work within the political-economy framework.

If we look to authors who work with the same concept of corporatism as we do here, there is more agreement that Scandinavian corporatism has been reduced. Jens Blom-Hansen (2000: 171, see also Blom-Hansen, 2001) reviews the literature up to the late 1990s and finds that 'traditional Scandinavian corporatism' has been weakened. Christiansen et al. (2009) conclude that the tradition of integrating interest groups in the preparation of public policies has been reduced significantly as measured by interest-group presence in policy-preparing committees. In the case of policy implementation, their results are more diverse. In the case of Denmark, they find a rather constant level from the 1990s and onwards – even if there is a drop in implementation corporatism in the 1980s. In contrast, Norwegian implementation corporatism follows the drop in the Norwegian corporatism in relation to policy preparation. The Swedish case is somewhere in between. It should be mentioned that while Denmark and Norway are quite similar in their approach to integration of interest groups in the policy-making process, Sweden deviates in some respects, for example, in the inclusion of interest groups in the boards of directors of the independent Swedish agencies.

The figures for the development in the Danish committees are shown in Table 1. As measured by the number of committees, Danish corporatism peaks at some point around 1980. There is a significant drop in the number of committees during the 1980s, a rise again in the second half of the 1990s, and a slight drop again in the first half decade of the 2000s. More interesting, perhaps, is the distribution of the remaining committees on functions. Only ten per cent of the committees in 2005 are primarily occupied with preparation of political decisions. In absolute numbers this corresponds to a little more that 40 committees. Compared to the around 260 policy-preparing committees in 1980 the Danish development is an almost dramatic example of a restructuring of the position of interest groups in the policy-making process. There has never been one way of policy-making in relation to interest groups, but one of the major roads – the inclusion of interest groups in policy preparing committees – is almost history. At least it is no longer a major road. In contrast, corporatism related to administration and implementation is as viable as during the so-called heyday of corporatism. The number of administrative committees dropped during the 1980s, but it rose during the 1990s. Contrary to the Norwegian case, the corporatist structures related to implementation and administration have not been significantly weakened in Denmark.

Table 1. State councils, committees etc. in Denmark. Function and interest group representation, per cent, 1965-2005

	1965	1975	1980	1985	1990	1995	2000	2005
Number of committees	673	667	715	516	388	368	513	434
Proportion devoted to preparation of decisions[1]	44	46	37	33	20	23	18	10
-proportion with interest organizations as members	51	50	70	70	74	71	60	87
Proportion administrative committees etc.[2]	56	54	63	67	80	77	82	90
-proportion with interest organizations as members	62	63	75	78	85	77	77	78

1. Committees etc. preparing legislation as well as other types of political and administrative decisions.
2. Committees etc. with administrative and advisory tasks.
Source: See Christiansen & Nørgaard (2003: 228ff; and update).

If interest groups are no longer present in earlier times' committee-supported policy preparation, where are they when the government or administration prepares new political decisions? Interest groups might be kept out of policy preparation and only be invited to comment on hearings when a proposal is ready or other kinds of last-minute participation. They might also be allowed access to the policy-formulation phase in all other ways than by participating in committees. The latter answer is closer to the truth than the former. Interest groups are still involved in the policy-making process prior to the presentation before parliament. Quantitative as well as qualitative studies have shown that interest groups have increased their contacts with administrators as well as with parliamentarians (Christiansen & Rommetvedt, 1999; Rommetvedt, 2005; Christiansen & Nørgaard, 2003: Ch. 5; Christiansen et al., 2004; Hermansson et al., 1997; 1999).

It has also been shown, at least for the Danish case – and there is no reason to believe that it is different in Norway and Sweden – that civil servants and ministers, who control access to the policy-making process, have sharpened their demands on interest groups that want to influence the process. The relationship between state actors and interest groups has always been a kind of exchange relation in which interest groups have been allowed influence on public regulation in exchange for legitimacy and knowledge (cf. Molina & Rhodes, 2002). Because of the changed environment of the policy process – of which major changes are the increasing role of the media, issue-voting instead of class-voting, and financial austerity – this exchange relationship has been sharpened. Interest groups must perform more explicitly than earlier (Öberg et al., 2009). With a pointed formulation, interest groups must be of some use to the minister or the ministry to be allowed significant influence on the political process (Christiansen et al., 2004: Ch. 12). If interest organizations cannot deliver to the minister or the ministry, or both, their political role in a given case will be minor.

If we used to think of the Scandinavian policy-making model as bearing the mark of openness, inclusion, and consensus, we might ask how these qualities are affected by the development of the relation between the state and organized interests through the last couple of decades. Several dimensions might be of interest, and in the following we shall concentrate on two of them: the structure of interest presentation, that is, the type of interests that are represented when political decisions are under consideration; and the degree of transparency related to the policy-preparation process. As we shall see, the two dimensions pull in opposite directions when we apply normative standards on the policy process.

The Structure of Interest Representation

The basic point about the structure of interest representation is that the structure of interests present in the policy-making process has become more diverse. In a way the Scandinavian countries are leaving the Scandinavian administrative model and in this respect approaching the Anglo-Saxon pluralist model (cf. Kickert, 2002; Veggeland, 2007). Data in Table 2 is from four Danish surveys to all nationwide interest organizations. The table shows the proportion of all organizations that have monthly or more frequent contacts with civil servants in ministries and agencies in Copenhagen and with MPs. In all groups, except consumer and patient organizations,[2] the proportion of organizations with frequent contacts has increased; for many groups even substantially. Especially it is clear that many more

[2] This is probably an effect of the sharp rise in the number of small patient organizations during the period. Many of these organizations probably focus more on services to their members than on affecting public policy-making.

organizations have frequent contacts with members of parliament. Seven per cent of the organizations in 1976 had frequent contacts with MPs compared to 24 per cent in 2000.

Table 2. Interest organizations with frequent contacts to the central administration and parliament, selected years 1976-2000, per cent

	Per cent with monthly or more frequent contacts							
	1976		1981		1993		2000	
	Administration	Parliament	Administration	Parliament	Administration	Parliament	Administration	Parliament
Employees, blue collar	41	19	66	32	71	53	89	69
Employees, white collar	39	8	51	1	55	22	67	26
Business organizations	23	6	30	8	41	17	50	27
Org. in education, science, culture	20	4	25	8	27	9	39	16
Charitable organizations	21	5	27	12	23	18	29	18
National and international org.	9	6	14	13	15	16	32	26
Consumer and patient org.	33	21	32	19	25	19	25	21
Org. for youth and leisure	20	8	25	5	17	9	30	18
Other organizations	48	30	61	37	56	42	58	42
Total	25	7	33	11	35	17	44	24
Standard deviation	12,6	9,2	18,0	12,2	19.9	14,9	21,4	16,8
Number of organizations	1890		1990		1316		1201	

Question: "How often does your organization have contact with public authorities?" Options: "Daily", "At least once a week", "At least once a month", "At least once a year", "Less/never". *Frequent contacts* are defined as "At least once a month" or more frequent.

Administration includes contacts with the minister, the department, agencies and councils and committees.

Parliament includes contacts with parliamentary committees, party groups and MPs.

Source: Christiansen & Nørgaard (2003: Ch. 5).

Put simply, more organizations have more frequent contact with decision-makers. Analyses of the different strategies and tactics used by interest groups suggest that more interest groups also appear more often in the media, although there is no definite evidence on this question (Binderkrantz, 2005). The presence of more different interests groups in the media increases the quality of the political discussion. However, there is no rose without a thorn: the standard deviations across the different types of organizations are steadily increasing over time, that is, the differences in contact frequency between the different types of interest organizations are increasing. This indicates that even if almost all groups increase their contacts, inequality also increases. Further analysis of these and other data, not shown here, points in the same direction (cf. Christiansen & Nørgaard, 2003: Ch. 7). We shall not pursue the question of equality and inequality further. We can also illustrate the increasing pluralism through case studies in the area of environmental policy. The following three cases are all related to environmental policy and are documented in Christiansen et al. (2004: 9-11). The environment entered the political agenda in Denmark in the late 1960s – phrased as pollution and pollution abatement – a little later than in Sweden, but at about the same time as in Norway (compare Christiansen, 1996; Jansen & Osland, 1996; and Lundqvist, 1996). The change from a liberal-conservative to a Social Democratic government in 1971 placed the issue on the decision-making agenda. A new ministry – the Ministry of Pollution Abatement – was established. The old environmental regulation, which was scattered and meagre, was gathered under the new ministry, but the ministry had to build an administration virtually from scratch. The new minister's masterpiece was the Environmental Protection Act, which was prepared from late 1971 through January 1973, when it was finally presented to and passed in parliament.

Back then, environmental policy did not enjoy the popularity it does today. It was not a given thing that the minister could come through with something even close to an efficient piece of legislation. The minister inherited the output of the Pollution Commission, which was established in 1969 – not so much to promote environmental regulation as to delay it. The minister and his civil servants quickly worked out a proposal for an environmental protection act. He invited the main interest groups from the manufacturing sector, from agriculture, and the two associations for municipalities and counties to a series of meetings – which in some respects had the character of a committee.

Environmental groups played no role whatsoever, partly because there were very few of them. Of the few that existed, some did not even try to influence the environmental protection act that was to shape Danish environmental policy and administration for many decades to come. Others tried to get access to the process, but were left outside the door. The reason environmental groups were not included was partly that they would only increase the complexity for the minister and that there was apparently only little public support for a special voice from the environment groups. All in all there was no significant political cost associated with keeping environmental groups outside the decision-making process. The environmental planning act was carried through with the endorsements from the largest interest organization within the manufacturing sector and from the two local and regional government organizations. The main agricultural organizations did not endorse the new environmental policy. In parliament the law passed with the votes of the Social Democrats and the Conservative Party, which traditionally had close relations to the urban industries, while the Liberal Party with its even stronger relations to agriculture did not support the bill in parliament.

The organizational landscape within the environmental sector looked dramatically different when 15 years later the then mature environmental protection act underwent a major revision on top of many minor revisions over the years. Environmental awareness had grown markedly in the general public, and environmental policy had become a political issue in which all political parties were competing for votes. When the issue of a major revision of the environmental protection act was put forward in late 1988, it was only two years after the Chernobyl disaster, the meltdown of a Soviet nuclear reactor that caused serious nuclear contamination of large areas in Europe. Denmark had been through a politically dramatic process related to a plan for the aquatic environment; Denmark was ruled by a weak Conservative-Liberal government that had to accept a series of defeats in parliament, among others in environmental policy; and finally, environmental policy had been institutionalized. By the late 1980s conditions for environmental policy-making were very different from those of the early 1970s and the old major piece of legislation that was the backbone of environmental administration and regulation needed revision. The manufacturing industry, agriculture, and the local and regional government organizations were again invited to take part in the policy process, just like in the early 1970s. But this time two other types of organizations were included with whom the minister and the civil servants deliberated on the reform: environmental groups and labour organizations. The Social Democratic government of the early 1970s did not grant the labour movement a privileged status in environmental policy-making, but 15 years later the Conservative-Liberal government did.

The ministry established a contact committee[3] with whom the minister and the civil servants could discuss the many issues involved in the reform. Ten interest groups were represented in the contact committee, among them two environmental groups and two labour union representatives, that is, four out of ten interest group representatives were not industry or municipal or county representatives. The organizations taking part in the reform decisions represent a significantly broader segment of possible interests compared to the early 1970s when only industrial and local and regional government organizations were given political influence.

The last environmental decision-making process to illustrate the political role of interest organizations took place a decade later. It was another major piece of legislation which regulated polluted soil. It was technically complicated because the regulation of soil pollution implies a clash between public and civil law, and because the law might have had quite massive consequences for ordinary house owners. The Soil Pollution Committee was established in 1994. The committee issued a report in 1996, but a bill was not presented to parliament until 1999 when it was passed with a broad majority.

Some members of the Soil Pollution Committee are known from the two cases above: the main organization for manufacturers is there, as are the two organizations representing municipalities and counties. The main environmental organization is there, and the labour unions are also represented. Missing are the agricultural organizations, but they are not represented because soil pollution in the countryside was to be dealt with in another way. However, a number of other organizations were also allowed to appoint a member of the committee, either alone or together with other organizations: the Danish Bar and Law Society, the Danish Association of Consulting Engineers, the Danish Construction Association, the Association of Soil Purification, of which the last three could appoint one member together. Finally, the Danish Bankers' Association and the Association of Danish Mortgage Banks could appoint one member together. Altogether the committee had 15 members.

Next to the minister and the ministry the main role in the committee's work and in the process following the submission of the committee report was played by the large industrial organization and the two local government organizations. The point is, however, that a large number of interest groups were involved in the creation of a new piece of regulation on soil pollution.

In sum, the three cases on environmental regulation illustrate that the structure of interests and the interests involved in environmental policy-making have developed significantly over the three decades that the cases cover. More types of interests and more finely tuned segments of the different types of interest groups became integrated in the

---

[3] The contact committee had a more ambitious goal than its name suggests, namely negotiation. From the outset, the ministry stated that it wanted to come to agreement with the organizations represented in the committee (Christiansen et al., 2004: 222).

decision-making process. In the early 1970s only industrial and municipal or county interests were privileged interests; in the 1980s environmental groups and labour-market groups gained a privileged status. These two cases are particularly interesting, because they cover the establishment respectively the revision of one law. In the case from the 1990s, more interest groups were represented in the policy-preparing committee.

Environmental policy is not a representative case, because it was new in the early 1970s, and because the environment is one of the major policy issues in which political parties compete for votes. However, no policy sector is typical of all policy sectors. All policy sectors have their own dynamics. The dynamics of politicized sectors such as the environment are partly created outside of the political system, because people and groups are involved in all kinds of activities, and partly by the political system itself, because policies create groups that are dependent on public policy (cf. Pierson, 1996, 2000). The environmental policy system may seem different from all other policy subsystems, but in terms of the dynamic between policy and interest groups environmental policy may very well be typical for other politicized policies such as those related to welfare provision – Ministry of Health, Ministry of Education, Ministry of Social Affairs. The gradual pluralization of the policy process is found in many policy sectors.

From a normative, democratic point of view increased pluralism is a positive development. More interests are infused into the policy process. More nuances and opinions are heard by the decision-makers. And more groups can blow the whistle if they think things are going the wrong way.

Transparency and Speed of the Policy Process

The growing role of interest groups is assessed as positive as far as the plurality of the policy process is concerned, but there are also drawbacks in the policy process, for example the increasing inequality among interest groups as indicated above. We shall not discuss that here, but rather look at another possible drawback, namely the lack of transparency of the policy process.

In OECD's definition of transparency 'refers to an environment in which the objectives of policy, its legal, institutional, and economic framework, policy decisions and their rationale … are provided to the public in a comprehensible, accessible, and timely manner' (www.oecd.org). Transparency is a core democratic aspect of the policy process, because the possibility for the public to scrutinize the policy process rests with a transparent policy process (OECD, 2008: 16). Interest groups relate to transparency because they can affect regulation in ways that are not easily detected until regulatory measures are implemented. Knowledge about who affects legislation helps the public in its assessment of the regulation.

We know that more interest groups have a voice in the policy process, but we also know that they are involved less often in the preparation of policy proposals through commissions compared to a couple of decades ago. If we accept the premise that policy-preparing committees imply that some interest organizations are allowed a privileged position in the policy process, the virtual abolition of the committee system leaves us with fewer immediate hints as to which organizations hold a privileged position. Without committees it is less clear *who*, *when*, and *how* different interest groups have been involved in policy preparation. Even with committees it is often difficult to know who affected policy decisions and who did not, but it is much more difficult without.

Transparency is a democratic need for a number of reasons. With today's complex public regulation it is often difficult to project how regulatory measures will perform when they meet the real world. Knowledge about how a piece of regulation has come into being is a hint for the considerations made by the authors of the regulation. Public regulation may not have visible consequences for years. Again, knowledge of the policy process may increase the possibility of forecasting the outcomes of public rule making. Western legal thinking requires rules to reflect general and public concerns, and not only those of rent-seeking interest groups. Transparency may increase the general public's trust in the purpose and implementation of public regulation.

Jørn Loftager (2004: 194ff.) shows that shifting governments during the 1990s and onwards increasingly carried through significant reforms as part of the annual settlements on the budget. Little or no public or political debate preceded policy changes of second or even third degree (according to Peter Hall's classification). There are several indications of not only the decline of transparency, but also the increased speed of the policy process (Togeby et al., 2003). High speed in the policy process may imply efficiency and the capacity for timely response to societal problems; it may, however, also imply scarce public discussion on policy issues. Reduced transparency and high speed in the policy process are democratic dubious.

It is not easy to document that the speed of the policy process has increased. We may all have the feeling that it is so, but that is not scientific evidence. We may also come up with comparable cases that show that the speed of the policy process is greater today that it used to be – this is actually so with the case discussed below. Still it is preferable also to have a quantitative measure. Table 3 reports the average time from a public committee[4] is appointed until it submits its report in selected two-year periods from 1957-58 till 2007-08. The absolute number of months of commission work is less interesting than the fact that the period from appointment to submission has almost halved over the last 50 years. Even if most other public decision-making processes are structured very differently than a public commission report, the table is a strong indication that the general public decision-making speed has gone up.

Table 3. Official commission reports. Number and production time, selected years 1957-2008

	1957-58	1967-68	1977-78	1987-88	1997-98	2007-08
Number of reports in two year period	41	84	69	66	40	12
Share of committees with interest groups	73	52	57	74	93	92
Number of months from appointment to submission	45,4	41,3	32,7	31,3	27,1	27,3

[4] In Denmark the committee system is not as institutionalized as in Norway and Sweden (cf. also above). Official reports here cover reports that are given a number in the series of commission reports. These reports or committees are a subset of all committees, cf. Table 1. Committees or reports given a number are generally believed to be more important than other committees. They are typically allowed more time for their job. Consequently, the numbers reported in Table 3 are a conservative estimate of the average time for a commission's work.

The cases that will be used to illustrate this development involve a high speed as well as a quite non-transparent decision-making process.[5]

Denmark had a major municipal and county amalgamation in 1970 followed by a major redistribution of public tasks to be implemented from 1970 and onwards. The ground for the reform was laid in 1958 with the establishment of the Municipal Commission, in 1966 replaced by the Municipal Reform Commission. A number of committees were established over the 12 years to deal with specialized issues. The result in 1970 was that the number of municipalities was reduced from around 1200 to 275 and the number of counties from 28 to 14. The new, large municipalities and counties were made ready to have tasks transferred from the state and to be responsible for the many new public tasks that were expanded or developed in these years. It was an impressive reform, thoroughly analysed, lengthy and followed by widespread public discussion (Pallesen, 2003).

A little more that 30 years later Denmark accomplished another major municipal reform with an equally impressive result. The number of municipalities was reduced from 271 (a few municipalities had been amalgamated in between the two reform periods) to 98; the 14 counties were replaced with five regions. The regions were stripped of most tasks, except hospitals, and of the right to levy taxes. The counties' tasks mainly went to the municipalities, but some former county as well as municipal tasks were transferred to the state. Again an impressive reform, but the timing was very different: the Commission of Administrative Structure was set up in late 2002 after a short public discussion. It had 12 members: four civil servants from four ministries, four experts, and four representing municipal and county interests, of which one member came from the Association of County Councils (ACC), another from Local Government Denmark (LGD), and one each from the municipalities of Copenhagen and Frederiksberg.[6] The commission's report was submitted in January 2004. The government released a proposal in late April 2004, and a political compromise – based on parties with only a narrow majority in parliament – was reached in late June 2004. Less than two years passed from the commission was formed until a political agreement had been reached. The reform was finally implemented by 1 January 2007. One of the largest public sectoral reforms ever was in place a little more than four years after the reform had entered the political decision-making agenda.

Not only was the speed of the policy process very high, it was also followed by very little public debate, not least during the period of political negotiations – at least if one by public debate refers to the chain between problems and the government's solutions the problems. The commission's report – issued in January 2004 – did not contain very many proposals; instead it came up with different models for the public governance structure in Denmark. They were widely discussed during the three months after the submission of the report. During these three months the government offered nothing concrete about its preferences in terms of the new institutional landscape, and its proposal, which was released in late April 2004, had very little relation to the models in the commission report. The opposition was shocked as were the counties and the Association of County Councils (ACC), which had traditionally been very closely integrated in the political and administrative decision-making

[5] The case is based mainly on Christiansen & Klitgaard (2008; 2009).

[6] The municipalities of Copenhagen and Frederiksberg had functions as both a municipality and a county before the recent reform. They were not members of ACC or LGD. Owing to an old tradition they were represented in many commissions by their own representatives.

processes (cf. also the environmental policy cases above). The government's proposal was a disaster for the counties, which ended up being stripped of their tasks in, among other areas, environmental administration, secondary education, and social policy. Since there were less than two weeks from the government released its proposal until political negotiations were to start, the ACC had no chance to mobilize a strong coalition against the reform. The government got it almost the way it wanted it, but its proposal was almost not discussed in public until after it had been passed.

The government's primary instrument was information control: no release of any kind of information on the government's intentions from January through April, and thus no involvement of ACC. However – and this was only known to a small circle of decision-makers – the CEO of ACC's sister organization, Local Government Denmark (LGD), was involved throughout the government negotiations, January through April. And by entering a strategic alliance with LGD, the government consolidated its near annihilation of the counties.

This case may be extreme. The combination of the inaccessibility, speed, and scale of the reform is unique. Even if the Scandinavian countries have a large reform capacity it is rare to see such large reforms carried through within such a short span of time. The case shows that involvement of a commission in public policy preparation is no guarantee that the involved interest groups are privileged in the political decision-making process. The case also illustrates that the state is prepared to use its means to privilege interest groups. Groups that may be useful to the government are closely included in the decision-making process. Groups that are estimated to counter government preferences are excluded. It is very unlikely that any government would have succeeded in the same exclusion of a traditional core actor such as the ACC 20 years ago – at least in an issue as serious as this. Finally the case illustrates that secrecy – Christiansen & Klitgaard (2008) call it a veil of vagueness – may be used as a strategic weapon to avoid anti-reform coalitions.

Pluralism, Transparency, and Scandinavian Corporatism

Interest groups have played a core role in the development of the Scandinavian countries. Without the peasants' and workers' movements and strong industrial groups the Scandinavian societies and democracies would have looked very different. Early on these organizations came to play a significant political role. If there ever was a Scandinavian model for the relationship between the state and organized interests, it was about privilege and inclusion of the most important interest groups in the formation and administration of public policy. Among the core consequences were a relatively peaceful labour market, a high level of societal and parliamentary consensus, and a gradual and broadly supported development of most public policies and political institutions. Interest organizations traded influence for endorsement, support, and consent.

Why could this not just go on? Somehow this trade arrangement did not fit into the preferences of those who have the power to set the conditions for trading, ministers and their civil servants. In Sweden in the early 1990s the employers' organization withdrew its representatives from the agencies' boards and from some administrative boards (Rothstein & Bergström, 1999), but it is usually the public decision-makers that set the terms for the institutions of interaction. Corporatist institutions must have effects that are less desirable today compared to some decades ago. Briefly, they may be that (1) corporatist institutions are time-consuming, and political decision-makers demand speed; (2) interest organizations no longer affect the vote of the electorate owing to decline in class voting; and (3) interest groups are difficult to involve in reforms that imply costs on their members. In some situations strong interest groups had *de facto* veto over political decisions. Public decision-makers' need for flexibility is no longer provided through traditional corporatist institutions. Consequently, they demand higher degrees of freedom in the policy-formation process.

We have left the good old model of policy-making in which the same organizations had a privileged status in the policy process for decades. More interest groups are around, more voices are heard, and decision-makers get inspiration from more sources. There is more pluralism in the policy process – at least until pluralism is overrun by the lack of transparency. Lack of transparency is the underside of the new way interest groups are integrated into the policy-making machine.

Where does this take us? Nothing would be easier than playing a song of doom: the Scandinavian model is gone, it will never come back, and consensual policy-making is about to be history too. This is to jump to conclusions. Interest groups are still there, only not on the same conditions as before. If the diagnosis is right, that the increased demand on interest groups to deliver in order to maintain a privileged position in the policy process is a consequence of their periodical inability to deliver, it is no big problem to demand more from interest groups. A fair counter-demand, then, would be that public decision-makers were more willing to tell us about who has been involved in the policy-making process, with what demands, and with what concessions. As Samuel Finer (1966: 145) has concluded as early as in the mid-1960s, based on studies of British interest group lobbyism in the 1950s: 'Light! More light!'

References

Binderkrantz, A. (2005). Interest group strategies: Navigating between privileged access and strategies of pressure. *Political Studies*, 53, 694-715.

Blom-Hansen, J. (2000). Still corporatism in Scandinavia? A survey of recent empirical findings. *Scandinavian Political Studies*, 23, 157-81.

Blom-Hansen, J. (2001). Organized interests and the state: A disintegrating relationship? Evidence from Denmark. *European Journal of Political Research*, 39, 391-416.

Christiansen, P. M. (1996). Denmark. In P. M. Christiansen (Ed.), *Governing the environment: Politics, policy, and organization in the Nordic countries* (pp. 29-104). Copenhagen: Nordic Council of Ministers. Nord 1996:5.

Christiansen, P. M. & Nørgaard, A. S. (2003). *Faste forhold, flygtige forbindelser: Stat og interesseorganisationer i det 20. Århundrede* [*Regular relationship, fluid connections: The state and interest organizations*] Aarhus: Aarhus University Press.

Christiansen, P. M. & Nørgaard, A. S. (2006). Whose agents? Non-governmental organizations in policy-proposing commissions: agents of government or opposition parties? In D. Braun & F. Gilardi (Eds.), *Delegation in Contemporary Democracies*. London: Routledge.

Christiansen, P. M., Nørgaard, A. S., & Sidenius, N. C. (2004). *Hvem skriver lovene? Interesseorganisationer og politiske beslutninger* [*Who is writing the laws? Interest organizations and political decisions*] Aarhus: Aarhus University Press.

Christiansen, P. M., & Rommetvedt, H. (1999). From corporatism to lobbyism? Parliaments, executives, and organized interests in Denmark and Norway. *Scandinavian Political Studies*, 22, 195-220.

Christiansen, P. M., & Klitgaard M. B. (2008). *Den utænkelige reform: Strukturreformens tilblivelse 2002-2005* [*The unthinkable reform: The creation of the structural reform*]. Odense: University Press of Southern Denmark.

Christiansen, P. M., & Klitgaard M. B. (2009). *Behind the veil of vagueness: Success and failure in the politics of institutional reforms*. Aarhus: Department of Political Science, Aarhus University.

Christiansen, P. M., Nørgaard, A. S., Rommetvedt, H., Svensson, T., Thesen, G., & Öberg, P. (2009). Varieties of democracy: Interest groups and corporatist committees in Scandinavian policy making. Aarhus: Department of Political Science, Aarhus University.

Compston, H. (1998). The end of national policy concertation? Western Europe since the Single European Act. *Journal of European Public Policy*, 5, 507-26.

Crepaz, M. M. L., & Lijphart, A. (1991). Corporatism and consensus democracy in eighteen countries: Conceptual and empirical linkages. *British Journal of Political Science*, 21, 235-56.

Finer, S. E. (1966). *Anonymous empire: A study of the lobby in Great Britain.* London: Pall Mall Press.

Hermansson, J., Svensson, T., & Öberg, P. (1997). Vad blev det av den svenske korporativismen? [What became of Swedish corporatism?] *Politica*, 29, 365-84.

Hermansson, J., Svensson, T., & Öberg, P. (1999). *Avkorporativisering och lobbyism* [De-corporating and lobbyism]. Stockholm: SOU 1999:121.

Jansen, A.-I., & Osland, O. (1996). Norway. In P. M. Christiansen (Ed.), *Governing the environment: Politics, policy, and organization in the Nordic countries* (pp. 181-253). Copenhagen: Nordic Council of Ministers. Nord 1996:5.

Kickert, W. J. M. (2002). Public governance in small Continental European states. *International Journal of Public Administration* 25, 1471-1491.

Knudsen, T., & Rothstein, B. (1994). State building in Scandinavia. *Comparative Politics*, 26, 203-20.

Lijphart, A. (1999). *Patterns of democracy: Government forms and performance in thirty-six countries*. New Haven: Yale University Press.

Loftager, J. (2004). *Politisk offentlighed og demokrati i Danmark* [*Political publicity and democracy in Denmark*]. Aarhus: Aarhus University Press.

Lundqvist, L. J. (1996). Sweden. In P. M. Christiansen (Ed.), *Governing the environment: Politics, policy, and organization in the Nordic countries* (pp. 259-337). Copenhagen: Nordic Council of Ministers. Nord 1996:5.

Molina, O., & Rhodes, M. (2002). Corporatism: The past, present and future of a concept. *Annual Review of Political Science*, 5, 305-31.

Nordby, T. (1994). *Korporatisme på norsk.* Oslo: Universitetsforlaget.

Nørgaard, A. S. (1997). *The Politics of institutional control: Corporatism in Danish occupational safety and health regulation and unemployment insurance, 1870-1995*. Aarhus: Politica.

OECD (2008). *Lobbyists, governments and public trust: Building a legislative framework for enhancing transparency and accountability in lobbying*. Paris: OECD.

Pallesen, T. (2003). *Den vellykkede kommunalreform og decentraliseringen af den politiske magt i Danmark* [*The successful municipal reform and decentralization of political power in Denmark*]. Aarhus: Aarhus University Press.

Pierson, P. (1996). The new politics of the welfare state, *World Politics*, 48, 143-79.

Pierson, P. (2000). Increasing returns, path-dependence, and the study of Politics. *American Political Science Review*, 94, 251-67.

Rommetvedt, H. (2005). Norway: Resources count, but votes decide? From neo-corporatist representation to neo-pluralist parliamentarism. *West European Politics*, 28, 740-63.

Rommetvedt, H., & Opedal, S. (1995). Miljølobbyisme og næringskorporatisme? Norske miljø- og næringsorganisasjoners politiske påvirkning [Environmental lobbyism and business corporatism? Norwegian environmental and business organizations' political influence]. *Nordisk Administrativt Tidsskrift*, 76, 270-302.

Rothstein, B. (1992). *Den korporativa staten* [The corporatist state]. Stockholm: Norstedts Juridik.

Rothstein, B., & Bergström, J. (1999). *Korporatismens fall och den svenska modellens kris* [*The fall of corporatism and the crisis of the Swedish model*]. Stockholm: SNS förlag.

Scruggs, L. (2002). The Ghent System and Union Membership in Europe, 1970-1996. *Political Research Quarterly*, 55, 275-97.

Siaroff, A. (1999). Corporatism in 24 industrial democracies: Meaning and measurement. *European Journal of Political Research*, 36, 175-205.

Togeby, L., Andersen, J. G., Christiansen, P. M., Jørgensen, T. B., & Vallgårda, S. (2003). *Power and democracy in Denmark: Conclusions.* Aarhus: Aarhus University Press.

Veggeland, N. (2007). *Paths of public innovation in the global age: Lessons from Scandinavia.* Cheltenham: Edward Elgar.

Veggeland, N. (2009). *Taming the regulatory state.* Cheltenham: Edward Elgar.

Öberg, P., Svensson, T., Christiansen, P. M., Nørgaard, A. S., Rommetvedt, H., & Thesen, G. (2009). *Disrupted exchange and declining corporatism? Government authority and interest group capability in Scandinavia.* Uppsala: Department of Government, Uppsala University.

In: Innovative Regulatory Approaches ...
Ed: Noralv Veggeland

ISBN: 978-1-60876-673-4

Chapter 6

EU REGULATION AND NATIONAL INNOVATION: THE CASE OF NORWEGIAN PETROLEUM POLICY

Ole Gunnar Austvik

INTRODUCTION

This chapter discusses to which degree a powerful interventionist policy of a nation-state can be adjusted to EU's more liberal way of organizing and regulating economic activities, while simultaneously maintaining nationally defined goals. Norway's integration with the EU and the impacts on her strong state policy in the oil and gas sector is used as an illustration or case.

The point of departure is that Norwegian petroleum (oil and gas) industry was developed as a political enterprise by the Norwegian state from the early 1970s. As a political entrepreneur, the state was engaged in the industry as production entrepreneur, as well as being a political and economic risk-taker. As a political entrepreneur the state could define social goals for activities and use regulative, legal and political measures to reach goals that private entrepreneurs do not have at their disposal. The Norwegian state did not limit itself to the regulation of activities on the Norwegian Continental Shelf (NCS), but instead took on the role of innovator and leader of economic change and development. After only a couple of decades Norway had become the third-largest petroleum exporter in the world after Saudi Arabia and Russia.

When Norway entered the 1990s and EU integration processes were increasingly evident, her petroleum policy and natural-gas strategy was under strong political control through a nationally developed system of institutions, regulations and direct engagements. The European Economic Area (EEA) agreement going into effect in 1994 made Norway a full participant in the EU Single Market in all areas except for agriculture and fishery. Through the 1990s the energy sector became part of the Single-Market liberal restructuration processes. A special focus was placed upon electricity and natural-gas markets, for which directives were eventually approved, and on the application of EU competition law. Strong pressure was put on the Norwegian petroleum model, and significant changes resulted in

2001/2002. The state now became more regulative than directly interventionist, but with substantial retention of control.

The EEA agreement, together with the degree and scope of economic, regulative, and market change within the EU, contributed to change the Norwegian model by taking away opportunities for policy-making, but also creating new ones. They contributed to the promotion of liberal ideological principles for economic activity, with an accompanying influence on Norwegian norms, institutions, and law.

This chapter analyses in which ways the EU system has influenced and contributed to change the strong Norwegian state system in the petroleum sector. In the first and theoretical half of the chapter, first, it is argued that the impacts from economic-integration processes on national policy-making must be analysed by the support of more than one discipline. The interaction between the chosen disciplines of economics and political science is made operational through multi-disciplinarity within an International Political Economy (IPE) framework. Secondly, the characteristics of the role of a state as political entrepreneur in developing a national industry are outlined. Thirdly, the multifaceted processes of how economic integration influences national policy-making are discussed.

Fourthly, in the second and empirical half of the chapter, the role of the EEA agreement in the Norwegian-EU relationship is outlined. Fifthly, a discussion of how the Norwegian state has acted as a political entrepreneur for her oil and gas sector is provided. Sixthly, the process of conflict, cooperation and adaptation in the bargaining between Norway and the EU about introducing EU directives and competition law in Norway is discussed. Seventhly, *de jure* and *de facto* effects on the Norwegian state's petroleum entrepreneurship from these changes are analysed. Eighthly and finally, some conclusions about the manoeuvring room for nation-state policy in a liberal international economic and political superstructure (as the EU) are drawn.

Economic Integration and Political Economy

The IPE approach in this chapter combines economics and political science analyses through multidisciplinarity. Multidisciplinarity is a non-integrative mixture of disciplines where each discipline retains its methodologies and assumptions, unaffected by changes and developments in other disciplines. Two disciplines may study various aspects of an object and integration is achieved by combining the two studies, or by taking conclusions from one discipline and using them as input factors in the research of the other.

In a multidisciplinary approach, disciplines are combined by aggregation. [The cooperation between the disciplines] ... may be mutual and cumulative but not interactive (Augsburg 2005:56).[1]

Using more disciplines in interaction rather than one single discipline in the analyses should increase the potential for reaching a comprehensive understanding of how changes in Norwegian *de jure* relations to the EU economic-integration processes *de facto* have influenced the Norwegian state's entrepreneurial manoeuvring room and policy choices in the oil and gas sector. The multidisciplinary choice is made owing to, first, the pressure that

[1] Interdisciplinarity, on the other hand, attacks a subject from various angles, and blends practices and assumptions of each discipline involved in a common core of concepts and methods (Klein 1996 and Klein 1990:19).

economic integration places for legal, political, institutional and ideological change; secondly, the mixed role of a political entrepreneur in industrial developmental processes; and thirdly, the politicization of the international energy industry and markets.

The academic boundaries of IPE are generally flexible, and along with acceptable epistemologies the subject of robust debate. Most scholars concur however that IPE is ultimately concerned with the ways in which political forces (states, institutions, individual actors, etc.) shape the systems through which economic interactions are expressed, being local, national or international – or by sector. Conversely IPE is also concerned with the effects that economic interactions (including the power of common markets and individuals acting both within and outside them) have upon political and administrative structures, actors and outcomes. Unlike conventional theories of international relations in political science, power in IPE is understood to be both economic and political, and interrelated in complex manners. Unlike conventional economics, market behaviour and market outcome is understood also in relation to the different strategic types in political and state behaviour and ideology, and not only among market participants.

Alternative ideological perspectives in IPE (such as the various types of liberalism, realism, structuralism, and constructivism) demonstrate how different ideologies can lead to different policy and economic strategies in a nation in situations which in other respects are considered the same. In addition, there are also different views on how to understand *de facto* European integration processes. The debate between liberal neo-functionalists, on the one side, and intergovernmental theorists, on the other, about whether or not the bargaining and consensus-building techniques of the Community method should be considered to be refinements of intergovernmental diplomacy, or an ultimate transfer of power to supranational EU institutions, is an important example (see for example Cini 2007). In addition to different perceptions about EU functioning, there are also variations in administrative and social traditions within a given formal international superstructure with resulting different outcomes to be understood, such as the divisions between the Continental, Anglo-Saxon, and Scandinavian models (Veggeland 2007).

Since ideology, perceptions, and traditions influence how a system *de facto* functions (and is designed) are echoed in different political practices, they must be understood to explain what happened in a specific area, why it happened, and what may happen in the future. The ability to innovate, develop, and design policy and economic strategy depends, on national as well as on EU level, on traditions and values related to development or the active creation of visions and ideology, or both. National adaptation depends *inter alia* on perceptions of how the system functions and how norms, traditions, and institutions lead development into specific paths (March and Olsen 1998:959, Keohane and Milner 1996:20).

Thus, when the Norwegian petroleum model met the EU model in the 1990s it represented a confrontation between two different systems of both economic, legal, political, institutional, and ideological factors and mechanisms. The Norwegian petroleum sector was developed by a strong and interventionist (and partly realist) state, while the principles for (liberal) European economic integration prerequisite a predominantly regulatory role of both the EU and member-state governments in economic activity and political practices.

The State as Political Entrepreneur

In this chapter the term *political entrepreneur* rather than just *state policy* is used for the type of activity the Norwegian state represented when developing her petroleum industry. This choice is made because the initiatives taken by the Norwegian state to create and maintain her petroleum industry, to control it, and to take most of the economic revenues from it resembles more an entrepreneur in an international market economy than a state that limits itself to encouraging or discouraging private economic actors to invest in and run an industry. Although ambiguous in the literature, in this article we focus on a political entrepreneur as a government or a state system that acts in an entrepreneurial way in order to create economic activities, with the private sector as full or partial commercially collaborating actors.[2]

Public sector entrepreneurship occurs whenever a political or governmental actor is alert to and acts on potential profit opportunities (Shockley, Frank and Stough 2002:12).

This type of political entrepreneur takes the initiative in an industrial-innovation process, rather than the private entrepreneur. Most studies of entrepreneurship are however concerned with private entrepreneurship with a limited focus on the political economy of entrepreneurship, not to say on political entrepreneurship itself (as for example demonstrated in Fagerberg, Mowery, and Nelson 2005). The characteristics of a political entrepreneur share many similarities with the private entrepreneur, as one who enters into the role of innovator and leader of economic change. However, while private entrepreneurs are mostly driven by the pursuit of their own profit, a political entrepreneur has social goals, in addition to company profit, for its actions. A social or political entrepreneur is concerned with values

… in the form of large-scale, transformational benefit that accrues either to a significant segment of society or to society at large (Martin and Osberg 2007:34).

Social goals include long-term concerns for society, and a more comprehensive view on economic activity in the country (or region or sector) that each company is too small and, hence, unwilling to internalize in their decision-making processes.

A political entrepreneur also has instruments and means to reach his goals not possessed by a private entrepreneur. The political entrepreneur can engage himself in a business directly, in a similar manner to a private entrepreneur and act as a production entrepreneur. Additionally, however, he can make use of interventionist or regulative measures in order to influence the economic, political and legal framework for economic activities in ways in which innovations take place (as a regulatory or interventionist entrepreneur). An entrepreneurial state can also be a substantial risk-taker in political as well as monetary terms.

The policies of the entrepreneurial state … include generation of venture capital for selected and growing businesses (Eisinger 1988:9).

Some projects can be of such a character that they would never be realized if political entrepreneurship was not exercised. It can be argued to be the case when a competitive national Norwegian petroleum industry was created following the discovery of the petroleum resources.

Entrepreneurship is generally about innovatively creating new economic activity. After a build-up period, the state has no longer the same entrepreneurial reason to directly control

---

[2] Austvik 2009b:40-42. See for example Taewook 2004, Schneider and Teske 1992:737, Abel 2003, Rickets 1987 for alternative definitions and understandings of the concept.

companies. However, other reasons for owning and controlling them can be important in a 'late-industrial' phase. In the petroleum sector it can be a desire to control the industry from a democratic perspective, to secure that long-term interests are ensured against the short-term time perspective of commercial businesses, to internalize positive and negative externalities in company decisions, and to perform an optimal resource management when such concerns are not easily regulated. The state can also remain a direct owner of an industry in order to collect more economic rent than what results from the corporate tax system, which is partly the case in the Norwegian petroleum sector.

There are however different degrees and scopes of political entrepreneurship depending on ideological perspective. Michael Porter (1990:131-175) emphasizes that forces that create the ability to innovate and consequently to provide for a country's competitive position, function as a dynamic system. He gives political actors and public authorities an explicit role in the improvement of the factors needed to make an economic system (or the 'diamond' as he calls it) competitive, and to innovate and function better. Such policy measures include first and foremost all infrastructural developments considered important for the areas where innovation may take place: roads, rail, broad band, research and development, culture, competition rules, and institutions.

While Porter argues strongly against public support for individual enterprises, he opens up for support to help sectors and geographical clusters through the use of such widely defined infrastructural measures. Bureaucracy in this context should ensure that the infrastructure functions properly. A bureaucrat is in this sense however not an entrepreneur because, '... in bureaucratic organizations those in charge are obliged to conform to the rules and statutes laid down by a higher authority' (Mises 1943:52).

Porter's (1990:680-682) liberal but active approach to the role of public authorities to a large degree resembles what the EU sees as her role in promoting economic development, such as in her Lisbon strategy (EU 2005). Governments have a role to play in shaping and promoting visions to help private and public actors work towards common goals. Clearly, if public authorities do not adopt this visionary and ideological role, the whole system will be weakened and somebody else will formulate goals, such as strong private entrepreneurs, in some countries the church or others.

The visions set up for the Norwegian petroleum industry however, such as in the 10 Oil Commandments (Report to the Storting 1970-71:76) greatly transcended this type of 'Porterian' policy roles for governments, also with respect to the role of bureaucratic functions on the ministerial level. The instruments used were also far more interventionist than what EU regulations promote, such as direct state participation, political interventions, preferential treatment of and regulation for national companies and a strong fiscal and regulatory regime to Norwegianize the industry, and to ensure that the state earned more rent from this sector than from any other.

A neo-Schumpeterian understanding of trade and international competitiveness supports the significance of (private) entrepreneurship and innovation in maintaining and creating competitive advantages (Fagerberg 2007). For a political entrepreneur, it is similarly the *relative* ability to develop policy that is important for a country to remain competitive in an economically integrated world. This parallels what Michael Posner (1961) has identified as respectively innovative and imitative countries and industries experiencing technological and commercial change, where the continuous ability to innovate is a force used by the leading country to maintain its advantage and achieve the highest economic standards.

Like Alice and the Red Queen, the developed region has to keep running to stay in the same place (Krugman 1979:262).

To which extent and how a country is *de facto* influenced by *de jure* common rules and regulations in an integration process depends consequently on whether it is even in political understanding and beneficial national adaptation, and whether it is able to influence the policies of integrating countries and superstructure so as to maintain advantages and freedom of action, compared to a potentially more passive (imitative) political attitude. The dynamism based upon the technological, commercial and political ability to innovate will be decisive for degree of *de facto* policy harmonization and adaptation.

Determining how to *measure* results of a particular policy and changes in entrepreneurship from exogenous change (introducing EU regulations in a national economy) is however a challenging task in itself. While there is considerable interest in entrepreneurship and innovation processes world-wide, there are, as of yet, no common concepts and definitions or an agreed upon list of key indicators that are required to improve the collective understanding of entrepreneurship and its impacts, although the need appears obvious. Entrepreneurial activity, firm creation, and business growth all occur within a complex, dynamic, and in our case politicized sector and economy. The measurement of political entrepreneurship can be considered even more complex than the challenges arising with the measurement of private entrepreneurship as it involves a wider set of objectives and instruments to be used. The Organization for Economic Cooperation and Development (OECD) however sets out that:

The practical definition and measure of entrepreneurship that one chooses will ultimately depend on the nature of the policy objective (OECD 2006:15).

Following this view as a point of departure we shall identify and measure impacts from Norwegian-EU and EU integration processes on the Norwegian state's petroleum entrepreneurship by changes in ability to reach goals, through changes in manoeuvring room and policy options, and to some extent by changes in the goals themselves. Put simply, if a new policy maintains the goals of the old policy, no change has actually taken place in the ability to reach entrepreneurial purposes.

A number of other forces for policy change than the integration processes confuse however the picture and the possibility to measure results from them. The way Norway and the EU defined interests and formulated energy policies in the 1970s and 1980s was conditioned and affected by the internal and external economic and political factors and actors at the time. Gradually, and in some important cases radically, these factors have changed. For example, with the 1991 collapse of the Soviet Union and the end of the bipolar world and diverging economic and political systems, the world became more politically integrated than before. Political systems changed and international affairs and trade relations became more globalized and in a situation of flux.

Furthermore, not only political factors influenced the situation. Neither EU energy markets nor the Norwegian petroleum industry were in their infant stages anymore in the 1990s and beyond. Different policy was needed for both as compared to in the 1970s and 1980s. Another aspect was changes in the profitability of the petroleum industry, which besides costs depends heavily on the price of oil. Relatively low oil prices in the period 1986-2001 led to a low attention to security-of-supply issues in the EU and elsewhere. Higher prices after 2001 have, on the other hand, brought back the attention to the profitability of the industry and long-term supply and prices, as in the period 1973-1985. The higher prices are the source of more income for producing countries and have political spill-overs that increase their influence, as well as provide an incentive for the EU to think more comprehensively about her energy policy.

Hence, part of the challenge in this chapter is to isolate impacts from economic regulatory integration processes on political entrepreneurship from other forces and factors. In some situations, changes from one force can be discrete and substantial in scope or strength, or both, or induce dynamic processes for incremental change. In other situations other forces can have the strongest impact, with accompanying changed constraints and opportunities for action for involved parties.

Economic Integration and National Manoeuvring Room

Going from lower to higher levels of integration means that more obstacles to trade are removed and more policy is harmonized. The research question in this chapter is concerned with in which ways international economic integration processes affect national policy-making. We shall discuss five main dimensions of this change.

1. Economic integration makes countries interdependent and redistributes wealth and activity within countries with social and political spill-over effects.

Often, two main benefits emanating from economic integration are emphasized, both central to the establishment and development of the EU. First, economic integration increased wealth at aggregated national levels, as demonstrated in international trade theory in economics. Secondly, economic integration makes countries mutually dependent, as demonstrated in interdependence theory in political science.

However, although all countries generally benefit from economic integration at an aggregated level, wealth and power within countries are redistributed. Those benefiting the most will usually become politically stronger compared to other domestic actors who lose from it. Business-oriented interests will in general be given a stronger say in policy formation in a more liberal economy. Also, as foreign policy through treaties becomes an explicit factor for the organization of industrial activities, a country's Foreign Ministry with its comprehensive contact with international organizations and other countries gains a *relatively* stronger say within the government, at the expense of other ministries. The focus of domestic policy will be directed towards aggregated national economic objectives of the integration process.

Because economic integration makes countries converge in their economic goals, it not only leads to the harmonization of costs and prices, but countries also become increasingly similar and converge in their design of economic and social policy. Both legal and competitive forces generate pressure towards the harmonization of political institutions, and in many cases force them to execute policies defined by agreements and common institutions. However, the complex interdependence arising from deeper integration can lead to both more and less options in national political manoeuvring room depending on the evolution of integrating processes, national interpretation, and adaptation by domestic political and commercial actors. Principles for non-discriminatory behaviour and reciprocity are clear, but situations and their practical implementation and understanding may vary.

2. International bindings vary across issues and international arrangements and practices.

The impacts from an international economic agreement come first through legal bindings. Common, or harmonized, laws and regulations increasingly bind national policy with higher levels of integration such as in a common market: more common rules and institutions result. The case of the independent central bank's control over monetary policy in the euro area is a case in point. Lower levels of integration, such as expanding the scope of a Free Trade Agreement (FTA) in the World Trade Organization (WTO), are, on the other hand, mainly concerned with reducing or eliminating traditional trade policy measures and negative integration, such as removing or reducing tariffs and quotas.

Hence, important to the scope and strength of an integrating process is *inter alia* the degree and scope of supranationality. *Ceteris paribus*, the manoeuvring room and policy options for a nation-state's policy are considered greater the fewer the federative aspects of the agreement. In EU studies, neo-functionalists and constructivists point to the potential for further integration and the role of a common decision-maker in Brussels. On the other hand, institutionalists and intergovernmentalists are more sceptical to both spill-overs and socialization. The institutional and policy integration are for them is less likely to change in the foreseeable future, and policy will continue to be defined through diplomacy and inter-state processes.

When domestic institutions are weak, the impact from exogenous change (integrating with other countries) will usually be more significant than if they are strong to a given international agreement. When institutions are strong, pressure for de-coupling from requirements in the treaty is more clearly also the product of institutions that shape (and maintain) local identities, norms, and preferences (Andersen 2006). The consideration of the EU as a 'weak' state structure resulting from intergovernmental bargaining opens a greater manoeuvring room for a national political entrepreneur, than if the EU is considered a neo-functional 'strong' state structure, in which member countries are compelled to follow a powerful (and entrepreneurial) EU Commission.

3. The integrating processes are dynamic and open for national interpretation, bargaining, and adaptation.

Within single sectors, countries try to reap the benefits of trade in general, and avoid the sectoral problems it creates at the cost of the other country, being exporter or importer. The struggle between open and restrictive trade continues after an agreement has been signed between two or more countries, which makes hidden and indirect barriers among the most important issues discussed in present trade talks. They are also central to the construction and maintenance of the Single Market.

Thus, in the Norway-EU relationship, both benefit from positioning themselves to favour free trade in general, and at the same time formulate (in parts) an independent policy as far as possible for sectoral and revenue interests, without breaking the overall deal. In this relationship, the EU appears to be far more powerful than little Norway. Small countries are however often more unified in defining preferences and policy (Katzenstein 1985). Clever adaptation can partly outweigh an obvious formal, economic, and political asymmetric interdependence when measured by the 'meat weight'.

4. De facto outcomes from similar de jure regulations may vary.

Policy change should be less frequent when national sectoral interests are strongly opposed to unfavourable international regulations. This is especially the case when opposing a change would not affect other domestic interests (such as losing a general election). A national system may not necessarily follow a neo-functionalist view which results in a situation with *de facto* common practices, even if rules *de jure* are the same, when strong interests are to be defended.

In some cases it is the form of national arrangements that are important and must be changed to make them legally comply with an agreement and its principles, in other cases it is the substance of an issue that is central. When it is the form (*de jure*), a national government has a chance to change for example an existing organizational model within the structure of the agreement, and simultaneously maintain its purpose. The more complex the situation becomes, the more difficult it will be to reach *de facto* comprehensive supra-national arrangements. Comprehensive formal arrangements may provide the opportunity for substantial autonomous national interpretation.

5. Domestic and international policy-making is interactive and dynamic.

The two-level game (Putnam 1988) shows, paradoxically, that the greater the degree of autonomy a country chooses in an economically integrated world, the less influence the country will possess over its own situation. International rules of competition and market mechanisms will in many situations *de facto* override national decisions, and the country will increasingly be left to adaptation.

Hence, the *de facto* degree and form of national-policy coherence, adaptation, and influence on international common rules depends on how able the government is continuously to interact simultaneously in domestic and international arenas. The definition of what is a 'national interest' is ambiguous and depends *inter alia* on the constellation of domestic actors. Domestic change takes place with international change and *vice versa*. The nation-state's ability to work at 'all tables' simultaneously and over time may in many cases be decisive for the *de facto* outcome of an international agreement. As with innovative processes in entrepreneurial activities, such policy coordination in economic integration processes may take place in an incremental manner, but it is sometimes also discrete or radical.

Different studies of EU and European integration processes, being uni-, inter- or multidisciplinary, include discussions about how participating nation-states are affected by economic integration. In the field of economics, discussions generally follow neo-functionalist and liberal market logics of how institutions and policies change when a country enters into deeper levels of integration with other countries. The political approaches often contrast or complement this view with various degrees of intergovernmental, institutionalist, and constructivist understandings of the political development of the EU. Such perspectives attempt to explain whether or not, and if possible how, nation-states influence the EU and *vice versa*.

Even though it is not a question of returning to laissez-fair economics and a totally politically passive state in industrial (and social) affairs, international economic integration is a step supporting an ideological view that the state should adopt a weaker and more regulative political hand on industrial (and social) policy as compared to more interventionist attitudes in Europe after World War II. A more liberal ideology and economic integration weaken the nation-state (Mann 1997). It has however long been argued that an effective state is an integral part of a successful competitive capitalist system (Evans and Rueschemeyer 1985). For developed economies, Mjøset and Andersson (1987) argue that

> … policies should aim to promote flexible specialization making the welfare state a comparative advantage in connection with industrial policies, by extending efforts at democratization of decisions concerning labor process organization and work environment.

In a "flexicurity" approach for welfare states, Noralv Veggeland (2007) similarly argues that flexible labour markets also '… depend, per se, on the continuing existence of universal social security and public neighborhood services'. High public-welfare expenses and a heavy tax burden can be 'compensated by high work productivity, low unemployment, flexible labor market, and encouraging subsidiarity policies' (ibid.).

As a consequence, there is a continuous debate about the formulation of social and industrial policy, and what will be the best for trade and fair competition within a liberal paradigm, with a focus on more than costs. John Maynard Keynes was for example also a liberal, but a rather interventionist one, compared to dominant present-day perceptions of the more passive role of the state in industrial policy. Debates over types of design of a liberal economic system and varieties of capitalism, as in Hall and Soskice (2001) and Mjøset and Clausen (2007), demonstrate that liberalism is not necessarily be orthodox. Possible variations in a liberal system are compatible with the basic ideology of the EU system, albeit in opposition to those suggesting a change to a non-liberal economic system (e.g., Elster and Moene 1989).

Taken together, the increased complexity of decision-making indicates that more, not less, political competence is required in comparison with the 1970s and 1980s, when national interests were defended among integrating countries. This challenge appears to be especially great for newer member countries to the EU, as well as developing countries in the poor world. But, it also exists for rich Norway with her (in some areas) diverging interests in the EU with respect to the petroleum sector. The ability and desire to interplay dynamically in the multifaceted integration processes is decisive for how they *de facto* affect national political manoeuvring room and policy-making.

The EEA Agreement

The EEA agreement was signed in 1992 and became operative on 1 January 1994. The European Free Trade Area (EFTA) Surveillance Authority (ESA) was set up to fulfil the control function towards EFTA participants in the EEA area (now only Lichtenstein and Iceland, in addition to Norway), similar to the control function of the EU Commission in relation to EU member countries. EU Single-Market regulations and law from this point onwards also became Norwegian regulations and law, even though Norway through the agreement gained no voting rights over policy-making.

The agreement made it possible for the three EFTA countries (Norway, Lichtenstein, and Iceland) that joined to participate in the Single Market in line with EU members. The main sectors exempted were agriculture and fishery. Another EFTA member, Switzerland, did not join the EEA agreement and deals with her relationship with the EU through bilateral agreements. The EEA agreement involves transferring sovereignty from the nation-states to ESA and the EFTA court, but not formally to the EU. The three countries can participate in preparing cases by participating in the EU committees that suggest new rules or changes in rules. The EU, however, makes the final decision without their involvement, that is, there is no vote from EFTA countries.

> The Agreement gives them the right to be consulted by the Commission during the formulation of Community legislation, but not the right to a voice in decision-making, which is reserved exclusively for Member States (EU 2007a)

EFTA countries must unanimously accept a rule, which means that a single country has a right to reserve itself by vetoing against its implementation in the EEA committee (Report to the Storting 2001-2002:27). So far, the right to veto has not been used by any EFTA country. This is partly due to the fact that, in case of a veto (reservation), the EU can take the entire area in question out of the agreement, which may incur substantial disadvantages for EFTA countries.

The EEA agreement is dynamic in the sense that new rules for the Single Market are designed and applied across the entire EEA area (the EU plus EFTA minus Switzerland). New subject areas can be introduced, and old ones can be taken out of the agreement. When the EU has expanded with new member countries the agreement has been renegotiated, implying mostly that EFTA countries had to pay more for market access, and to support financially the poorest countries in the EU.

The EEA agreement is such a fragile construction which probably is more important for Norway and the other EFTA countries to keep alive than it is for the other signatories (Arnesen 1995:663, my translation).

For many EFTA countries it became evident that the EEA agreement would not be satisfactory, and they regarded it as a stepping-stone to full EU membership, rather than as a permanent alternative. Finland, Sweden, and Austria joined the EU as full members in 1994, while Switzerland chose neither to become an EU member nor to sign the EEA agreement. Only Liechtenstein, Iceland, and Norway remained. The three EEA states have taken on board some 4000 legal acts of the EU Single-Market regime as of 2009 and implemented them into national law; the EU is the policy-maker and the EFTA countries are the policy-takers.

According to the EEA agreement EU regulations for the Single Market must be applied for the whole EEA area, such that the free movement of products and services, labour and capital are promoted. While Norway has the right to reserve herself against the domestic implementation of, for example, an energy directive in Norway, she cannot veto against its implementation in the EU area. General rules, as, for example, in the practice and application of competition law, however, cannot be vetoed, and are handled by supranational organs such as the ESA and the EFTA court (Graver 2000).

The situation for Norway is that she ended up as a full participant in the Single Market, but not as a full member of the Union. This means that she has achieved a position, as many other countries, where scope and strength of integration with the EU is different to the position of the core EU countries. However, the EEA agreement was for Norway not designed to defend petroleum interests, but for the interests of the rest of her economy. Strictly speaking, Norway did not need an EEA agreement to sell oil and gas to the EU. It was the rest of the economy that had or has a major economic interest in securing market access and rules of fair competition. *Ceteris paribus*, it would have been better for Norway not to have petroleum activities included in the agreement, if the only goal had been to maintain as large as possible manoeuvring room for the national petroleum entrepreneurship. However, the integrating process required that singular interests were balanced against other economic interests.

With the EEA agreement's passive character for Norway, her influence on EU policy is more limited compared to that of member countries. If Norway becomes an EU member and gains the right to influence the formulation of regulations, she might seek to shape them in her favour. If a trade agreement was the alternative, as in the case of Switzerland, she could explicitly try to exempt natural-resource management as far as possible. Both membership and the trade-agreement alternatives appear as better political frameworks for the manoeuvring room for the state's petroleum entrepreneurship than the EEA agreement.

Norway has, as a consequence, also put herself in a different situation than Europe's (and the world's) largest combined oil and natural gas exporter, Russia. Norway and Russia, on the other hand, to a large extent share interests in natural-gas market developments, besides being competitors. Norway has also an interest in what the Russians as market leaders do domestically, as well as in her relations with the EU in the energy sector. European-integration processes, market liberalization, and diverging economic interests between producers and consumers especially in the field of natural gas have offered the Norwegian state a new dimension in her relation to Russia.

The Norwegian State as Petroleum Entrepreneur

From its very start in the early 1970s, Norwegian authorities had high political ambitions about controlling the petroleum industry and the international oil companies, as expressed in the 10 Oil Commandments in 1971 (Hanisch and Nerheim 1992). To begin with however, neither the Norwegian state, nor Statoil or other Norwegian companies possessed sufficient competence to develop petroleum activities on their own. Norway needed the assistance of international companies' competence, and also their capital. Industrial and technological cooperation with the internationals was important (Nore 1979, Noreng 2004). Through access to advanced technology and knowledge, Norwegian companies should after a learning period, become more independent of the internationals. For example, Mobil was replaced by Statoil after 15 years as operator at the Statfjord field in 1987. As the then head of Statoil claimed, 'You cannot learn to drive by sitting in the back seat' (Ask 2006, quoting Statoil head Arve Johnsen when the takeover took place)

The system established that while the oil companies were able to provide ideas and do the practical work, the government was to (understand and) approve all steps on all levels of activity. In order to promote both competition and cooperation, licenses were awarded to a group of companies, rather than to a single company, in general with Norwegian ownership dominance. Companies were chosen from geological and technological expertise, financial strength, and previous experiences. The idea was that they would share ideas and experiences, as well as costs and revenues from the license. Through competition and cooperation, the value of each license would be maximized. At the same time, the licensees acted as a controlling system, as each company had an interest in securing that the work of the chosen operator was undertaken in the most cost-effective way (Ministry of Petroleum and Energy (MPE) annual). All taxes went to the state, except for local property taxes where a terminal was built on land. The Ministry of Finance (FIN) managed to introduce a special tax on petroleum activities to capture most of the rent. Later arrangements with the State's Direct Financial Interests (SDFI) ensured that the entire rent from these shares went to the state.

The Norwegian state used several instruments in a combination to reach the established goals: regulations, direct participation and political interventions, and preferential treatment of Norwegian companies. Policies were developed with high ambitions with regard to national sovereignty and control of the industry, an optimal resource management, and to capture as much rent as possible through taxation and direct participation. In addition to being the regulator, legislator, and policy-maker, the state became itself an industrial actor, and in periods also a substantial financial contributor to developments. Governmental policy and industrial structures changed as the industry matured, and markets, international affairs, and technology changed. The state not only ensured the establishment of the industry, but maintained its role as a driving force looking after and contributing to change and evolution, to the intended benefit of the industry and the state itself.

The establishment phase with a strong state entrepreneurship represented a radical innovation in Schumpeter's terms. It was a mixture between a strong state and private companies, and was different from how the petroleum sector was organized in other countries. From nothing, the state built a new company (Statoil), and protected the Norwegian supply industry in its coupling with international companies. The system of companies, institutions, regulations, and politics should provide a 'Porterian' type of dynamism in the national petroleum cluster, making it internationally competitive as soon as possible. The direct interventions went however far beyond Porterian type of policy.

The special Norwegian policy created and developed was based on a strong desire to control the value chain from the reservoirs and as far as possible down to consumers; in practical terms this largely meant to the borders of downstream importing countries for natural gas, and from export terminals (platform or onshore) for crude oil. Important policy measures were the establishment of a state oil company (Statoil), the regulation and optimization of production levels to favor Norwegian companies when awarding licenses, protecting the supply industry, controlling the transportation infrastructure and maintaining concentrated gas sales.

To begin with Statoil to a large extent implemented policy together with the MPE. Later, the MPE's direct engagement increased at Statoil's expense. The ownership of Statoil's oil and gas fields was also split into a larger share to the State's Direct Financial Investments (SDFI) and a smaller one to Statoil. *Forsyningsutvalget* (FU, the Supply Committee) and *Gassforhandlingsutvalget* (GFU, the Gas Negotiation Committee), supervised directly by the MPE, replaced and supplemented important Statoil policy-functions in the gas sector.

The GFU gained from 1986 responsibility for selling all Norwegian gas independently of who owned it. The purpose of centralized gas sales was to maintain a strong market position in relation to European buyers who had organized themselves as a monopsony. In this phase the big transmission companies on the Continent (such as Ruhrgas, Gasunie, and Gaz de France) collaborated as buyers ('the consortium'). To prevent these companies (through their owners) sitting on both sides of the table in gas negotiations, foreign companies were not allowed to participate in the GFU.

The FU was established in 1993 as a counselling body for the MPE, this time with foreign companies as participants. The FU evaluated developments in individual fields and considered which fields should supply each contract. The FU's goal was to secure the exploitation of scope economies and optimal resource management across fields, and between oil and gas production. The MPE was to make the final decision concerning whether a gas contract was to be ratified, and which fields were to supply the contract (these were 'supply contracts' as opposed to 'depletion' or 'field' contracts from the 1970s).

As the leader of the GFU, Statoil remained in a strong bargaining position vis-à-vis foreign buyers, but Hydro and Saga also increased their influence, and the MPE obtained more direct insight into and control of negotiations. Together, the GFU/FU system, SDFI ownership, and Statoil, all under the control of the MPE, represented a 'Norwegian Gas factory' where national policy instruments made it possible to achieve lower costs through economies of scope, better resource management, and a strengthened market position for Norwegian gas production and its sale.

The state model was made in the interplay between domestic and international factors and actors. A political consensus across party lines supported a state-controlled entrepreneurship domestically. Discussions were not about whether or not the state should be engaged in the industry, but rather how. The nationalization of multinational oil companies in the 1970s supported a strong national policy. Significant price variations and the politicization of the European gas market changed the external framework for policy in the 1980s. The US embargo of Soviet gas in 1982, with a desire that Norwegian gas should replace Soviet gas (Jentleson 1986, Austvik 1991), and the British rejection of the Sleipner deal in 1984 were examples of external political pressures (Stern 1986). Domestically, a gradual maturation of the industry and a new balance between political parties modified the situation. The model was eventually adjusted in the mid-1980s, but its state controlled style was retained.

The strong state control was in line with the social democratic spirit and Scandinavian administrative traditions dominant after WWII, and with the state occupying more roles as owner (Grønlie 1990). The state had from early in the twentieth century exerted strong control over, for example, hydro-power developments and many other industries considered to be public utilities. The relatively loose international framework for trade at the time, as expressed in the General Agreement on Trade and Tariffs (GATT) and EFTA cooperation, provided an international framework that made it possible to discriminate in favour of Norwegian companies.

Public ownership and engagement in the energy sector was however not a particularly Norwegian or new phenomenon. Since 1914 a number of states had participated actively in the oil industry as part or full owners of companies (Yergin 1991). In 1970 however, state-owned companies represented only six per cent of international oil trade (Noreng 2000). The nationalization of the petroleum industries in OPEC countries in the 1970s implied a dramatic increase in state participation in the oil companies in most producing countries. The nationalization made it difficult for the outside world to criticize Norway in building her own national oil company. With the establishment of Statoil, the control mechanisms became however so strong that 'the limits for what a capitalist state can do if it wants to remain capitalistic' were approached (Olsen 1989:104, my translation).

Although state control was essential to the Norwegian model it was different to models of nationalized oil industries, as both Norwegian and international private companies were invited as important partners to acquire capital, competence, and technology. The model was as such not an imitation of other countries' practices, but an innovation in itself, combining state control with market principles. The innovative solution in between complete nationalization (as in most OPEC countries) and more or less free-market principles (as in the United States) were unique at the time.

National control of a very profitable petroleum industry was important to most oil-producing countries through the 1970s and until prices fell in 1985-1986. Lower profit margins made companies stronger in relation to the state, but the situation also showed more clearly than before that the state and the companies had many interests in common. A general understanding of the need for more foreign technological competence evolved (Ryggvik 1997:61-62). The Norwegianization policy led to employment, growth, and competence in Norwegian companies and regions (Olsen and Reiersen 1991:9-20). However, the lower profit margins weakened the state's power to require that the companies should also satisfy national (industrial policy) goals (Nerheim 1996).

The Petroleum Fund, established in 1991 and the first deposits were made in 1995, also had significant effect on oil and gas production policy. The Fund ensured that annual public budgets were no longer directly influenced by fluctuations in oil and gas revenues.[3] What was not used of revenues was to be accumulated in the Fund. When petroleum revenues were not changed into Norwegian krones, the pressure for an appreciation of the currency was strongly weakened, and domestic demand would be kept under control. A Norwegian Dutch Disease was avoided.[4] The Fund is administered in a separate section of the Central Bank (NBIM = Norges Bank Investment Management), and the Parliament decides upon how much of it should be used in the annual budgets.

Not only earnings and expenditures were however decoupled, but also activity level on the NCS and macroeconomic concerns, despite the impact from the huge oil and gas investments in themselves on the Norwegian economy. FIN had a strong constraining role on production levels in the 1970s, but has in public not said much on the issue after the Fund was established.

---

[3] The net cash-flow (net government take) from the petroleum sector is at present dominated by a 78 per cent tax on companies' economic profit (28 per cent general corporate tax plus 50 per cent special tax) and 100 per cent of net revenues from the SDFI shares (representing 59 per cent and 36 per cent of total net cash flow, respectively, in 2008). In addition, the government receives a dividend from Statoil profits and royalties, area fees, and CO_2 tax (4 per cent and 1 per cent of the total, respectively, in 2008). The combined net cash-flow amounted in the year 2008 to 416 Billion Norwegian krones, BNOK (some 50 billion euro or 70 billion USD). Under the SDFI arrangement, the state pays its share of investments and costs, and receives a corresponding share of income from a production license. The expenditures are accounted for when they occur, so are also revenues (no depreciation). Through the SDFI the state takes all costs and the risk, but also all the economic rent. Typically, the SDFI holds the largest shares in the biggest and most profitable fields (MPE annual).

[4] The term 'Dutch Disease' was used first time in an article in *The Economist* ('The Dutch Disease' 28 Nov. 1978:82-83). It was soon established as the diagnosis on the problems a country can get from domestic use of petroleum revenues.

The establishing of the Petroleum Fund was another radical innovative step and obviously wise from a macroeconomic and financial point of view. Without the Fund, production increases making Norway the third biggest combined oil and gas exporter in the world would have been most difficult from a macroeconomic point of view, and would most likely have been resisted by the FIN. The removal of production restraints increased the domestic manoeuvring room, as well as for consuming countries that were able to pressure Norway for higher production. This implied that the Win-Set (Putnam 1988) for Norway was expanded; with the Fund in place it became more difficult for Norway to reject pressures for increased production, for example, from the EU, if she has available resources.

The coupling between structural changes in the Norwegian petroleum industry, the changed role and maturity of Statoil, and the establishment of the petroleum Fund is important in understanding the de-politicization of policy and adjusting to an increasingly more liberal economic international world. With the alliance with British Petroleum (BP) in 1989 Statoil also started to internationalize the company in countries like Angola and Azerbaijan. Technological change and international expansion should now gradually bring progress for the company, more than domestic developments.

Hence, the de-politicization of the role of Statoil came gradually before its privatization in 2001. It was Statoil's own initiative to become partly privatized. Its main arguments were that it had become a mature enterprise, and wanted to grow more internationally than domestically. After the privatization, Statoil was to carry on with what had become an industrial entrepreneurship for the company, with the goal of becoming a strong international oil company. Privatization made the company freer in its business decisions. The state was to take the back seat as the biggest owner, but with the opportunity to intervene in decisions, if it was willing and considered it necessary.

EU And Norway: From Conflict to Cooperation and Innovative Adaptation

The first adjustment of Norwegian petroleum policy to EU regulations came in the early 1990s, when the EEA agreement challenged established preferential arrangements for Norwegian supplies to the sector. At the time, however, most of the supply industry had become competitive and the industry itself did not any longer consider continued protection an important issue. Access to markets in other countries was considered more important. The EU Concession Directive (EU 1994) appeared eventually as rather uncontroversial for the industry. However, it provided a signal that the EU had become an important force in Norwegian petroleum policy-formation. National policy now had to be made according to EU rules and their interpretation by the ESA and not only to the defined national interests. The price transparency (EU 1990) and the electricity (EU 1997) directives did not qualify much for a Norwegian policy adaptation either, because she was not affected much (the transparency directive) or had already implemented similar policies (the electricity directive).

The gas directive (EU 1998) introduced in 2002 and revised in 2003 (EU 2003)[5] represented however political decisions that wanted to create a more liberal European gas

[5] A proposal for a new revision of the directive was put forward in 2007 (EU 2007b).

market. In the highly concentrated structure of the European gas market, gas was (and to a large extent still is) sold and resold many times on its way from the fields of production to the final user, often between monopolies (or oligopolies) and monopsonies (or oligopsonies). Generally, producers (exporters) sold gas to transmission companies (pipelines) who act both as transporters and merchants in the market. The gas the pipelines buy at its entry, they resell at its exit at the city-gate to their customers; local distribution companies (LDCs), power plants and large industrial users. The LDCs also act as both transporters and merchants, as pipelines do, and resell the gas to final consumers (end-users) in private households and businesses. In general, producers and pipelines have written long-term Take-or-Pay (TOP) contracts (up to 20 years), while pipelines signed medium-term contracts with its customers (one to five years). The gas directive intended to change this imperfect structure and to separate activities throughout the gas chain. The directive was considered far more important than the other petroleum-related directives and threatened, together with EU competition law, the structure of the Norwegian petroleum cluster (Stern 1998:164-170).

Statoil's privatization took place at the same time as the EU demands, and was adjusted to these. With privatization, the company could no longer take care of the same functions for the government as before. Privatization required a clearer definition of the role of the state in taking care of its own interests, and new ways of promoting efficiency, distribution, and political and social aspects of petroleum activities in line with EU ideology, rules, and practices. Hence, the substantial reorganization of Norwegian oil and gas activities in 2001/2002 must be understood as the result of three factors: the privatization of Statoil and the twin pressure from the EU to make her adapt to EU competition law and the gas directive, respectively.

The GFU and FU arrangements and existing transportation solutions were long defended from a Norwegian national point of view. The arguments were that 'free competition' in production and sale between companies might contribute to weaker resource management, a larger supply of gas in the market and put pressure upon prices, particularly in the short and medium term. The impaired possibility of exploiting economies of scope by opening the Norwegian pipelines through a Third Party Access (TPA) arrangement might technically make things more complicated and expensive. The advantages of scope between Norway as a gas seller and the large transmission companies on the Continent, expressed through the long-term TOP contracts, were also pointed out. The GFU was regarded as part of the Norwegian resource management system and the MPE (1997) did not 'consider the EEA agreement applicable to the establishment and functioning of the GFU'.

Maintenance of the model would assure that Norway was still able to appear as a stable supplier of gas with 'factory gates' in Emden, Zeebrügge, Dunkerque and St. Fergus, the MPE argued. A change in joint management might put long-term investments at risk and through that weaken the supply of gas, which would be a disadvantage, also to purchasing countries in the long-run.

The argument about maintaining market power through the GFU was clearly contrary to the principles of a liberalized gas market, as well as the direct interests of consumer countries (EU member states). On the other hand, the principles for how FU worked were not automatically at variance with EU's Single-Market principles, as long as MPE did not discriminate between who was to receive licenses on the NCS. The Norwegian arguments for optimal resource management and the exploitation of economics of scope are something that the EU also should take into consideration and furthered in their liberalization efforts.

At the same time, it was not obvious that the GFU maintained in its old shape was an organ that was sufficiently dynamic to safeguard Norwegian interests when many smaller and more short-term contracts were evolving in the market. The market had been undergoing fundamental changes for some time through an extensive growth and infrastructural developments. A changed role for the GFU could have been in Norwegian interests anyway. Both market developments and political efforts pointed towards that producers increasingly should sell gas directly to the customers of gas. The buyers of 'new' Norwegian gas (new contracts) would not (only) be the same as before (the transmission companies), but also the transmission companies' customers (distribution companies, the industry and gas power plants). Future gas contracts were to be made on a more fragmented basis than before.

A similar tension over legal aspects concerning Norwegian petroleum policy emanating from the EEA agreement as with GFU/FU issues, arose when Norway decided to support OPEC efforts to reduce production, in order to stabilize prices in 2001, although not equally controversial. In the OPEC case, the European Commission charged Norway with contravention of Article 12 of the EEA Agreement, which prohibits quantitative restrictions on exports, as well as competition provisions of the EEA agreement. Norwegians, however, considered that

> ... petroleum produced on the NCS should (consequently) not be regarded as an EEA product. ... Non-discriminatory regulations of production (and exports) should not conflict with EEA rules (Arnesen 1995: 528, 530-539, my translation).

Nevertheless, the Commission wanted to highlight Norway's failure to notify its action to the appropriate EEA forum. The situation did not lead to a case before the EFTA Court, 'since the EU itself has an interest in oil price stability' (Emerson, Vahl, and Woolcock 2002:13).

This tension in Norway's relations to the EU might, however, return to haunt a weak oil market situation at a later point in time. Norway desires the freedom to interplay with OPEC, as she has done since 1986 (Austvik 1989), 'while it is very formally associated with the EU. There can be times when the two relationships do not ride well together' (Emerson, Vahl, and Woolcock 2002:13).

Any similar interplay with Russia in the future with the goal of stabilizing European gas prices in a weak-market situation would certainly be met with much harsher reactions from the EU than was the case in the OPEC example.

Norway resisted moving towards a more open and flexible transportation solution on the NCS and the abolishment of GFU/FU arrangements. Eventually, however, she was forced to follow the gas directive and to introduce TPA on the NCS. She was also forced to abolish the GFU and FU arrangements according to the interpretation of EU competition law and moved from a position of conflict to a position of cooperation with the EU. The actual outcome of the changes was however more à-la-Norvége, and implied that most goals of the political entrepreneurship could be maintained.

To take care of the SDFI, the new fully state-owned company *Petoro* was created. The company assumed responsibility for administering the ownership interests of the state, monitoring Statoil's production and sales activities, and doing the accounts for the SDFI. In order to secure an open access for transportation of gas on the NCS, the new fully state-owned company *Gassco* was established. Gassco took Statoil's role as operator for transmission systems to the Continent and the U.K. These systems had different tariff practices and were organized as separate companies, where each could deny third parties' access to their systems. The *Gassled* system offered in principle equal tariffs for everyone using the system, as an adjustment to the EU gas directive (MPE 2002).

Within this new framework the Norwegian government (including the bureaucracy in the MPE) showed high competence in giving the Norwegian structure a new form, while at the same time maintaining control. Important part of the solution was increased direct state participation (Gassco and Petoro); another part was new regulations (Gassled). EU principles and regulatory requirements were translated into a form that made it possible to maintain important policy goals. The negotiating position towards the buyers was weakened, but not in a fundamental way. Downstream markets had also become more open than before, on the positive side, as seen from a Norwegian perspective.

The MPE appeared through the changes again with increased relative political power, as Statoil was in a position to act more (or only) commercially. With its privatization, the perspective for Statoil became more short-sighted as the capital market, rather than political decision-making, was to guide corporate strategy. As the dominating owner, the state would now prioritize Statoil profits and shareholders value. Statoil's responsibility for the SDFI shares, transportation and processing of the oil and gas systems, and other political consideration and factors that were not directly related to Statoil's own interests, were taken over by state organs, new companies, and regulatory agencies.

Statoil continued however as the single seller of the SDFI and Petoro oil and gas. The links between state and company remained strong, partly because the state maintained its position as majority owner with some two-thirds of the shares. Government policy and structures changed with industrial and market maturation, in addition to the impacts from Norwegian-EU integration. The state gained a more regulative than interventionist role, but remained the main rent collector in the sector, and could continue in a role as a political industrial entrepreneur and innovator when considered necessary, albeit with changed political tools.

The EEA Agreement and Norwegian Petroleum Policy

The EEA agreement's impact on the Norwegian petroleum industry represents a broader political change. The agreement aimed at bringing the petroleum sector more in line with how other sectors are managed politically. It implied, 'as other international agreements, that the state is not only the regulator, but is also object for regulation' (Arnesen 1995:659, my translation). What previously had been a 'political question about which rules should be in force in Norway, was now to be … a judicial question about the content of policy' (ibid.).

While being strongly focused on the role of the entrepreneurial Norwegian state as an explanation for market imperfections in her petroleum sector, the EEA agreement has not challenged the role of the state as the dominant owner, the main capitalist in the sector and the establishment of more state agencies. The heavy taxation system and the arrangement with the SDFI to capture a maximum share of the economic rent for the state have been maintained. The agreement strongly affects however domestic competition policy. It ended for example the policy of choosing developmental concepts and materials specifically designed to fit the Norwegian supply industry (Arnesen 1995:343-393), which actually was a *de facto* protectionist measure in favour of Norwegian suppliers.

The agreement sets limits for the content of normative political measures; non-discriminatory restrictions are allowed, while discrimination between firms and persons is not allowed, independently of whether it is a state or a private firm that runs the business. What changed was that national goals could no longer be reached by normative political means alone, but must be complemented by the state as an actor and regulator, respectively, in relevant situations. The result of the EEA agreement is that more decisions are made by independent market actors, but there can also be more state involvement through state ownership or regulatory intervention in markets and private actors' behaviour, or both.

The EEA agreement also contributed to changing the constellations of domestic actors relevant for petroleum policy-formation. Within the government the Ministry of Foreign Affairs (MFA) returned as a more important ministry, as it was in the 1960s and 1970s when the processes around the law of the sea contributed to the development of the emerging Norwegian petroleum sector at the time. The Ministry of Justice and its sub-organs have in the areas where the EEA agreement largely applies, gone from being a domestic law-maker to an external law-taker, and in relevant cases override what the MPE otherwise would have done in the petroleum sector. Before the EEA agreement came into effect, the MPE would have rather asked the Ministry of Justice to make laws that supported her policy objectives.

Both privatization and EU pressure induced new government-company relationships and made Statoil more independent from the government. As the company became 'only commercial', questions gradually re-emerged, as in the early 1980s when the company was wing-clipped, of whether the government had also become the 'junior partner to business' (Wood 2001) in petroleum policy. One example was when Statoil and Hydro, and not the government, took the initiative to merge in 2006/2007. Statoil even suggested that it should claw back the SDFI shares that were taken away politically in 1984, in order to become internationally competitive. It would have made it the fourth biggest oil company in the world in terms of production at the time.

In the establishment phase of the Norwegian petroleum industry it was clear that business was a 'junior partner to government' (ibid.). As the roles of Statoil as an instrument for the state was wing-clipped and the company eventually privatized, it became a Norwegian multinational oil company with engagements in many countries. This coincided with a strong increase in international trade and direct foreign investments. Now the Norwegian state supports StatoilHydro's international engagements in countries such as Azerbaijan, Angola, Algeria, Libya, Russia, and Venezuela. At the same time, Statoil is promoting its interests at home in an expansion on the NCS (as for example through an increase in Troll production, rejected by the MPE in the fall of 2007). As the company has become 'only commercial', questions have once again been asked about whether the government has become a 'junior partner to business' (a principal-agent problem), as it was in the early 1980s. The political wing-clipping and privatization have offered Statoil greater freedom in how to influence policy and to act as grown cuckoo at home.

The formal position of the government was however not changed in 2001-2002, other than that she was still able to exercise strong authority over domestic petroleum policy through the new institutions and regulations, as well as towards StatoilHydro as a company, if she so desires. The ESA's evaluation of the GFU system was coloured by formality, but also by the interests of Norway and her bargaining with the EU system. The StatoilHydro merger, which formally increased seller concentration of Norwegian gas, and the company's continued sales of SDFI gas, were not met by criticism from the ESA. Taken together, to date EU regulations in this sector have in sum *de facto* ended up being more about form than substance. This conclusion is supported by a number of downstream impediments on the Continent compared to the purposes of the gas directives and EU competition law (Austvik 2009a). The regulations to a large extent represents changes where,

> 'fuzzy liberalization' – universal free-market rules that are open to a wide range of interpretations by governments, companies and the courts – is becoming the norm, even when there is broad agreement on liberal market principles (Andersen and Sitter 2009).

Dag Harald Claes studied how four types of cumulative factors influenced how Norway has adapted to the EU energy sector in the Single Market: affectedness, policy similarities, bargaining opportunities, and legal proceedings. He found that

> there is considerable variation in domestic adaptation to the EU even within the case of Norwegian energy adaptation ... [due to] variations in the policy fits and misfits, but more interestingly due to the dynamic interactions between actors' interests and the institutional aspects of the adaptation processes (Claes 2002:306).

The price transparency, concessions, and electricity directives did not qualify much for a Norwegian policy adaptation because of either low affectedness bargaining opportunities or (existing) policy similarities. The gas directive however represented a strong conflicting interest between Norway and the EU, especially when Norway did not obtain bargaining opportunities. Norway did however to a large extent manage to adapt to the new situation. In spite of her legal 'defeat', she did not lose the essentials of the petroleum model's entrepreneurial purpose when it was reorganized to comply with EU directives and competition law.

The complexity of the petroleum sector implies that when a judicial review of whether a measure is necessary to take care of the concerns in which it is anchored, doubtfully will be very intense. … [The] ESA will most doubtfully be able to deal with other than striking violation of rules (Arnesen 1995:662, my translation).

To some extent this is also true in the EU itself:

> The 'fuzziness' of the rules have meant that even court cases against national import/export monopolies are only met with partial success (Andersen and Sitter 2009).

The integration with the EU modified however the nationally defined ideological platform for industrial and social goals of Norwegian petroleum policy. The move was towards more liberal ideas, as compared to the interventionist and realist attitudes in the 10 Oil Commandments, and as practised in the 1970s and 1980s. However, already in the early 1990s, attitudes that the state should hold a weaker and more regulative political hands-on industrial policy began to inform policy in Norway. At the same time, as the EEA agreement was signed, a government report stated that state control should 'mainly be executed through laws, provisions and other administrative measures, rather than through direct interventions' (Report to the Storting 1993-1994:26). The process of integration with the EU strengthened liberal ideology and an emphasis on a New Public Management (NPM) type of policy. The tradition in Norwegian petroleum policy had been to look for broad compromises across institutions and political parties and a bureaucracy that formulated policy. Only in foreign and security policy areas were otherwise consensus procedures explicitly sought. Initiatives for changing the petroleum sector were taken by companies of interests and the EU. This occurred in what was a radically changed liberal ideological environment. While the OPEC revolution gave strong support for independent national policy-making in the 1970s, the liberal sphere of the 1990s provided disincentives.

A relevant counterfactual question is what would have happened if Norway had not entered the EEA agreement, and instead chosen the Swiss model or full membership, respectively, for her EU relations. To answer this question it is important to note that independently of the EEA agreement, in the 1990s, both the international and domestic situations were substantially changed for Norway, as compared with the early years when it was the state that took the initiatives to create Statoil, separate out the SDFI shares, and make the GFU and FU arrangements.

> Many changes in Norwegian politics would most likely have also taken place without the EEA agreement (Claes and Tranøy 1999, my translation).

In addition, how EU regulations and rules can be translated (Veggeland 2009) into domestic policy changes over time and depends on the situation. The domestic impacts of any exogenous change tend to be heavily coloured by incumbent ideology and governmental institutions. This path-dependency includes strong elements of stability, predictability and sustainability:

> ... history is path dependent in the sense that the character of current institutions depends not only on current conditions but also in the historical path of institutional developments (March and Olsen 1998:959).

In the long run the EEA agreement may continue to weaken the state's ability to intervene in oil and gas affairs. But the debate over the degree and scope of policy that best serves a liberal society's competitive situation will continue, not to say that the liberal idea as such of framing economic and political affairs may be modified. In the case of petroleum, the difference to a Swiss model and full membership would for Norway most likely have been of modest significance. This demonstrates that the distinction between the different perspectives on international affairs and international political economy often cover aspects of the same story:

> The sharp disagreement between realism and liberal theory is overstated. In fact, the two approaches can be complimentary (Nye 1988:238).

The state gained a more regulative than interventionist role caused by integration with the EU, but also owing to industrial and market maturity. The scale and scope of the *de facto* results from policy depended on the Norwegian state's understanding of the situation and eventually interplay with the EU as international superstructure. Most interestingly is that it appears to be the hostile perceptions of and attitudes towards the integrating processes that was more decisive for outcomes and the ability to maintain policy goals than the scale and scope of *de jure* new regulations.

CONCLUSION

As political entrepreneur the Norwegian state combined several instruments when creating and developing her petroleum industry. Measures were regulative as well as interventionist, and Norwegian companies received preferential treatment in the infant stage. From the very start, the state also engaged itself directly in the industry through its own company. Important goals were to defend national control of the petroleum sector, to optimize resource management, and to capture as much rent as possible. With substantial political and financial risks the state managed not only to establish the industry, but to also be the driving force in taking care of and contribute to change and evolution. Without these efforts Norway, as many other resource rich countries, could have been another victim of elements of the resource-curse paradox (Auty 1993).

> Being blessed with large petroleum resources is not enough to assure that their management will lead to social well-being (Estrada 2006).

Through several discrete and incremental innovative changes the state managed to create a competitive Norwegian petroleum industry from nothing in only a couple of decades, and to take most of the profits from the activities itself. *Ex post facto*, policies turned out to be largely successful.

Many factors have contributed to this success, but it is the mixture of strategies that seems to have worked (Gordon and Stenvoll 2007).

The EEA agreement challenged and contributed to change the Norwegian petroleum enterprise. Her government, however, succeeded in entrepreneurial re-regulation and finding new ways of intervening in the sector within the new legal framework. The new policy could largely maintain the goals of the old policy in a context of industrial and market maturity and competitiveness. Norway would however have had great difficulties building a national petroleum industry from nothing if the resources were found now and not in the 1970s. It would under the agreement be difficult to give Statoil the best licenses and not at the outset to more efficient foreign competitors. It would be especially difficult to discriminate to the advantage of the Norwegian supply industry. A government cannot any more address support towards specific companies, a situation different to the 1970s. Political measures must in terms of single companies be neutral.

This neutrality does however not mean that policy today must be neutral to economic growth, employment or regional development. In Norway it is difficult to avoid the state becoming an important participant in one way or another in the development of large industries. First, as in any other country, the state must be an important actor as a 'Porterian' infrastructural provider. Secondly, the Norwegian state owns the now enormous Petroleum Fund and possesses the largest bulk of financial resources in the country. Thirdly, the state owns about 40 per cent of combined Norwegian industries. When the government has expressed desires for a larger and more efficient private ownership to act as entrepreneur in Norwegian industry (as in the Report to the Storting 2002-2003:22) the state must remain an important partner different from the state in many other market economies.

Today the possibility of the state following an innovative industrial policy within the EU economic paradigm appears to apply to the case of 'normal' industries and does not equally well appear to fit a situation when the economy experiences an exogenous shock, as through the discovery of the huge petroleum reserves, and the subsequent desire of the state to build a national industry to deal with such an event. Many of the state entrepreneurial efforts from the 1970s and 1980s would today be in conflict with present international trade regulations (EU and the WTO).

On the other hand, even if the national political tool-box is changed, it is not empty when dealing with discrete and powerful exogenous change. One example is the tremendous growth in the Norwegian Petroleum Fund after 2001, which can today be considered a new exogenous shock to the Norwegian economy and society, parallel to the discoveries of the petroleum resources after 1969. Norway has not put down labour or capital to create the Fund (it is the accumulation of economic rent from the NCS and returns on international financial investments), nor did she do anything to bring the resources under the bottom of the North Sea millions of years ago. To use part of the Fund's foreign earnings to long-term building of alternative domestic sectors through support of 'Porterian' infrastructure in a wide sense is possible within the new international framework; social security, roads, rails, air, harbours, education, research and development, culture, etc. Some of these investments could even be state (or publicly) run. Should she learn from the petroleum enterprise acting to the best for Norwegian state and society, such (massive and) discrete investments could be considered a responsible response to this second exogenous petroleum gift, and possible within the existing international and European economic superstructure.

Within an orthodox liberal framework, governments should not however have roles in the form of direct involvement in business activities, in terms of policies that favour certain business or branches, or through massive infrastructural investments based on public money. We argue, however, that such an approach to the role of a government is unrealistic in a complex economic system, where a myriad of regulations and programs are in place, particularly in the petroleum sector.

Under such circumstances, talk of substituting global governance for the primacy of the national state is in vain (Gilpin 2001:402).

Hence, the scope and scale of the national political manoeuvring room depends on how the EU itself evolves. The EU represents today a regulated market economy (and not a laissez-faire) system. Entrepreneurship and innovation is however about individuals taking actions on their own. But the EU has changed much over the past decades, and it may continue to change in the future. If the EU allows for more national interventionism and political innovation in economic activities it will not necessarily break with the overall idea of the Union. A liberal economic model can be interpreted within the 'variety of capitalism' literature, with different state-industry mixtures and optimization purposes.

How the EU develops further depends on circumstance, ideological perspective, and intra-EU developments, and will contribute to defining the manoeuvring room and policy options for the Norwegian state, as well as in economic activity in general. It will be important for any European state with the aim of promoting national economic interests to follow how EU's economic, political and *de jure* regulations and practices will change with ideological change. The resulting *de facto* national political manoeuvring room within these developments is eventually determined by each country's innovative ability to interpret, adapt, and influence the processes.

REFERENCES

Abel, F. (2003). The political entrepreneur and the coordination of the political process: A market process perspective of the political market. *The Review of Austrian Economics*, 16:2/3. pp.153–168

Andersen, S.S. (2006). The mosaic of Europeanization: An organizational perspective on national re-contextualization. In From & Sitter (Eds.), *Europe's nascent state: Public policy in the European Union.* Oslo: Gyldendal Akademisk

Andersen, S.S. & Sitter, N. (2009). The European gas market: Differentiated integration and fuzzy liberalization. In Ferman (Ed.): *The political economy of energy in Europe.* Berlin: Berliner Wissenshafts Verlag.

Arnesen, F. (1995). *Statlig styring og EØS-rettslige skranker* [*State streering and EEA legal barriers*]. Oslo: Universitetsforlaget

Ask, A.O. (2006). *Mennene som skapte oljegiganten: Statoils historie er også beretningen om Olje-Norge* [*The men who created the oil giant: Statoil's history is also the story of Oil-Norway*]. www.e24.no

Augsburg, T. (2005). *Becoming interdisciplinary: An introduction to interdisciplinary studies.* New York: Kendall/Hunt Publishing

Austvik, O.G. (Ed.) (1989). *Norwegian oil and foreign policy.* Oslo: NUPI / Vett and Viten

Austvik, O.G. (1991). Norwegian energy in an international context: The U.S. embargo of Soviet gas in 1982. In Austvik (Ed.), *Norwegian gas in the new Europe: How politics shape markets.* Oslo: NUPI / Vett and Viten

Austvik, O.G. (2009a). EU natural gas market liberalization and long-term security-of-supply and demand. In Ferman (Ed.), *The political economy of energy in Europe.* Berlin: Berliner Wissenshafts Verlag. pp. 61-94.

Austvik, O.G. (2009b). *The Norwegian state as oil and gas entrepreneur: The impact of the EEA agreement and EU gas market liberalization.* PhD Thesis. Saarbrücken: VDM Verlag

Auty, R.M. (*1993*). *Sustaining development in mineral economies: The resource curse thesis.* London: Routledge.

Claes, D.H. (2002). The process of Europeanization: Norway and the internal energy market. *Journal of Public Policy,* 22, *3*: 299–323

Claes, D.H. and Tranøy, B.S. (Eds.) (1999). *Utenfor, annerledes og suveren? Norge under EØS-avtalen* [*Outside, different and sovereign? Norway under the EEA agreement*]. Bergen: Fagbokforlaget

Cini, M. (Ed) (2007). *European Union politics.* Oxford: Oxford University Press

Eisinger, P.K. (1988). *The rise of the entrepreneurial state: State and local economic development policy in the United States.* Madison WI: The University of Wisconsin Press

Elster, J. & Moene, K. (1989). *Alternatives to capitalism.* Cambridge: Press Syndicate of the University of Cambridge

Emerson, M., Vahl, M. & Woolcock, S. (2002). *Norway, the European Economic Area and the European Union.* Brussels: Centre for European Policy Studies (CEPS).

Estrada, J. (2006). *The Norwegian petroleum model and its benefits.* Mexico City: Analitica Energetica S.C.

EU, European Union (1990). *Council directive of 29 June 1990 concerning a community procedure to improve the transparency of gas and electricity prices charged to industrial end-users.* CEL-Title: 90/377/EEC. Brussels: EU

EU, European Union (1994). *On the conditions for granting and using authorizations for the prospection, exploration and production of hydrocarbons.* Council Directive 1994/22/EC, 30.5 1994. Brussels: EU

EU, European Union (1997). Restucturing the community framework for the taxation of energy products: Proposal for a council directive COM (97) 30 Final 97/0111 (CNS) 12.3.1997. Brussels: EU

EU, European Union (1998). *The single market for natural gas.* IGM Directive 98/30. Brussels: EU

EU, European Union (2003). *Common rules for the internal market in natural gas and repealing Directive 98/30/EC.* Council Directive 2003/55/EC, 26.6.2003. Brussels: EU

EU, European Union (2005). Working together for growth and jobs: A new start for the Lisbon Strategy. COM(2005) 24 final Brussels, 2.2.2005. Brussels: EU

EU, European Union (2007a). *The European Economic Area (EEA): Overview.* Legal notice. October. Brussels: EU

EU, European Union (2007b). *Common rules for the internal market in natural gas.* Proposal for a Directive of the European Parliament and of the Council amending Directive 2003/55/EC of the European Parliament and of the Council of 26 June 2003. COM (2007) 0529. Brussels: EU

Evans, P.B. & Rueschemeyer, D. (1985). The state and economic transformation: toward an analysis of the conditions underlying effective intervention. In Evans, Rueschemeyer & Skocpol (Eds.), *Bringing the state back in.* Cambridge: Cambridge University Press

Fagerberg, J., Mowery, D.C. & Nelson, R.R. (Eds.) (2005). *The Oxford handbook of innovation.* Oxford: Oxford University Press

Fagerberg, J. (2007). The dynamics of technology, growth and trade: A Schumpeterian perspective. In Hanusch & Pyka (Eds.), *Elgar companion to neo-Schumpeterian economics.* Cheltenham: Edward Elgar Publishing

Gilpin, R. (2001). *Global political economy: understanding the international economic order.* Princeton NJ: Princeton University Press

Gordon, R. & Stenvoll, T. (2007). *Statoil: A study in political entrepreneurship.* Policy Report. Texas: The James A. Baker III Institute for Public Policy, Rice University

Graver, H.P. (2000). *Supranationality and national legal autonomy in the EEA agreement.* Working paper no 23. Oslo: Arena

Grønlie, T. (1990). *Statlig industrietablering som politisk reiskap: Norge i vest-europeisk samanheng* [*Establishment of industry by the state as a political tool: Norway in a western European context*]. Notat no. 1. Bergen: LOS-senteret

Hall, P. & Soskice, D. (2001). *Varieties of capitalism: the institutional foundations of comparative advantage.* Oxford: Oxford University Press

Hanisch, T.J. & Nerheim, G. (1992). *Norsk oljehistorie: Fra vantro til overmot?* [*Norwegian oil history: From disbelief to arrogance?*] (vol. I) Oslo: Leseselskapet

Jentleson, B. (1986). *Pipeline politics: The complex political economy of east-west energy trade.* Itacha NY: Cornell University Press.

Katzenstein, P. (1985). *Small states in world markets: Industrial policy in Europe.* Itacha NY: Cornell University Press.

Keohane, R. & Milner, H. (1996). *Internationalization and domestic politics*. Cambridge MA: Cambridge University press

Klein, J.T. (1990). *Interdisciplinarity: History, theory, and practice*. Detroit: Wayne State University

Klein, J.T. (1996). *Crossing boundaries: Knowledge, disciplinarities, and interdisciplinarities*. Charlottesville VA: University Press of Virginia

Krugman, P. (1979). A model of innovation, technology transfer and the world distribution of income. *Journal of Political Economy* 87, 253-266

Mann, M. (1997). Has globalization ended the rise and rise of the nation-state. *Review of International Political Economy* Vol 4, No 3

March, J.G. & Olsen, J.P. (1998: The institutional dynamics of international political orders. *International Organization* 52, 4

Martin, R.L., & Osberg, S. (2007). Social entrepreneurship: The case for definition. *Stanford Social Innovation Review*

Mises, L.von (1943). *La Bureaucratie* [*Bureaucracy*]. Paris: Librairie de Médicis.

Mjøset, L. & Andersson, L. (1987). The transformation of the Nordic models. *Cooperation and Conflict*, 22, 227-243

Mjøset, L. & Clausen, T.H. (2007). *Capitalism compared. Comparative Social Research* (vol. 24). Amsterdam: Elsevier

MPE, Ministry of Petroleum and Energy (annual). *Fact sheet*. Oslo.

MPE, Ministry of Petroleum and Energy (1997). *Memorandum on the establishment and functioning of the GFU*, January 20. Oslo.

MPE, Ministry of Petroleum and Energy (2002). *Draft Royal Decree regarding amendments to Regulations to Act relating to petroleum activities of 27 June 1997 No. 653* and *Draft of new Regulations for determining tariffs*, September 2002. Oslo.

Nerheim, G. (1996). *Norsk oljehistorie. En gassnasjon blir til.* [*Norwegian oil history: A gas-nation comes into existence*] (vol. 2). Oslo: Leseselskapet.

Nore, P. (1979). *The Norwegian state's relationship to the international oil companies over North Sea oil, 1965-75*. London: Council for National Academic Awards

Noreng, Ø. (2000). Statsselskap – et gode for nasjonen? Internasjonale erfaringer – Statoil som norsk tilfelle [State company: Good for the nation? International experiences – Statoil as a Norwegian case]. Presentasjon på PETROPOLs seminar: *Privatisering av Statoil og SDØE's framtid* [*Privatization of Statoil and the State's direct financial interest (SDØE)*] Oslo 23. oktober.

Noreng, Ø. (2004).Norway: Economic diversification and the petroleum industry. *Middle East Economic Survey*. Nicosia. VOL XLVII no. 45.

Nye, J. (1988). Neorealism and neoliberalism. *World Politics* 15(2): pp. 235-51

OECD, Organization for Economic Cooperation and Development (2006). *Understanding entrepreneurship: Developing indicators for international comparisons and assessments*. STD/CSTAS (2006)9. Paris: OECD

Olsen, J.P. (1989). *Petroleum og politikk – det representative demokratiets møte med oljealderen* [Petroleum and politics: Representative democracy's meeting with the oil era]. Oslo: TANO.

Olsen, O.E. & Reisersen, J.E. (1991). *Svart gull på alles fat? Oljevirksomhetens regionale fordeling* [Black gold in everyone's barrel? Regional distribution of oil activity]. Oslo: Kommuneforlaget.

Porter, M. (1990). *The competitive advantage of nations*. London: Macmillan Press Ltd.

Posner, M.V. (1961). *International trade and technical change.* Oxford Economic Papers 13: 323-341

Putnam, R.D. (1988). Diplomacy and domestic politics: the logic of two-level games. *International Organization*, 42(3). pp. 427–460.

Report to the Storting (1970–1971).*Undersøkelse etter og utvinning av undersjøiske naturforekomster på den norske kontinentalsokkel m.m.* [*Search for and extraction of undersea natural deposits on the Norwegian Continental Shelf*, etc.] Oslo: Industridepartementet Nr. 76

Report to the Storting (1993-1994). *Utfordringer og perspektiver for petroleumsvirksomheten på kontinentalsokkelen* [*Challenges and perspectives for petroleum activity on the Norwegian Continental Shelf*]. Oslo: Nærings- og energidepartementet, Nr. 26.

Report to the Storting (2001-2002). *Om EØS-samarbeidet 1994-2000* [On EEA co-operation: 1994-2000]. Oslo: Utenriksdepartementet 26 April 2002. Nr. 27.

Report to the Storting (2002-2003). *Et mindre og bedre statlig eierskap* [*A smaller and better state ownership*] Oslo: Nærings- og handelsdepartementet, nr. 22

Rickets, M. (1987). *The new industrial economics*. New York: St. Martin's

Ryggvik, H. (1997). Norsk oljepolitikk mellom det internasjonale og det nasjonale [Norwegian oil policy between the international and the national]. In Olsen and Sejersted (Eds.), *Oljevirksomheten som teknologiutviklingsprosjekt* [Oil activity as a project of technological development]. Oslo: Ad Notam.

Schneider, M. & Teske, P. (1992). Toward a theory of the political entrepreneur: Evidence from local government. *American Political Science Review* Vol. 86 No.3

Shepsle, K. (979). Institutional Arrangements and Equilibrium in Multidimensional Voting Models. *American Journal of Political science* 23. pp. 27-59.

Shockley, G.E., Frank, P.M. & Stough, R.R. (2002). Toward a theory of public sector Entrepreneurship. *The school of public policy, George Mason University* NCIIA 7th Annual Meeting: Big Ideas in a Small World March 20-22 Boston, Massachusetts.

Stern, J. (1986). After Sleipner: A policy for UK gas supplies. *Energy Policy* vol 14 no.1.

Stern, J. (1998). *Competition and liberalization in European gas markets: A diversity of models*. London: Royal Institute of International Affairs

Taewook, C. (2004). Promoting a northeast Asia economic integration policy. *Korea Focus*, vol 12, no 2.

Veggeland, N. (2007). *Paths of public innovation in the global age*. Cheltenham: Edward Elgar Publishing

Veggeland. N. (2009). *Taming the regulatory state.* Cheltenham: Edward Elgar Publishing

Wood, S. (2001). Business, government, and patterns of labour market policy in Britain and the Federal Republic of Germany. In Hall and Soskice (Eds.), *Varieties of Capitalism.* Oxford: Oxford University Press.

Yergin, D. (1993). *The prize: The epic quest for oil, money and power*. New York: Simon and Schuster.

In: Innovative Regulatory Approaches ...
Ed: Noralv Veggeland

ISBN: 978-1-60876-673-4

Chapter 7

THE NORWEGIAN PENSION FUND:[1] AN ETHICAL 'GOLD STANDARD' FOR INTERNATIONAL CLIMATIC INVESTMENTS?

Kristian Alm

Carbon assets can be likened to subprime
lending in terms of financial risk.
(Al Gore)

INTRODUCTION

'Sustainable development' is a new expression that has spread throughout the world since the United Nations World Commission introduced it in the report, 'Our Common Future', in 1987. The Commission developed 'sustainable development' as a strategic answer to a new challenge and a new risk. This report showed for the first time that the sum of human interventions in nature risked the irreversible destruction of the global environment. It made a major contribution in placing environmental questions on the international political agenda. However, this report did not manage to convince the centres of power in the international community that our planet was on its way towards a climatic crisis. Nor did it contribute to fundamental social change. Nevertheless, the Commission's focus on the close relationship between environmental, social, and economic development formed a basis for subsequent political discussions on environmental questions.

The UN climatic reports (2007) have presented research and analyses of the climatic crisis that are more disturbing than any earlier scientific reports. The UN Climate Panel has determined that there is a substantial risk that we are unable to create sustainable development for nature, the economy, and society. We are on the brink of destroying nature's capacity to absorb the effects of human activities because of global warming, caused by human beings

[1] Formerly called the Norwegian Petroleum Fund.

over the last 250 years. Humans are the principal cause of global warming, not the different mechanisms that exist in the natural world. The UN reports have established inroads in many parts of the world, and insights into the dramatic climatic change have altered significantly the public's attitude in many countries. But there are still substantial differences along the political spectrum, not least in the United States.

According to Malka (2009), increased knowledge about global warming in the US has been linked to an increased level of concern, but this is only among people who trust scientists to provide reliable information about the environment and among Democrats and Independents. Among people who are sceptical about scientists, and among Republicans, more knowledge has generally not been associated with greater concern. Despite this substantial difference, the US public has been through a considerable change compared to attitudes two or three decades ago. One of the most significant causes behind this change is most likely that the UN Climate Panel has based their reports on scientific inquiries of the highest quality.

This change both in the US and in several other democracies may in particular be due to the fact that the UN presents scientific-based disaster scenarios. People are scared. The apocalyptic images have disturbed social actors and convinced them that there is a high risk of an irreversible climatic disaster. We know now that the global sea level may rise at a rate faster than ever before and threaten many cities and coastal communities. This will force many people into dramatic life circumstances, both financially and socially. We know that the glaciers in the Antarctica, the Arctic, and in other parts of the world are melting at an alarming rate. People living on small islands in the Pacific are afraid that the ever rising ocean will destroy their communities. Such scenarios are not only visualized in popular cultural phenomena such as Al Gore's movie *An Inconvenient Truth*, but the UN has also based their apocalyptic images on already existing scientific inquiries, carefully controlled by the international scientific community. These apocalyptic images have, therefore, caused deep concern.

But it is one thing to be convinced; it is quite another thing to translate this into action with sufficient effect. There is still no international agreement on climatic change that would bind the nations of the world to implement effective countermeasures. The US and China have a large part of the responsibility for this. Nevertheless, the risks are being recognized in society after society, sector after sector. This means that governments throughout the world know now that they should quickly place climate-related risks on the agenda to avoid a dramatic destruction of nature and its strike-backs on our societies. Important has international research been for bringing forward knowledge in the field and thereby contributed to intensify the pressure for political action.

The financial markets are no exception in this context; this challenge affects them too. The financial markets share responsibility for combating climatic change through investments and lending to the business community. Some parts of the financial markets are starting to orient themselves towards more environmentally friendly operations. Many of the major institutional investors in the world, especially pension funds and sovereign wealth funds, are looking for methods of promoting sustainable development. This strategy is in their self-interest. Sustainable development is necessary in order to achieve an acceptable return in the long term. The risk is clear: they can be drawn into an environmental crisis that is *not* sustainable financially. The traditionalism of financial markets may add to this problem by slowing the speed at which necessary change needs to occur.

Institutional investors have increasingly pursued ethical investments with environmental criteria in order to help limit climate-related risks. The so-called ESG (Environmental, Social, Governance) criteria have become key to many major funds (Vandekerckhove & Leys 2007). One of the largest government investment funds in the world, the Norwegian Government Pension Fund – Global (GPF-G, formerly called the Government Petroleum Fund), is no exception in this regard. For many institutional investors, the Fund has become a model and a pioneer for ethical investments, especially because the ethical work carried out by the Fund is so thorough. In the decisive passages in the Ethical Guidelines[2] from 2004, we find formulations with a noticeable affinity to the UN's 'Our Common Future'.

The Government Petroleum Fund is an instrument for ensuring that a reasonable portion of the country's petroleum wealth should benefit future generations. The financial wealth must be managed with a view to generating a sound return in the long term, which is contingent on sustainable development in the economic, environmental and social sense.

In the eyes of many Norwegians, the proper management and control of the financial risk associated with the Pension Fund is one of Norway's most important contributions to the international battle against the threat posed by climatic change.

Norwegian Government Pension Fund – Global

The Government's ambitions with regard to the management of the Fund are lofty. The Norwegian press has placed a critical focus on these plans since the establishment of the Ethical Guidelines in 2004 (Alm 2007), partly owing to the political aspirations behind this document. The Norwegian state wants the Fund to be the best managed in all respects, including the combat against climatic change. These demands prompt the following question:

> Has the Norwegian government established an international gold standard for financial investments in an attempt to regulate the Fund's climate-related financial risk?

This question will be the guiding element of this chapter. In general, I shall focus on the potential gap between the image of the Fund as a paragon for other institutional investors and the concrete realities of managing the portfolio. Is the Fund exposed to criticism for proclaiming itself as an ethical model for investment management in the financial market, but is in reality failing to live up to its own standards, even in the core of its investment universe? When I refer to the ethical investment model as a supposed "a gold standard" I simply see the term as an indication of idealistic investment behaviour.

My interpretations draw on insights from the research on socially responsible investments (SRI). This research has mainly classified SRI as investments of four different types (Vandekerckhove & Leys, 20007) based on criteria of categorical exclusions, for example, an investor's policy excluding the armaments sector as a whole. The 'best-in-class' investments are another type of SRI where assets are invested in a percentage of credited companies in a special sector, based on social, environmental or ethical criteria, or any combination of them. The third type links the investment to an engagement with the management of the portfolio-company on non-financial issues (e.g. child labour) in order to encourage changes in

[2] The Ethical Guidelines appear in Appendix 1.

corporate practice. SRI might also refer to investments which aim to sustain alternative economic projects that would not be supported by normal market forces.

This chapter seeks to expand this commonly accepted notion of SRI by including an ethical judgement of the financial criteria embedded in an investment philosophy. The quest for SRI ought to include an assessment of the classical investment criteria of a funds portfolio, that is, the criteria for diversification. Does the Norwegian Pension Fund use these classical financial criteria in a responsible way by facing the challenge of climatic change? Do these specific financial criteria enable the Fund to regulate the climate-related financial risks as part of a climate-related conscious investment strategy?

To begin, I shall briefly describe the major ideals of the Government for the management of the Fund. Since the establishment of the ethical guidelines in 2005, these aspirations have gradually intensified. Next, I shall consider whether the Government has been successful in establishing a gold standard in its efforts to control the Fund's climate-related financial risk. I shall discuss this risk as a paradoxical result of the application of internationally financial indices. This discussion will benefit from the major consultative process on the ethical guidelines that opened on 1 January and ended on 15 September 2008. The last part of the chapter will consider if the Fund is able to reduce this risk on the basis of the use of four measures: environmental criteria for real estate investments, a 'green' index as part of the Financial Times Stock Exchange (FTSE) index, a special environmental fund, and an active ownership strategy.

A Gold Standard?

In the first quarter of 2009 the total asset base of the Fund was estimated at USD 321.7 billion, making the Fund one of the largest state-owned institutional investors in the world. The investments are exclusively linked to financial markets outside Norway in fixed income securities and equities, and have their primary basis on an even flow of capital. This capital flow is the income from extractions of petroleum from the oil fields beneath the North Sea. The Fund received USD 178.9 billion from 1995 to 2005.

The primary aim of the Fund's ethical guidelines is for the wealth to yield good returns now and far into the future. The Minister of Finance, Kristin Halvorsen from the Socialist Party, has talked about a fund with a time scale of many hundreds of years. At the Norwegian Central Bank they joke that they intend to manage this wealth for eternity. Not only current and but also future Norwegian generations are to benefit from the Fund because the latter are regarded as equal owners as well. The Government also channels portions of the return yielded by the Fund into the fiscal budget to cover the Government's debt. However, the Fund's actual principal remains untouched. The reasons for this cautious approach are the concern about over-stimulating the national economy and the desire to respect future generations as owners with a status equal to those who are living today. The upper limit for annual use in the real economy is the entire return, which has been about 4 per cent on average during recent years until the financial crisis. The Minister of Finance has referred to this economic policy as 'generational solidarity'. Economists (Matsen 2001) have called this mechanism the 'budgetary rule' to describe the disciplined, long-term use of the returns from the Fund. The Stoltenberg government originally introduced the practices of the 'budgetary rule' in 2001.

A management of the Fund that yields a good return in the long term is the actual means of achieving this solidarity with future generations. On several occasions the Government has expressed that it has very lofty goals, not just for the ethical management of the Fund but also for the management of the entire structure. These ambitions began to take shape already in the Graver Commission's report 'Management for the Future' (NoU 2003:22). The report presented a proposal for the Fund's ethical guidelines, and this proposal was adopted in its entirety. The Commission stated that it wanted to make the Fund one of the best investment funds by management in the world with regard to collaboration between financial goals and ethical values.

After the Norwegian Parliament adopted the ethical guidelines at the end of 2004, the Ministry of Finance regularly expressed these high aspirations to the Norwegian press. The Minister of Finance published an article in *Dagsavisen* on 28 April 2006 under the title, 'UN Follows up Norwegian Ethical Principles'. Here the Minister writes:

> The Government Pension Fund has drafted principles for responsible investment activities after an invitation by the UN Secretary General Kofi Annan. The result of this work was six principles [...] and this represents yet an example of how Norway through its work on ethical guidelines emerges as an international pioneer in this area.

In Report no. 16 (2007-2008) to the Parliament, the Ministry of Finance sharpened its goals. The Ministry maintained repeatedly that the goal of the Fund was to be the best in the world by ethical management. This ambition must be seen in the context of the already existing ethical guidelines. This theme repeated itself during the consultative process on the Fund in 2008. The Ministry of Finance initiated this consultative process with a conference in February 2008 on the theme 'Investing for the future'. Several of the participants here claimed that Oslo had become the world's capital of ethical investment. The conference attracted international experts both in fund management and in the exercise ownership rights, researchers, the press, and representatives from voluntary organizations.

The Minister of Finance again outlined the ambitious plans during a consultative meeting on 18 June 2008 to a group of commentators, who were invited to participate in the consultative process. The Ministry of Finance's consultative paper (2008) was along the same lines. This paper also outlined the parts of the Fund's ethical management where the Government wished for critical input. Once again, following the consultative process, the Ministry of Foreign Affairs stated that 'Norway has become a world leader with regard to taking ethical considerations into account in the management of the Norwegian Government Pension Fund' (Ministry of Foreign Affairs' consultative paper, 2008).

There can be no doubt in other words that key parts of the Norwegian government have particularly high aspirations for the management of the Fund. Right from the run-up to the political consensus on the establishment of ethical guidelines in the Parliament in 2004 and on until the consultative process in 2008, there has been a belief that it was and it still is possible to realize the ethical goals of the Fund. This belief has gradually taken root in the Government.

These ambitions have started to receive international recognition. International commentators have stated that the Fund's ethics represent the gold standard among major institutional funds (*Time* 2008). Immediately after the meeting of the World Economic Forum held in Davos in January 2008, the Norwegian radio station, NRK P2, interviewed the Minister of Finance. Halvorsen maintained that the Fund has become a model for other oil nations that also want to build up this kind of government fund. She pointed out that politicians from many countries have come to Oslo to learn. She told the listeners that the Russian authorities wanted more or less to establish an exact copy of the Fund. The International Monetary Fund (IMF) also stated that the Fund is exemplary (2008). It appears, then, that the perception of the Fund as being a gold standard for the financial markets has begun to take root in Norway and abroad.

Yet, despite the multitude of positive and ambitious assertions, we should do well to wonder about the validity of these statements. One weighty question is whether it is the case that the Fund is managed ethically also from an environmental point of view. To begin answering this question, let us take a look first at what emerged with regard to climate-related risk during the major consultative process in ethical management from 2008, the year in which the current financial crisis emerged.

Consultative Process

The financial crisis has changed this sanguine outlook. The annual report for 2008 paints a picture of a fund portfolio that had been exposed to extreme risk precisely during the period when everything was apparently so positive. The Norwegian press has been very critical of the fact that portfolio's overall value fell by 23 per cent or NOK 633 billion (USD 98.1 billion) in 2008 (Reinertsen, 2009). This loss represents around three-fourths of Norway's fiscal budget. The Central Bank's equity investments fell by 40.7 per cent, which was relatively close to the fall in the global equity market. The bank's investments in bonds also dropped by 6.6 per cent, which was considerably worse than the index used for comparison (Norwegian Central Bank's Annual Report 2008). The debate in the Norwegian media on the Fund's losses during the financial crisis has focused especially on these numbers, in addition to the fact that the active management in 2008 was responsible for around NOK 70 billion (USD 10.6 billion) of the NOK 633 billion in losses.

The Fund's official documents have given the impression for many years that the Norwegian Central Bank has had the Fund's financial risk well under control. The annual reports from the Central Bank from 2000 to 2007 consistently provided the readers with reassuring information on risk control. Yet, some researchers have been questioning this rosy picture even before the financial crisis. Veggeland (2009) has underlined that significant challenges were kept outside the scope of the risk assessments, such as the regular cycle of global economic crises and the connection between global warming and CO_2 emissions from petroleum activities. As a consequence, according to Veggeland, the Fund's notion of actual market risk has been 'far too narrow'.

Moreover, the Albright group, led by former US Secretary of State, Madeleine Albright, won a competition about evaluating the level of ethical management from an international point of view. The Albright group presented a criticism which reflected their experience and ability to analyse the inner dynamic of global organizations. Commentators from the Central Bank, however, defended themselves, pointing to the fact that the Government initiated this process of consultation only after a short period of ethical management, from 2005 to 2008. They felt perhaps that they had not received enough time to do the job properly. The reasons behind the Government's consultative process seem to have been the high aspirations of the ethical guidelines and a corresponding political will to use the results of the consultation to strengthen the Government's position before the election in the autumn of 2009.

Criticism

Key contributions to this process of consultation focus precisely on the fact that the Fund is still exposed to a high level of financial risk, specifically climate-related risk. In spite of various proposed solutions, there is a general consensus among the critics that the climatic crisis is the greatest financial challenge the Fund will ever face. If we look at all of the 53 consultative papers as a whole, the climatic crisis is the financial problem that receives the most intensive criticism. The critics maintain that the financial crisis may prove to be a minor glitch compared with the global financial crisis that may arise in the aftermath of climatic disaster. Many of the consultative papers focus their critical attention on a single issue – the Fund as an index fund.

The intensity of the criticism differs from one institution to the other. It is perhaps not surprising that three famous Norwegian Non-governmental organizations (NGOs) have presented the sharpest criticism of the Fund's investment strategy. These NGOs are well known for their critical attitude to a wide range of governmental practices. In recent years when the Government has acted as a large successful investor at the Norwegian Stock exchange, the NGOs have taken on the role as watchdog, trying to disclose potential violations of human rights in the supply chain of state-owned Norwegian companies. This scrutiny is especially trained on those companies operating in low-cost countries. The issues of child labour and corruption have been among the most controversial themes.

The contributions to the consultation by the NGOs must be understood in such a context. Based on the more or less articulated assumption that the Fund's overriding pursuit is to maximize profit and that it does not sufficiently take into account ethical considerations, the NGOs have agreed with the intense criticism that Fund does not take global environmental problems seriously. Against this background the consultation ought to be interpreted as one way in which the NGOs have expanded and deepened their criticism of the state as an investor that neglects non-financial criteria.

According to one of the most well known Norwegian NGOs, Bellona, the UN believes that global investments in the magnitude of USD 15-20 trillion will be required in the coming 20-25 years to promote sustainable development and to avoid an out-of-control climatic crisis. The criticism from Bellona focuses on the fact that 'green' companies in the Fund's portfolio are not credited from a financial point of view. If Norway is to be a credible advocate of sustainable development, the Fund must be an instrument that contributes to this transformation of the global economy. The goal of the investment philosophy must be to make contributions to what the Intergovernmental Panel on Climate Change (IPCC) believes to be necessary to avoid a climatic catastrophe: an 85 per cent reduction in the emission of greenhouse gases by 2050. Integration of a new environmental strategy in the selection of portfolio companies requires, however, that the Fund changes its use of traditional indices as a basis for the definition of a benchmark portfolio. As it stands, the Fund's traditional indexing entails 'business as usual'. The Fund invests in resource-intensive enterprises, but this practice results in substantial financial risk. Portfolio companies that have yielded good returns, even if they have been responsible for substantial emissions of greenhouse gases, will find it difficult to survive in a new economy in which the emissions are priced correctly. The value of these companies may fall dramatically, and lead to a corresponding effect on the Fund's global portfolio. Even if this criticism from an NGO could be characterized as a categorical and one-sided, their point of view still points to a crucial problem at the very foundations of the Fund's construction.

Another well known Norwegian NGO, the Future in Our Hands (FIOH), has pointed out that 11 per cent of the Fund's equities were issued by companies with operations related to oil, gas or coal in 2007, while only 0.15 per cent of the investments related to companies engaged primarily in renewable energy. The three largest shares are in three of the world's oil giants: BP, Shell, and Total. FIOH points out that the Fund's returns will be dependent precisely on whether such companies will be allowed to continue with their emissions of CO_2 into the atmosphere.

The third NGO, Greenpeace, has referred to its consultative paper to the British Government's Stern Review. According to this report, 'business as usual' will result in an annual reduction in the global GDP by 5-20 per cent. With the Fund's global profile, such a risk could have a dramatic impact on long-term returns. Greenpeace regards the fact that the Fund has not invested in companies that produce renewable energy or that are adequately energy-efficient as particularly problematic. In addition, the Fund has probably invested in companies that knowingly contribute to the emission of greenhouse gases, such as those that build coal-fired power plants or invest in new sources of fossil fuels, such as oil sands or oil shale.

Compared with the sharp criticism from the NGOs, the consultative papers from the University of Oslo and the Norwegian Ministry of the Environment have a more friendly tone. The academics agree with the NGOs in content but not in form. According to the Centre for Development and the Environment at the University of Oslo, financial markets do not take adequately into account the risk factors associated with environmental and climatic problems in the criteria on which the financial indices are based. A carbon-intensive portfolio based on such indices can thus represent a serious financial risk in the future. The climate-related risk in the market must be understood as being closely related to industrial emissions. Industrial pollution is concentrated in only a few sectors; companies engaged in oil, gas, mining, steel, electricity, and tourism account for 85 per cent of the global climatic pollution, even if they only account for 29 per cent of the companies in the FTSE 100. The companies in the world that emit the most greenhouse gases, which represent a substantial portion of the portfolio, represent a serious financial risk to the Fund. The Ministry of the Environment is even more diplomatic in its criticism of the climate-related financial risk. It is stated here that the Fund is not only responsible for its own monetary returns, but also for how the investments affect the environment. The Ministry points out that the Fund's proportion of investments in environmentally friendly companies and in companies with a substantial potential for improvement is less 'than is desirable'.

NGOs and public institutions are not the only critics of the Fund's investment strategy. Also one of the SRI pioneers in Norway, Carlos Joly (who started the first SRI fund in Norway in the middle of 1990, as part of the portfolio of the insurance company, Storebrand) has produced a profiled consultative paper. His criticism is at least as intensive as those from the NGOs. Joly points out that climate-related risk is not adequately reflected in the equity and bond markets. This criticism also applies, then, to the index model on which the Fund is based. The Ministry of Finance has used the FTSE equity indices and Lehman Brothers' bond indices for defining the Fund's benchmark portfolio, that is, the core of the Fund. No critical distance has accompanied the use of these indices, as the incorrect pricing inherent to the indices indicates. The benchmark portfolio is a virtual portfolio that follows the risk management that has been proven *historically* to be the best for equities and bonds, namely index-based management. The climatic crisis entails, however, that what has yielded the best returns historically will not continue to do so. It is likely that large parts of the market are making a gigantic mistake by failing to recognize the unsustainability of certain companies and pricing them accordingly, and with a deep discount. Joly concludes: 'In protecting its capital, the GPF-G would not want to find itself saddled with a large chunk of assets that the market will one day realize are overvalued from a sustainability point of view. Conversely, in seeking good returns, it will want to recognize which of today's mid caps will become tomorrow's large caps' (p. 135).

The consultative process on the ethical management of the Fund has brought NGOs, individuals, and the authorities together in a common criticism of the Fund's inadequate commitment to environmental investments. The critics point out, with varying degrees of intensity, that the global financial market will have to redefine its criteria for the determination of financial value if the Fund and the market are to overcome the financial risk that the climatic crisis represents. The consultative process indicate that today's relatively low pricing of companies with sustainable production is just as unacceptable as the high valuation of companies that are among the greatest contributors to the emission of greenhouse gases.

This process raises many questions. How will the Government act on this criticism? Will the management of the portfolio take a more sustainable direction as a result of the consultative process? Will the Government do something about the fundamental problem the consultative process has articulated, namely the fact that the international indices the portfolio uses are devoid of environmental criteria?

BENCHMARK PORTFOLIO

In many ways, the Government is continuing with 'business as usual'. Even after the consultative process, the Government still bases the global portfolio on international indices for equities and bonds, which lack essentially any environmental criteria. This is evident in the document in which the Government has given an account of how it will make use of the consultative process, Report no. 20 (2008-2009) to the Norwegian Parliament, p. 145.

The climatic crisis is indeed taken more seriously in this document than any earlier official document concerning the Fund. That is perhaps a promising sign. This document mentions most notably plans for environmental criteria for real estate investments, making an environmental strategy a key part of active ownership, and the allocation of funds for a special environmental fund. In addition, the Ministry of Finance has decided to prepare a major international report on what effect the climatic crisis will have on the financial markets.

Here, the Stern Review will serve as a model. The Fund's report may play a key role in the international debate on financial market's contribution to combating the climatic crisis.

In spite of these promising statements, the Ministry supports the idea that the Fund will be broadly diversified in a very traditional manner, based on indices that are devoid of dynamic environmental criteria. The Ministry of Finance points out in the report that the Fund will still be a passively managed index fund with limited active management 'at the top'. The belief that the broadest possible diversification is the best counterweight to substantial financial risk predominates. As one of the Fund's academic supporters, Eckbo (2006) points out with this illustrative understatement, 'Don't place all your eggs in one basket'. This method seems to be the best way to avoid the problem of concentrating risk, would lead to vulnerability.

The Ministry of Finance uses financial indices to build the actual foundation for the Fund: the so-called benchmark portfolio, a globally invested virtual portfolio. The Fund has invested in all the major markets in the world, including the so-called emerging markets, of which China, India, and Brazil are the most important. The benchmark portfolio establishes decisive guidelines for the actual investments that the Norwegian Central Bank makes through its day-to-day management. The Central Bank receives large sums of money from the Ministry of Finance after selling Norwegian oil and gas on the international market.

The Central Bank invests the capital that is transferred annually based on the standards established by the Ministry of Finance in the benchmark portfolio. The Central Bank's opportunity to deviate from the benchmark portfolio standards is severely restricted. The Fund can, of course, 'concentrate more on certain investments', but this is a low-scale activity. The Fund is nevertheless to be a universal investor as long as it exists (Syse & Gjessing, 2007). In spite of this 'concentration', the Fund is expanding its investments in new markets significantly (Alm, forthcoming) in accordance with index-based managerial principles. The Fund emerges, therefore, as a global investor under surveillance of the Norwegian Central Bank.

FTSE Global Equity Index Series All Cap is the index for determining what equities the Fund should invest in. This index covers 8000 companies in 48 different countries and includes 98 per cent of the equity markets that the Fund can invest in. Even if the Ministry of Finance has developed a modified version of this equity index, essentially it has been copied almost in its entirety. For equities the benchmark portfolio in 2007-2008 was invested in 7000 companies in 46 countries. The benchmark portfolio consists also of bonds that are included in the indices Barclays Capital Global Aggregate Bond Index and Barclays Capital Global Inflation Linked Index. The benchmark portfolio for bonds consists of 10 000 bonds from 1600 companies in 21 countries (Report no. 20 (2008-2009) to the Norwegian Parliament, p. 145).

This global investment profile raises precisely the financial, climate-related risk on which the consultative process has focused. Due to its heavily index-based profile, the Fund is deeply interwoven with the risks in the global economy that are responsible for the global emission of greenhouse gases. This is most clearly evident in the Fund's use of indices for equities and bonds.

Real Estate and the Environment

With regard to the planned investments in real estate, the picture is more encouraging. The ongoing climatic challenges are taken more seriously. Here, there is no global real-estate index. The Ministry will not, therefore, prepare a benchmark portfolio for real estate. They have, on the other hand, prepared an investment mandate for real estate, which has a management function similar to an index. This mandate controls the five per cent share of the wealth that the government has decided to invest in real estate. This share will be heavily diversified. The portfolio was indeed already invested in a number of listed fund units and listed real-estate company shares, as well as bonds issued against security in real estate, prior to this change in 2008. The change entails that the portfolio will also be invested in real estate as a separate asset class, that is, real estate that is *not* listed.

The Ministry's reason for introducing this new asset class is that it will contribute to improving the 'diversification of risk' (Report no. 16 to the Parliament on the Management of the Government Pension Fund, p. 88). The portfolio will be invested in a number of countries in this new asset class as well. However, the nature of this diversification of risk will differ from the current diversification of risk for equities and bonds. The Ministry of Finance has included new environmental criteria in the real-estate investment mandate. The Ministry stated in Report no. 16 (2007-2008) to the Parliament that, according to the UN Climate Panel, annual CO_2 emissions from the construction sector, including emissions attributed to energy consumption, account for around one-fourth of the total emissions in 2004:

The design and management of buildings has a major impact on the environment . . . Through major ownership interests in real-estate management, Norges Bank could have a greater influence as a manager on the requirements that apply to the underlying assets in the portfolio than through the management of the equity and fixed income portfolio. This points towards special environmental considerations in real-estate management. This will apply in particular to the areas of energy efficiency, water consumption and waste management. The Government Pension Fund – Global should follow and contribute to development of the best practice for the integration of environmental considerations in the management of real estate (p.91).

It appears that the Ministry believes that the government will be a major owner and actor behind the overall global greenhouse gas emissions with an investment of five per cent of the petroleum wealth in the global real-estate market. A greater influence over the climatic crisis and the financial risk it creates is, therefore, more feasible as a real-estate investor than it is through the active management of the equity and bond portfolios.

This perspective places attention on the Fund as a mean of combating climate-related financial risk. What is of decisive importance here is not to focus on what happens *after* an investment has been made, i.e. exercising active ownership and influencing the portfolio of companies to operate in a more climate-friendly manner. What is critical here is the focus on the reasons for choosing to invest, that is, the formulation of ethical environmental requirements *prior* to investing. We do not yet know what such an ethically ambitious investment mandate for real estate will look like. It is apparently still under development in the Ministry and the Central Bank. There was no mention of it in Report no. 20 (2008-2009) to the Storting on the Management of the Government Pension Fund on 3 April 2009.

All the same, the planned real-estate investment mandate emerges as a dynamic environmental force compared with the lack of action that characterizes the index-based investments in equities and bonds. Such an ethical environmental mandate for investments in office buildings, shopping centres, industrial buildings, and housing complexes represents an ambitious new orientation of the Fund's investment philosophy and indexing practice.

ACTIVE OWNERSHIP

What is surprising about the management of the Fund is the conspicuous lack of consistency in its management as a single entity. One part of the Fund creates a problem that other parts of the Fund are required to solve. As a result of the use of equity and bond indices, thousands of companies that are among those responsible for the greatest greenhouse-gas emissions in the world are included in the portfolio. The objective of the planned real estate investments and exercise of ownership is to solve exactly this problem. In other words, there is a great deal of tension within the Fund with regard to the regulation of climatic risk. This inconsistency has not been a topic in any of the Fund's official documents, perhaps because it could be embarrassing to an owner striving to be 'the best in class'.

The Central Bank is addressing the climatic challenge as one of its most important tasks in its efforts to influence the companies in which it has invested. After the Fund's assets are invested in the global market, the Central Bank exercises active ownership of the companies. This influence is based, for example, on the world's foremost environmental documents, namely the UN climatic reports and the Stern Review.

A principal strategy for the years 2007-2010 calls for combating the environmental lobbying of companies based in the US. It is well known that US companies lobby Congress in order to promote their interests. As Ripetto (2007) shows, corporate lobbying on public-policy issues is not always in the best interests of shareholders. Lobbying activities are often overlooked in the annual report of leading companies. The lack of transparency with lobbying is a challenge for the Fund's relation to several portfolio-companies, not least when it comes to the question of their role in adding to the climatic crisis. The Fund has, therefore, demanded an extensive elaboration on these issues in these companies' annual reports.

It is also well known that US energy companies use a great deal of resources to fight attempts by the US authorities to introduce regulations and acts that are intended to help reduce greenhouse-gas emissions. These companies are also in the Fund's portfolio. The Fund has entered into a number of dialogues with US companies in order to prevent them from interfering with the Fund's long-term financial interests. The goal is to influence them to cease impeding the authorities in the US from adopting laws that would require a significant reduction in the emission of greenhouse gases. The Central Bank has conducted an analysis of 100 companies and has been in dialogue with around 20 companies, especially companies in the transport and energy sector. In order to change the attitude of these companies, the Central Bank's policy is to talk directly with the management face to face.

Research shows that institutional investors have been very successful in influencing companies through direct dialogue, especially if it is made clear that a proposal for change will be presented at the general meeting if the dialogue is not successful (Smith 1996, Wahal 1996, Carlton et al. 1998). For the time being, however, the Central Bank does not have any examples of such dialogues leading to specific cuts in the companies' emissions. The Fund remains hopeful of helping to limit the large share of global emissions from the US with this strategy. The Central Bank's annual report has not, of course, mentioned this aspect as an explicit strategy, but it has emerged during an interview with the former manager of the Ownership Department who originally initiated this strategy (2007). A reduction in global emissions for which the US is responsible will enable a reduction in financial risk in the global market, and thus the Fund's global portfolio as well.

The Central Bank's Ownership Department has selected this strategy because they believe it reflects an overlapping consensus among Norwegian politicians: the owners' representatives. Responding to the intense public debate on climatic issues in Norway since 2007, they have undoubtedly found an area of consent among the owners. Far from Madeleine Albright's (2008) portrayal of the Central Bank's supposed solipsistic tendencies, the Fund's strategy from the very beginning of the ethical management in 2005 has been to base all aspects of the ethical guidelines on precisely this overlapping consensus. The works of John Rawls (2005) have inspired the fundamental orientation stated in the guidelines. Rawls has underlined that in a pluralistic democracy there are large and permanent differences between several groups with respect to ethical and political views. Despite this challenging fact, it is possible to find a small area of deep agreement 'outside' this dimension of deep disagreement. The Fund calls this 'a stable, overlapping consensus'. In order to demonstrate its content, they refer to such international agreements as the Human Rights Declaration, the OECD's norms for multinational companies, and UN's Global Compact.

In the annual reports for 2006 and 2007, the director of Central Bank's Ownership Department (CPOD) pointed out that long-term financial development can be secured through a climatic strategy.

> … serious climate change may have a substantial negative effect on NBIM's(CPOD) global portfolio. In this context it is natural to make reference to the IPCC reports and the Stern Review, which point out that a proactive implementation of measures to reduce greenhouse gases will entail substantially lower costs for global society than the probable costs that will result from inactivity.

The IPCC reports and Stern Review have, in other words, become an important part of the Central Bank's ideological foundation for management. Still, how long will it be acceptable that these environmental documents have an effect on only one part of the Fund and not the entirety? How long can the Ministry of Finance ignore these environmental documents while accepting the financial market's equity and bond indices indiscriminately? How long can the Fund sustain its conflicting activities?

The Central Bank does not have the authority to intervene in the Ministry of Finance's strategy for the benchmark portfolio and to change the criteria used there to make them consistent with these environmental documents. The Central Bank is not in a position to make the investment criteria selected by the Ministry of Finance come into line with the Central Bank's climatic strategy. Only the Ministry has the final authority and power over the Fund's investment philosophy and is able to change the adopted fundamental values, by order of the Parliament's political majority, the most obvious political sign of the overlapping consensus.

The Central Bank's climatic strategy does not, however, encompass the bond portfolio, which is 40 per cent of the wealth (Alm 2008). Ownership of bonds does not entitle one to influence the companies that issue those bonds. The companies can simply use the debt they have raised to invest in or to furnish credit to companies that worsen the climatic crisis, without the Fund being able to influence this kind of practice by means other than withdrawal from the bond investment. The agreement the Fund enters into with a bond-issuing company does not recognize any right to stipulate requirements on how the company can use the loan.

It is, in other words, only specific portions of 60 per cent of the portfolio that will be subject to a climatic strategy. In practice, this will probably mean that some of the largest shareholder companies in the world are the targets. However, the Fund is implementing one more measure to combat the climatic problem and to safeguard long-term returns.

A Climatic Fund

The Fund will invest in an environmental programme. The environmental programme will consist of investments in infrastructure and unlisted equity submarkets, so-called environmental bonds, and the opportunity to invest portions of the listed equity portfolio in accordance with the environmental index. The investments are to be aimed at environmentally friendly assets or technology that is expected to provide a clear environmental benefit, such as climate-friendly energy conservation, carbon capture and storage, water technology or waste and pollution management. Investments in infrastructure will be aimed in particular at environmentally friendly technology (Report no. 20/2008 to the Parliament, pp. 63).

The Ministry points out that the environmentally friendly investments that are expected to yield the greatest return in the years to come are investments in technology that contributes to a reduction in the emission of greenhouse gases. A reference is made to the UN Climate Panel, which believes that a large and rapid reduction in emissions is necessary if we are to limit the concentration of greenhouse gases in the atmosphere at a level that does not entail a high risk of extensive environmental destruction globally.

In spite of the affirmation of a substantial reduction in emissions will require 'a complete restructuring of the world's energy consumption and energy supply' (Report no. 20/2008 to the Storting, p. 63), the Ministry has nevertheless decided only to invest a small share of the Fund's overall wealth in this environmental programme, NOK 20 billion. This capital does not represent more than around one per cent of the total wealth, which was over NOK 2 000 billion in 2008.

Still, this investment will far exceed other major investment funds with which the Fund's managers like to make comparisons. Other major funds have made environmental investments in a number of asset classes, such as environmentally friendly bonds, listed equities, unlisted equities, and infrastructure. The largest pension fund in the US, CalPERS, has allocated USD 500 million (around NOK 3.25 billion) to investments in listed equities based on environmental criteria. They have also allocated USD 600 million (NOK 4.2 billion) to investments in unlisted equities in environmentally friendly technology. CalPERS's combined investments of NOK 7.45 billion are substantially lower than the Norwegian investments of NOK 20 billion, however.

Even though the Norwegian environmental investments will be around three times as much as CalPERS, using only per cent of the Norwegian portfolio for specific environmental investments is akin to a drop in the ocean. It must be added that the environmental investments in real estate will eventually reach five per cent. Moreover, the Ministry of Finance (Report no. 20 to the Parliament, p. 65) has pointed out a little-known fact. As much as six per cent of the value of the Fund's benchmark index for equities already has a green profile. The benchmark index for equities is defined by a 'green' index, the FTSE Environmental Opportunities All-Share Index, among others. The selection criteria for this 'green' part of the benchmark index require that the companies have more than 20 per cent of their earnings from environmental activities related to energy, water, pollution or waste.

The sum total of the Fund's environmental investments is five per cent if we include the existing investments. As the Fund gradually invests in a special environmental fund and real estate, investments based on specific environmental criteria will increase to 12 per cent.

Conclusion

In this chapter I have pointed out that there is no evidence that the Norwegian government has introduced a gold standard in its efforts to regulate the Fund's climate-related, financial risk. This lofty ideal is just that, rather than an accurate description of reality. National and international claims that the management of international public investment funds worldwide ought to be in line with ethical guidelines do not change the presence of weak control measures. The Norwegian government has indeed implemented certain minor measures to regulate the climate-related financial risk. There are essentially four measures: environmental criteria for real estate investments, a 'green' index as part of the FTSE index, earmarked funds for a special environmental fund, and a special ownership strategy for 2007-2010.

Overall, these measures have little impact compared with the Fund's mechanism of index regulation. Rather, they are best interpreted as parts of a new environmental *ideal* than a significant environmentally friendly practice. They can by no means be said to solve the climatic problems created by the indexing measures. The Fund has instead become intertwined with the global economy's role in the climatic crisis due to the use of indices, and it is not possible to change this practice through these measures. They appear, therefore, to be relatively superficial.

The use of equity and bond indices is not subject to any effective environmental control. The equity and bond indices essentially lack non-financial criteria that can contribute to a reduction of the Fund's adverse effects on the climate. That this risk is not taken seriously is a symptom of the market. The largest portion of the portfolio (95 per cent today, 88 per cent in the near future) is not regulated with respect to climatic risk. The climate-related financial risk in the largest portion of the Fund's investment universe will remain uncontrolled in the years to come. There is, in other words, a large gap between the Fund's ambitions and its actual climatic efforts. In sum, ideals and reality do not match each other with this type of risk control.

REFERENCES

Albright, M. & Chesterman, S. (2009). Assessment of implementation of Articles 3 and 4 of the Ethical Guidelines for the Government Pension Fund – Global. D. Social and Environmental issues. http://www.regjeringen.no/upload/FIN/Vedlegg/aff/Albright_Group_Ethical_Guidelines.pdf

Alm, K. (2008). Etiske utfordringer for en global investor [Ethcial challenges for a global investor]. Contribution to the 2008 assessment of the Government Pension Fund – Global. Ministry of Finance 2008. http://www.regjeringen.no/upload/FIN/etikk/h_uttalelser/alm.pdf

Alm, K. (2007). Challenges to investment ethics in the Norwegian Petroleum Fund: a newspaper debate. *Philosophica, Special edition, 80,* 21-45.

Alm, K. (forthcoming). The Norwegian Government Pension Fund – Global: Patriotism, complicity and ethical management. (forthcoming, in the review process, *Journal of Business Ethics*)

Bellona (2008). Consultation statement on the ethical management of the Government Pension Fund – Global. *http://www.regjeringen.no/nb/dep/fin/dok/hoeringer/hoeringsdok/2008/horing---evaluering-av-de-etiske-retning/horingsuttalelser.html?id=517313*

Consultation Paper: Evaluation of the Ethical Guidelines for the Government Pension Fund – Global. Ministry of Finance h*ttp://www.regjeringen.no/upload/FIN/Vedlegg/aff/hoeringsdokument_etiske.pdf*

Consultation statements (2008). http://www.regjeringen.no/nb/dep/fin/dok/hoeringer/hoeringsdok/2008/horing---evaluering-av-de-etiske-retning/horingsuttalelser.html?id=517313

Carleton, W., Nelson, J. & Weisbach, M. (1998). The influence of Institutions on Corporate Governance through Private negotiations: Evidence from TRIAA-CREF. *The Journal of Finance LIII (4),* 1335-136.

Eckbo, E. (2006) Corporate Governance – i et nøtteskall [in a nutshell], *Penger og Kreditt 34(2)*, 87-99.

Ethical Guidelines for the Government Pension Fund – Global. (2005). http://www.regjeringen.no/nb/dep/fin/tema/Statens_pensjonsfond/etiske-retningslinjer/Graverutvalget/Graverutvalget-og-etiske-retningslinjer.html?id=434926 FTSE Global Equity Index Series All Cap http://www.ftse.com/Indices/FTSE_Global_Equity_Index_Series/index.jsp

Future in Our Hands. (2008). Consultation statement on the ethical management of the Government Pension Fund – Global. *http://www.regjeringen.no/nb/dep/fin/dok/hoeringer/hoeringsdok/2008/horing---evaluering-av-de-etiske-retning/horingsuttalelser.html?id=517313*

Graver Commission's report (2003). Forvaltning for fremtiden [Administration for the future]. Proposal for ethical guidelines for the Government Petroleum Fund. NoU 2003:22

Greenpeace (2008). Consultation statement on the ethical management of the Government Pension Fund – Global.

http://www.regjeringen.no/nb/dep/fin/dok/hoeringer/hoeringsdok/2008/horing---evaluering-av-de-etiske-retning/horingsuttalelser.html?id=517313

Halvorsen, K. (2006). UN follows up Norwegian ethical principles. *Dagsavisen*, 28 April 2006.

IMF. International Monetary Fund. (2008). *http://www.imf.org/external/pubs/ft/survey/so/2008/POL070908A.htm*

IPCC: Climate Change (2007) *http://www.ipcc.ch/*

Joly, C. (2008). Response to the Norwegian Ministry of Finance consultation paper. Evaluation of the ethical guidelines of the Norwegian Government Pension Fund – Global. Ministry of Finance, Oslo. *http://www.regjeringen.no/upload/FIN/etikk/h_uttalelser/joly.pdf*

Malka, A., Krosnick, J.A. & Langer G. (2009). The association of knowledge with concern about global warming: Trusted information sources shape public thinking. *Risk Analysis: An International Journal, (29) 5,* 633-647.

Matsen, E. (2001). Om sammenhengen mellom den finanspolitiske handlingsregelen og forvaltningen av oljefondet [On the connecion between the financial political trading rules and the administration of the oil fund]. *Økonomisk forum, 55 (8),* 15-17.

Ministry of the Environment. (2008). Consultation statement on the ethical management of the Government Pension Fund – Global. *http://www.regjeringen.no/nb/dep/fin/dok/hoeringer/hoeringsdok/2008/horing---evaluering-av-de-etiske-retning/horingsuttalelser.html?id=517313*

Norges Bank's Annual Reports 2005, 2006, 2007

Rawls, J. (1999). *A theory of justice*. Cambridge, Massachusetts. Belknap Press of Harvard University Press, 1971. The revised edition.

Reinertsen, M. (2009) I Gjerdrems hjerne [In Gjedrem's brain]. *Morgenbladet*, 13-19 March 2009.

Repetteo, R. (2007). The need for better internal oversight of corporate lobbying. *Challenge, the Magazine of Economic Affairs. 50 (1),* 76-96.

Report no. 16 (2006-2007) to the Norwegian Parliament on the management of the Government Pension Fund – Global

Report no. 20 (2008-2009) to the Norwegian Parliament on the management of the Government Pension Fund – Global.

Smith, M.P. (1996) Shareholder activism by institutional investors: Evidence from CalPERS. *The Journal of Finance 51(1*), 227-252.

Syse, H. & Gjessing, O. P. (2007). Norwegian petroleum wealth and universal ownership. *Corporate Governance: An International Review, 15 (3),* 427-437.

Time Magazine (11 June 2008). *http://www.time.com/time/magazine/article/0,9171,1813509,00.htm*l

Vandekerckhove, W. & Jos, L. (2007). Information asymmetries in socially responsible investment. *Philosophica, 80,* 5-19

Veggeland, N. (2009). *Taming the regulatory state.* Cheltenham, UK: Edward Elgar.

Wahal, S. (1994). *Public pension fund activism and firm perfomance*. Working paper. Chapel Hill, N.C.: University of North Carolina

CONTRIBUTORS

Kristian Alm is Doctor of theology , University of Oslo, and Associate Professor of Ethics, Institute f or Strategy and logistics, Centre for Ethics and leadership, BI Norwegian School of Management, Norway. Scholarship holder 1986, Deutsche Academische Austaschendienst.

Editor and Secretary: The Norwegian Government Commission on Human Values (Verdikommisjonen), 1998-2001. His academic publishing is on the intersection between philosophy, theology and ethics with special emphasis on the development of the ethical management of the Norwegian Government Pension Fund.

kristian.alm@bi.no

Ole Gunnar Austvik is Doctor of Philosophy in International Political Economy from University of Oslo and is the Head of Research at Lillehammer University College, Norway. He holds a master's degree in economics from University of Oslo and in political economy from John F. Kennedy School of Government, Harvard University. He has previously worked at the Norwegian Institute of International Affairs (NUPI) and Norwegian School of Management (BI). Austvik has written numerous articles and books within the fields of international petroleum economics, political entrepreneurship, energy security, and European integration.

Homepage: www.oga.no. ole.gunnar.austvik@hil.no

Peter Munk Christiansen is Professor at the Department of Political Science, Aarhus University, Denmark. He has previously held professorships at the University of Aalborg and the University of Southern Denmark. He was member of the executive board of the Danish Power and Democracy Study (1998-2004), and he is currently chairman of the Danish Social Science Research Council. He has published widely on the political role of interest groups, the recruitment and development of elites, administrative reforms, and public policy, especially environmental policy.

pmc@ps.au.dk

Christel Elvestad is currently a researcher at Nordland Research Institute, Bodø, Norway, where she has conducted and participated in numerous projects of research project. She is also a doctoral student at the Department of Political Science, University of Tromsø,

Norway. International governance within the fields of resource regulation and management and trade with a particular focus on the important food sector are her main areas of research.

christel.elvestad@nforsk.no

Olivier Thomas Kramsch is Senior Lecturer at Nijmegen Centre for Border Research (NCBR), and Director, External Relations, Dep. of Human geography, Radboud Universiteit, The Netherlands. Dr. of Philosophy in Urban Planning, University of California. He has published widely on border issues, and is Contributor and Editor of numerous books. He is currently a Member of NORFACE Workshop, 'Globalization and Borders, Theorizing European Transformation', and a Member of the Editorial Board, 'Cuadernos de Investigación del CEINLADI'.

o.kramsch@fm.ru.nl

Tor Helge Pedersen has a PhD in Political Science, University of Tromsø, and currently he is an Associate Professor at Lillehammer University College, Norway. He has previously worked as a senior lecturer at Hedmark University College. His main fields of expertise, and latest research and publications, are on comparative public administration, organizational design, and the translation, diffusion, and application of organization ideas. He is also studying with administrative traditions and institutional path-dependence related to historical transformation.

tor.helge.pedersen@hil.no

Frode Veggeland has a doctoral degree in political science from the University of Oslo, Norway. He is currently Senior Researcher at the Norwegian Agricultural Economics Research Institute, Oslo, and has also held positions as associate professor at the Department of Political science, University of Oslo, and as senior researcher at

Centre for European Studies (ARENA). His main research field is global and European governance and regulation, with a particular emphasis on the WTO, the EU, and food and trade policies. He has published widely on these topics.

frode.veggeland@nilf.no

Noralv Veggeland is Professor in Social Sciences at Lillehammer University College, Norway. He is a former Director of the Nordic Institute of Regional Policy, Copenhagen, Denmark. He has served as Visiting Research Fellow (1980), Visiting Lecturer (2006) at the University of Massachusetts, Amherst, United States, and Research Visitor at the European University Institute (2009), Florence, Italy. He is also currently a member of NORFACE Workshop, 'Globalization and Borders, Theorizing European Transformation. He has published more than twenty academic books and numerous other publications, and is profiled in *Who's Who in the World*, edition 2010.

noralv.veggeland@hil.no

APPENDIX 1

ETHICAL GUIDELINES

(This translation is for information purposes only. Legal authenticity remains with the original Norwegian version.)

THE NORWEGIAN GOVERNMENT PENSION FUND – GLOBAL

Issued 22 December 2005 pursuant to regulation on the Management of the Government pension Fund - Global, former regulation on the Management of the Government Petroleum Fund issued 19 November 2004.

1. Basis

The ethical guidelines for the Government Pension Fund - Global are based on two premises:

- *The Government Pension Fund - Global* is an instrument for ensuring that a reasonable portion of the country's petroleum wealth benefits future generations. The financial wealth must be managed so as to generate a sound return in the long term, which is contingent on sustainable development in the economic, environmental and social sense. The financial interests of the Fund shall be strengthened by using the Fund's ownership interests to promote such sustainable development.
- *The Government Pension Fund - Global* should not make investments which constitute an unacceptable risk that the Fund may contribute to unethical acts or omissions, such as violations of fundamental humanitarian principles, serious violations of human rights, gross corruption or severe environmental damages.

2. Mechanisms

The ethical basis for the Government Pension Fund - Global shall be promoted through the following three measures:

- *Exercise of ownership rights* in order to promote long-term financial returns, based on the UN Global Compact and the OECD Guidelines for Corporate Governance and for Multinational Enterprises.
- *Negative screening* of companies from the investment universe that either themselves, or through entities they control, produce weapons that through normal use may violate fundamental humanitarian principles.
- *Exclusion* of companies from the investment universe where there is considered to be an unacceptable risk of contributing to:

- Serious or systematic human rights violations, such as murder, torture, deprivation of liberty, forced labor, the worst forms of child labor and other child exploitation
- Serious violations of individuals' rights in situations of war or conflict
- Severe environmental damages
- Gross corruption
- Other particularly serious violations of fundamental ethical norms.

3. The Exercise of Ownership Rights

3.1.

The overall objective of Norwegian Central Bank's exercise of ownership rights for the *Government Pension Fund - Global* is to safeguard the Fund's financial interests. The exercise of ownership rights shall be based on a long-term horizon for the Fund's investments and broad investment diversification in the markets that are included in the investment universe. The exercise of ownership rights shall mainly be based on the UN's Global Compact and the OECD Guidelines for Corporate Governance and for Multinational Enterprises. Norwegian Central Bank's internal guidelines for the exercise of ownership rights shall stipulate how these principles are integrated in the ownership strategy.

3.2.

Norwegian Central Bank shall report on its exercise of ownership rights in connection with its ordinary annual reporting. An account shall be provided of how the Bank has acted as owner representative - including a description of the work to promote special interests relating to the long-term horizon and diversification of investments in accordance with Section 3.1.

3.3.

Norwegian Central Bank may delegate the exercise of ownership rights pursuant to these guidelines to external managers.

4. Negative Screening and Exclusion

4.1.

The Ministry of Finance shall, based on recommendations of the Council on Ethics for the *Government Pension Fund - Global*, make decisions on negative screening and exclusion of companies from the investment universe.

The recommendations and decisions shall be made public. The Ministry may, in certain cases, postpone the time of public disclosure if this is deemed necessary in order to ensure a financially sound implementation of the exclusion of the company concerned.

4.2.

The Council on Ethics for the *Government Pension Fund - Global* shall consist of five members. The Council shall have its own secretariat. The Council shall submit an annual report on its activities to the Ministry of Finance.

4.3.

Upon request of the Ministry of Finance, the Council issues recommendations on whether an investment may constitute a violation of Norway's obligations under international law.

4.4.

The Council shall issue recommendations on negative screening of one or several companies on the basis of production of weapons that through their normal use may violate fundamental humanitarian principles. The Council shall issue recommendations on the exclusion of one or several companies from the investment universe because of acts or omissions that constitute an unacceptable risk of the Fund contributing to:

- Serious or systematic human rights violations, such as murder, torture, deprivation of liberty, forced labor, the worst forms of child labor and other forms of child exploitation
- Serious violations of individuals' rights in situations of war or conflict
- Severe environmental damages
- Gross corruption
- Other particularly serious violations of fundamental ethical norms

The Council shall raise issues under this provision on its own initiative or at the request of the Ministry of Finance.

4.5.

The Council shall gather all necessary information at its own discretion and shall ensure that the matter is documented as fully as possible before making a recommendation regarding negative screening or exclusion from the investment universe. The Council may request Norwegian Central Bank to provide information as to how specific companies are dealt with in the exercise of ownership rights. Enquiries to such companies shall be channeled through Norwegian Central Bank. If the Council is considering recommending exclusion of a company, the company in question shall receive the draft recommendation and the reasons for it, for comment.

4.6.

The Council shall review on a regular basis whether the reasons for exclusion still apply and may against the background of new information recommend that the Ministry of Finance revoke a decision to exclude a company.

4.7.

Norwegian Central Bank shall receive immediate notification of the decisions made by the Ministry of Finance in connection with the Council's recommendations. The Ministry of Finance may request that Norwegian Central Bank inform the companies concerned of the decisions taken by the Ministry and the reasons for the decision.

INDEX

A

B

C

D

E

F

G

H

I

J

L

M

N

O

P

Q

R

S

T

U

V

W

Y